Every Day's a HOLIDAY

VALUE-BASED THEME UNITS FOR INDIVIDUAL CALENDAR DAYS

Abraham Resnick

Margaret Pavol

Helen Pappas

Fearon Teacher Aids

Simon & Schuster Supplementary Education Group

Editor: Barbara Armentrout

Copyeditors: Diane Sovljanski and Lisa Schwimmer

Illustration and Design: Rose Sheifer

ISBN 0-8224-6372-5

Printed in the United States of America
1. 9 8 7 6 5 4

Contents

Introduction

Every Day's a Holiday is a quick-reference mini-unit and activity book for teachers. It's designed for use by classroom teachers, curriculum coordinators, and principals. Each mini-unit can be readily converted into a workable lesson plan.

As a practicing educator, you are well aware of the excitement that can be generated in the classroom when holidays, festivals, and special days are imaginatively observed. The celebration or remembrance of a special event, historical anniversary, or birthday can also become a catalyst for integrating positive citizenship themes—such as patriotism and appreciation for our rich cultural heritage—into the instructional program. Commemorative days can provide an array of motivational opportunities for furthering your students' social development, skill mastery, understanding, and creative expression.

The events and people featured in the mini-units in this book were selected in order to give you, the teacher, opportunities to

- accentuate pride in our country's heritage, ideals, democratic institutions, and accomplishments
- examine the exemplary characteristics of the role-model being honored
- elicit proper codes of conduct for life through the study of and commemoration of historical episodes, and
- encourage understanding and appreciation of the customs and cultures of diverse peoples.

How to Use This Book

Every Day's a Holiday is a compendium of interesting information and instructional ideas. The book is clearly presented and arranged. There are twelve monthly calendars that list

at least one holiday or anniversary for every day. Following each monthly calendar for September through June are mini-units for six to eight selected days in each month.

Each mini-unit includes the following components, which can be adapted to the needs, interest, and abilities of your class:

- Themes and Thoughts
- Fascinating Facts
- Activities for Students
- Questions for Class Discussion
- Key Vocabulary
- Related Career Education Terms

Themes and Thoughts lists value themes that can be highlighted by the mini-unit. This feature also includes quotations that are by or about the person commemorated or that express the values being taught. Class discussions of the meanings of the quotations might prove worthwhile.

Fascinating Facts provides a summary of information about the person or event commemorated. You can use this information in the manner most appropriate for your students. For younger classes, you might simply choose a few of the most basic or interesting facts to convey verbally. For older classes, you might duplicate the entire passage for the students to read.

The activities and discussion questions will help promote learning through a broad array of "think and do" offerings. You might provide your class with the entire list of *Activities for Students,* or let them choose among a handful. Each unit's list of activities provides suggestions for a wide variety of learning experiences—from research to art to special celebrations and community projects. To maintain high enthusiasm, it is important to vary the methods of recognition and celebration throughout the year. Many of the learning experiences suggested for a particular observance can be adapted for other special days. For example, many of the activities for National Grandparents' Day (first Sunday after Labor Day), Mother's Day (second Sunday in May), and Father's Day (third Sunday in June) are interchangeable, with minor adaptations.

Competent reading is a complex skill that requires continual exercise and practice. Because the *Questions for Class Discussion* include questions in each of the four basic comprehension categories—literal, interpretive, critical, and creative comprehension—they provide practical applications of reading skills and reinforce classroom instruction. Many of these questions are open-ended. They don't necessarily have "right" answers and are primarily intended to stimulate curiosity and discussion.

You can tailor the *Key Vocabulary* list to fit your class. This list includes not only key words in the "Fascinating Facts" passage, but also words that are likely to be encountered in more thorough discussions of and readings about the topic. You might use the list for a dictionary skills assignment. Because some of the words have multiple meanings, students could be asked to find only definitions related to the topic, or they could study all of the meanings and discuss their similarities.

The *Related Career Education Terms* can be discussed after the students are familiar with the topic. Such discussions can be valuable in widening your students' knowledge about the world of work.

Your class' observance of special days will be more effective if you

- correlate the subject with other areas of the curriculum
- center the activities around a value theme
- involve the students in the planning of and participation in the commemorative activities
- introduce the topic at an appropriate time prior to the day of the observance, and

- relate the topic to local points of reference, current events, and community activities.

ADDITIONAL IDEAS

The Daily Greeting. At the start of each day, before the usual announcements, you (or a student reporter) might acknowledge the day's anniversaries (as listed on the monthly calendar pages in this book) and then salute the class with a greeting such as "Have a . . . Marvelous Monday, Terrific Tuesday, Wonderful Wednesday, Tremendous Thursday, or Fabulous Friday." Students can enhance their vocabulary development by providing their own alliterative adjectives. Each day's greeting and the list of the day's anniversaries could also be posted on a bulletin board.

The Mystery Commemorative Day. Have individual students or small groups choose a special event in advance of the calendar date listed in this book. They'll research the event and then, about a week before the date, begin to reveal a clue each day, using "Who Am I, What Am I, Where Am I?" questions. Their classmates—or even the rest of the school—can try to guess what the event in question is.

The clues (which should be helpful, but not give away the answer) can be posted on the chalkboard or a bulletin board or even announced over the school intercom system. The solutions can be placed in an answer box in the library or the classroom. Students who answer correctly can be recognized by having their names added to a school or class "Special-Day Puzzle-Solvers Honor Roll." Students submitting mystery clues can also be honored.

THE ORIGIN OF HOLIDAYS

Originally a holiday was a "holy day." Thousands of years ago, people held feasts and performed rites to acknowledge their dead or to pay homage to their gods and goddesses. Members of major religions still observe holy days and customs that have their origins in these early times.

Today, holidays are days that are singled out by a religious body, a government, a national or ethnic group, or an organization to honor some highly cherished ideal, the contribution of a great person, or a memorable episode in history. There are many different purposes for special celebrations. Holidays may be religious (such as Christmas), patriotic (such as Washington's Birthday), legal (such as Election Day), special days (such as Arbor Day), traditional (such as Mother's Day), days to celebrate our heritage (such as American Indian Day), or days to recognize a particular ethnic group (such as St. Patrick's Day).

A NOTE ABOUT DATES

Although we have made every effort to ensure that the dates in the monthly calendars and the "Fascinating Facts" are accurate, your students may discover discrepancies when doing research on some of the topics. These discrepancies may be due to lack of conclusive historical records, disagreement among reference materials, or differences in defining an event (for example, some references may give as the date for an invention the date when it was patented or introduced to the public rather than the date when it was created in a laboratory).

Your students may also discover discrepancies between the "real" date of a holiday and the date on which it is observed. Some of these discrepancies are due to the federal "three-day-weekend" law that went into effect on January 1, 1971. Since then, Washington's birthday (February 22) has been observed on the third Monday in February, Memorial Day (May 30) on the last Monday in May, and Columbus Day (October 12) on the second Monday in October. In 1986, the third Monday in January was designated as Martin Luther King, Jr., Day, although his birthday is actually January 15.

September

First Week:

National Highway Week
National Square Dance Week
National Child Safety Week

1

National Dog Day
World War II began, 1939

2

U.S. Department of Treasury established, 1789
Eugene Field, "the children's poet," born, 1850

3

* Labor Day first celebrated as legal holiday, 1894 (now the 1st Monday in September)
Treaty of Paris officially ended Revolutionary War, 1783
Viking II landed on Mars to collect scientific data, 1976

4

Transcontinental television service began with telecast of Japanese Peace Conference, 1951
George Eastman received patent for first roll camera, 1880

5

First Continental Congress met at Carpenters Hall, 1774
Jesse James, desperado, born, 1847

6

President William McKinley assassinated, 1901
Jane Addams, pioneer social worker and Nobel Peace Prize winner, born, 1860
Marquis de Lafayette, French patriot, born, 1757

7

Brazil became an independent nation, 1822

*A teaching unit is included on the following pages for each starred entry.

Every Day's a Holiday

Second Week:

National Hispanic Heritage Week (including September 15 and 16)
* National Grandparents' Day (the 1st Sunday after Labor Day)

8

Pledge of Allegiance published, 1892
St. Augustine, Florida, the oldest city in the U.S., was founded, 1565
International Literacy Day

9

California admitted to the Union, 1850

10

Oliver H. Perry, U.S. naval officer, won Battle of Lake Erie, 1813
Elias Howe patented sewing machine, 1846

11

* Henry Hudson sailed up the Hudson River, 1609

12

Richard Hoe, inventor of rotary press, born, 1812
Soviet Union launched first rocket to the moon, 1959

13

Walter Reed, conqueror of yellow fever, born, 1851
Commodore John Barry, father of the U.S. Navy, died, 1803
Milton S. Hershey, candy maker, born, 1857

14

* National Anthem Day—Francis Scott Key wrote "The Star-Spangled Banner," 1814
American Philatelic Society formed, 1886

15

World Peace Day
James Fenimore Cooper, author of tales of frontier life, born, 1789
William H. Taft, the only man in U.S. history to be both President and Chief Justice, born, 1857

Third Week:

National 4-H Club Week
Constitution Week (September 17–23)
American Newspaper Week
Press Sunday, tribute to freedom of the press and to first newspaper published in the U.S.
  (3rd Sunday)

16

Mayflower Day—Pilgrims sailed from England on the *Mayflower,* 1620
James J. Hill, financier and railroad builder, born, 1838

17

Citizenship Day
Baron von Steuben, German military officer who fought in American Revolution, born, 1730

18

President Washington laid cornerstone of the Capitol, 1793
The New York Times established, 1851
Samuel Johnson, English author and dictionary maker, born, 1709

19

Washington's Farewell Address published, 1796
International Day of Peace, declared by United Nations, 1981

20

Alexander the Great born, 356 B.C.

21

Louis Joliet, French fur trader and explorer, born, 1645
* First day of autumn (traditional date)
Great hurricane swept the Atlantic Coast, 1938
World Gratitude Day

22

Michael Faraday, English scientist and pioneer in electricity, born, 1791
Nathan Hale put to death as a spy by the British, 1776

23

Augustus Caesar, first Roman emperor, born, 63 B.C.
Captain John Paul Jones captured the *Serapis,* 1779
William McGuffey, compiler of *McGuffey's Eclectic Readers,* born, 1800

Fourth Week:

* American Indian Day (the 4th Friday in September)
Kids' Day (4th Saturday)
Good Neighbor Day—to promote understanding and good relations among peoples and
    nations (4th Sunday)

24

U.S. Supreme Court created, 1789
John Marshall, U.S. Supreme Court Chief Justice, born, 1755
"Black Friday" gold panic in New York, 1869
Devils Tower, Wyoming, became first national monument in the U.S., 1906

25

* Vasco Núñez de Balboa sighted the Pacific Ocean, 1513
Alfred Vail, who helped develop Morse Code, born, 1807
Christopher Columbus sailed on second voyage to America, 1493
Benjamin Harris published first newspaper in America, 1690

26

Federal Trade Commission established, 1914
John Philip Sousa, march composer, performed his first concert, 1895
* Johnny Appleseed Day—John "Johnny Appleseed" Chapman born, 1775
National Gold-Star Mother's Day

27

Samuel Adams, American Revolutionary–era hero, born, 1722
Thomas Nast, editorial cartoonist, born, 1840

28

Al Capp, cartoonist and creator of "Li'l Abner" born, 1909

29

First telephone message sent across the continent, 1915
Enrico Fermi, Nobel Prize winner in physics, born, 1901

30

Ether first used as anesthetic, 1846
First hydroelectric power station opened, 1882

Better Breakfast Month

THEMES AND THOUGHTS

Fitness, Strength, Health

Tell me what you eat, and I will tell you what you are.
—*Anthelme Brillat-Savarin*

Eat to live, and not live to eat.
—*Ben Franklin*

Good health and good sense are two of life's greatest blessings.
—*Publius Syrus*

FASCINATING FACTS

Breakfast means "to break the night's fast." It is the first meal of the day.

Your body cannot store proteins or most vitamins and minerals, so you need to give it fresh fuel every day. Most nutritionists today agree that breakfast should include about one-third of the day's total nutritional requirements. It should be as large, or almost as large, a meal as lunch or dinner.

Any food can be served for breakfast as long as it is wholesome and nutritious. Breakfast should include

- some protein
- other energy source, such as carbohydrates
- vitamins B-complex and C
- minerals, especially calcium, iron, and phosphorus
- roughage
- appetizing foods

How much breakfast you should eat depends on how old you are and how active you are. An active, growing child needs to eat a much larger breakfast than does an older adult who leads a rather inactive life.

The American colonists brought special customs and recipes from the various countries from which they immigrated. They often had to make do with the foods that were available, however. In the early days, a typical colonial breakfast consisted of bread and milk or cider-flavored water. Later, the colonists' breakfast menu was expanded to include hasty pudding and baked apples or berries. After the Revolution, a wealthy colonist might breakfast on hot breads, cold meats or bacon and eggs, fried apples, and batter cake.

The twentieth century has given birth to the brunch. The word *brunch* is a combination of the words *breakfast* and *lunch*. Brunch is a hearty breakfast served anytime between 10:00 A.M. and 1:00 P.M. and can include desserts. A typical English brunch might be bacon, omelettes, veal croquettes, fish, toast, oat cakes, stewed apples, tea, coffee, and milk.

Breakfast menus have varied throughout history, and they vary from country to country. The following menus are typical in various parts of the world. Most of the countries with long menus serve breakfast buffet style; the diners don't eat every food, but rather choose from among them.

❦ AUSTRALIA

fresh or stewed fruits

dry cereal in summer, oatmeal porridge in winter

eggs in the shell

buttered toast

milk

grilled tomatoes

bacon

❦ BRAZIL

large crusty roll of white bread

warm milk flavored with coffee

wheel-shaped salty cheese

butter

❦ CHINA

rice gruel

eggs

fried fish

salted turnips

fermented bean curd

❦ CONTINENTAL (EUROPEAN) BREAKFAST

coffee, tea, or milk

a brioche, roll, or croissant

jam or preserves

❦ DENMARK

smörrebrod (open-faced sandwiches of roast pork, roast beef, sardines, or cheese)

pastries

coffee

❦ EGYPT

brown beans

eggs cooked in butter

soft white bread (1/4 loaf per child)

white cheese

marmalade

black olives

buffalo milk

❦ ISRAEL

bagels and rolls with butter or cream cheese

cooked cereal

radishes, turnips, and other vegetables

cheeses

yogurt

smoked fish and herring

fried, scrambled, or boiled eggs or omelette

assorted pastries

coffee, tea, or cocoa

❦ JAPAN

rice

miso (fermented soybean soup)

❦ NORWAY

porridge

rye or wheat bread

herring or fish

smoked meats

potatoes

bread

cheeses

coffee

❦ POLAND

rye bread

butter

kielbasa (Polish sausage)

hard-boiled eggs

paczki (sweet coffeecake made with prunes or poppyseeds and honey)

❦ SPAIN

churros (crisply fried fritters)

chocolate, coffee, or tea

ACTIVITIES FOR STUDENTS

Art and Visual Aids

1. Collect breakfast-food cartons, juice containers, wrappers, and other visual aids that can be used for planning a variety of nutritious breakfast combinations.
2. Make a breakfast tray and dishes from colored paper. Cut out pictures of foods for a good breakfast and paste them on the dishes.

Information Gathering and Sharing

3. Compile a list of a variety of foods that would represent a good breakfast.
4. Invite a resource person, such as a dietitian, cafeteria manager, or school nurse, to speak to the class about the need for and the types of nutritious breakfasts.
5. List all the nutrients (carbohydrates, proteins, minerals, and vitamins) contained in your breakfast. Record the calories. Research the activities that it would take to burn off those calories.
6. As a class, take a survey of what people usually eat for breakfast. The results can be charted on a graph, using categories of age, gender, occupation, and so on.
7. Look up and list breakfast habits of children of other lands.
8. List as many occupations as you can think of that are involved in producing and getting your breakfast to the table.

Critical Thinking

9. Keep a list of your breakfasts for one week. Analyze and discuss your list in terms of nutrition. Also identify those foods that are not recommended for wholesome eating.
10. Discuss the problem of world hunger and why people are starving in some parts of the world. Brainstorm what can be done to lessen world hunger and to lessen the problem of hunger, if it exists, in your community.

Writing and Language Arts

11. Write a "good breakfast" slogan.

12. Write a television or radio ad for a "good breakfast" campaign.
13. Write a breakfast jingle or poem, such as

    Jack be nimble, Jack be quick,
    Eat a good breakfast, and don't get sick!

14. As a class, discuss the advertising value of bumper stickers. Create breakfast bumper stickers. Bumper-sticker slogans need to be short and snappy—"Be a Breakfast Eater" or "Breakfast Gives You Energy," for example.
15. As a class, compile and publish a cookbook of breakfast menus and recipes. The cookbook could be organized according to the types of breakfast people eat in various regions of the country.

Cooking

16. As a class, plan and cook a brunch.
17. Concoct an original breakfast dish that could be offered in a restaurant. List the ingredients.
18. Plan and prepare a nutritious breakfast for your family. Solicit comments from your family members about the breakfast. The comments and menus may be displayed on a bulletin board.

QUESTIONS FOR CLASS DISCUSSION

1. What criteria do we use to judge a breakfast?
2. In what ways does a poor or a good breakfast affect you?
3. Why is breakfast important to your diet?
4. Name some cereal grains. Why are they good for us?
5. What are the basic food groups? Why do we need certain amounts of each group every day?
6. What does the expression "Eat breakfast like a king, lunch like a prince, and dinner like a pauper" mean?
7. Why has the traditional family breakfast become less important today?
8. What are some advantages and disadvantages of having coffee breaks on the job?

9. What factors determine the type of breakfast foods a particular nationality or ethnic
   group eats?
10. Why is there a trend today to eat breakfast
    out?

KEY VOCABULARY

appetite	grain
beverage	malnutrition
breakfast	manners
calorie	menu
carbohydrate	mineral
cereal	nourishment
cholesterol	nutrition
diet	portion
digest	proper
energy	protein
enriched	taste
fast (noun, verb)	utensil
food value	vitamin

RELATED CAREER EDUCATION TERMS

advertising manager	manufacturer
baker	market researcher
cafeteria manager	nutritionist
chef	produce developer
cook	purchasing agent
dairy farmer	quality controller
dietitian	restauranteur
farmer	truck farmer
grocer	waiter
hostess	waitress

Labor Day

THEMES AND THOUGHTS

Work, Reward, Ambition

All work is as seed sown; it grows and spreads, and sows itself anew.

—*Thomas Carlyle*

Life is work, and everything you do is so much more experience.

—*Henry Ford*

★★★ THE TRIBUNE ★★★

| NEW YORK | MONDAY, SEPTEMBER 3, 1894 | TWO CENTS |

PRESIDENT CLEVELAND PROCLAIMS LABOR DAY!

WASHINGTON, D.C.— President Grover Cleveland proclaimed the first national observance of Labor Day, henceforth the first Monday in September. In 1882 Peter J. McGuire, founder of the United Brotherhood of Carpenters, first suggested a day to honor workers. That year, on September 5, the Knights of Labor held the first "Labor Day" parade in New York City. The organization repeated the parade the next two years. In 1884 it adopted a resolution declaring the first Monday in September to be Labor Day.

The Knights of Labor campaign for national recognition of the holiday succeeded ten years later. On June 28 of this year, congress passed the bill to make Labor Day a holiday in the District of Columbia and for all federal workers in the states.

FASCINATING FACTS

In 1894, all the industrial nations, except the United States, Canada, and Italy, observed a labor holiday on May 1. Because the 1894 law applied only to the District of Columbia and federal workers in the states, each state had to enact its own Labor Day legislation. Eventually, all the states and territories put the law into operation, and Labor Day became truly a national holiday.

The word *labor* is derived from Latin and means "to be tired." Labor can be physical or mental toil. Today, the word *labor* usually means physical exertion for the purpose of supplying material wants.

ACTIVITIES FOR STUDENTS

Information Gathering and Sharing

1. As a class, list and discuss community helpers. Compile a directory by categories.
2. With your class, take a tour of the school building or the neighborhood, and then list

the kinds of workers you see and their activities.

3. As a class, take 15 minutes to list as many occupations as you can for each letter of the alphabet. Then discuss your list.

4. As a class, identify and classify types of production workers and service workers. Use the yellow pages in the telephone book and the classified ads in newspapers as resources.

5. Tell what kind of work the members of your family do.

6. Survey and report on the type of occupations held by members of your family. As a class, put all your results into categories and plot them on a graph.

7. List in chart form the kinds of work children can do to benefit others at home, at school, in the neighborhood, in the community, in the nation, and throughout the world.

8. Interview an adult about his or her occupation. Your interview may be taped or presented orally to the class. Or invite a worker to visit the classroom and talk about his or her occupation.

9. Research and prepare a written or oral report about one of the following topics:

   • how hours and conditions have changed for working people

   • the purpose and programs of a major labor union or the contributions of an important labor leader

   • the need to recognize how working people contribute to society

   • the history of working women

   • the types of workers that will be needed in the year 2025

Dramatics and Role-Playing

10. In a small group, role-play a family or work situation.

11. Bring in the classified ads from a local newspaper and select a job you would be interested in pursuing. Specify the reasons for your choice and describe the requirements for the position. Choose a partner and play the roles of the applicant and the personnel manager in an interview for the position.

Writing and Language Arts

12. Write and illustrate a story about workers. As a class, gather your stories into a book entitled "Community Helpers I Know."

13. Write a business letter. As a class, discuss the difference between business letters and other types of letters, such as friendly letters and thank-you notes.

14. Develop an application form. Your teacher can display samples of applications from businesses on a bulletin board.

Art and Visual Aids

15. Bring in pictures clipped from magazines and booklets for a class picture-file of workers. As a class, choose a picture editor to organize and mount the pictures to add to your classroom's collection of visual aids.

16. Make illustrations of the occupations held by the members of your family. A class collage could be made with all of the illustrations.

17. Make a diorama (using a shoebox) to depict a community helper at work. Cut out figures and foliage and other objects to make your diorama look realistic.

18. As a class, develop a filmstrip on school workers, such as custodians, secretaries, aides, and cafeteria workers. The narration for the filmstrip could be put on a cassette. The filmstrip could become part of the library media-center collection.

Special Projects

19. Have a career-day fair. This could be handled in two ways. Your class could invite resource people from various occupations to staff booths and give brief talks and hand out informative literature about their jobs. Or the class members could research occupations and become the "experts" and each design a booth and handouts. Other classes could be invited to visit the fair.

20. As a class, develop a list of classroom jobs, including the responsibilities and skills needed for each one. Each class member can then apply for one of the jobs by completing an application, indicating appropriate skills and interests. Fill the jobs on the basis of the applications.

QUESTIONS FOR CLASS DISCUSSION

1. Explain why we observe Labor Day by not working. What does your family do on Labor Day?
2. What are some good things that have happened to you after working hard? Explain.
3. How have conditions changed for workers since the colonial era? Since your grandparents' time?
4. What is a good worker? When are you considered to be a good worker? Why do we admire good workers?
5. What contributions have labor unions made to higher living standards in our country?
6. What are some laws regulating labor? Why do we need labor laws?
7. What types of work can children perform to help others?
8. Who are some famous people noted for their ability to work hard?
9. What kinds of workers are found in your community?
10. What does the expression "All work and no play makes Jack a dull boy" mean?
11. Why is it important to develop good schoolwork habits?
12. What is a skill?
13. What are some kinds of professional workers?

KEY VOCABULARY

adopted	local (noun)
AFL	management
apprentice	mediator
arbitration	negotiate
benefit	overtime
brotherhood	picket
career	ratify
CIO	resolution
congressional bill	salary
contract	skill
demonstrate	strike
dispute	teamster
federation	trade
hourly	union
industry	wage
journeyman	walkout
labor	worker

RELATED CAREER EDUCATION TERMS

artist	laborer
community worker	professional
craftsperson	service industry
Department of Labor	trade union leader
employment agency counselor	unemployment counselor
government worker	

National Grandparents' Day

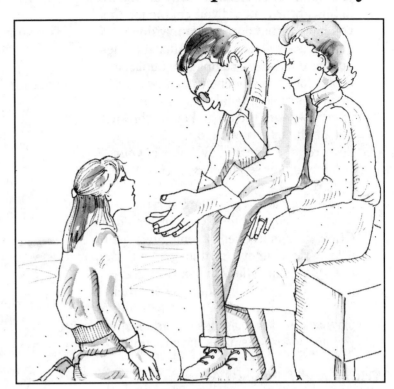

THEMES AND THOUGHTS

Honor, Love, Compassion, Respect, Appreciation

The people whom the sons and daughters find it hardest to understand are the fathers and mothers, but young people can get on very well with their grandfathers and grandmothers.
—*Simeon Strunsky*

Age is a matter of feeling, not of years.
—*G. W. Curtis*

When grandparents enter the door, discipline flies out the window.
—*Ogden Nash*

FASCINATING FACTS

Just as we set aside special days to honor our mothers and our fathers, we honor our grandparents also.

Nowadays, the prefix *grand* means a relative two generations older or younger. In speaking of them as "grandparents," we give our parents' parents a rank of special distinction, usually as a sign of respect for their age.

Today, some grandparents live with their families, and others choose to live in their own homes or in retirement villages. Wherever grandparents choose to live, they have a special place in their family and should be remembered often, especially on their own special day.

In the year 1900 the average life span in the United States was 47.3 years. A baby born in the United States in 1985, however, can expect to live 74.7 years. Life expectancy was estimated in 1985 at 78.2 years for girls and 71.2 years for boys. Now it is even greater. A larger percentage of people in the United States are living longer each year. Some of them join organiza-

tions like the American Association of Retired Persons to see that their interests are protected. Others join organizations that speak out for the causes of older people, such as the Gray Panthers.

In many cultures, the older members of a family or a community are highly respected and honored for their age-proven wisdom.

ACTIVITIES FOR STUDENTS

Information Gathering and Sharing

1. Create a family tree. Interview your parents, grandparents, and other relatives for information. See how far back you can trace your family tree. Older students may want to chart their family, using a line chart.
2. As a class, create a Family Interview Sheet.

Formulate questions to ask each person in your family. For example, Why do you live in this town? How did you get the job that you have? What does our family do together as special customs? After the questionnaire has been completed, duplicate copies for each student. Interview some members of your family and share the interviews with the class. You might want to tape the interviews, too.

3. Research the activities available in your community for senior citizens. List them on a chart.

4. Oral history is the recording of remembrances verbally rather than written down. Grandparents frequently remember seeing or experiencing events of long ago. Formulate specific questions to ask your grandparents or older neighbors. Record their impressions on a portable tape recorder for playback in class. Discuss the oral history you and your classmates have recorded.

Writing and Language Arts

5. Write an essay or a poem entitled "Those Special People—Grandparents." If you do not know your grandparents, write about "My Ideal Grandparents." These compositions can be shared orally with the class.

Art and Visual Aids

6. Make a "kinship" mobile showing your relationship to five relatives. Use a coat hanger for the base. Cut out figures from construction paper and decorate them with felt and fabric for clothing. Display all the mobiles in the classroom.

7. Design a coat of arms for your family. It should use symbols to show that members of your family were, for example, sailors, farmers, and teachers. You can construct the coat of arms from oak tag and colored construction paper. Explain the significance of your coat of arms. Display all the coats of arms in the classroom.

8. Make a "thumbprint family." Have each person living in your home make a thumbprint on a piece of paper. Ink their thumbs with a stamp pad. Make a stick figure person out of each thumbprint, adding hair, limbs, and articles of clothing. You might add background scenery and show your family doing an activity you enjoy together.

Special Project

9. As a class, plan a special grandparents' tea. You can bake cookies and make punch. Send out invitations to all your grandparents. Class members who do not have a grandparent in town can invite an older friend or neighbor as their "adopted" grandparent for the event.

QUESTIONS FOR CLASS DISCUSSION

1. Think about the statement "My son or daughter's children are twice my children." What does this statement mean?
2. How can we learn from the experiences of our parents and grandparents?
3. What does *retirement* mean? Do people stop working completely when they retire?
4. What activities and services should a retirement community include for those who live there?
5. What are ways to show honor and respect for our grandparents? Why is respect important?
6. Why are some grandparents lonely?
7. What are some of the common problems faced by grandparents and older people?
8. In what ways do grandparents prove they are "grand parents"?
9. It is said that grandparents tend to spoil their grandchildren. Why might this be so?
10. What can grandparents do to make their lives useful after they retire?

KEY VOCABULARY

age	derivation
ancestor	descent
background	elderly
birthright	endowment
custom	estate

KEY VOCABULARY CONTINUED

extraction
family
family tree
folks
friend
genealogy
generation
genes
geriatrics
grandparent
heir
heirloom
heritage
inherit
inheritance
kindred
kinfolk
kinship
legacy
line
lineage
maturity
offspring
parentage
pedigree
pension
relative
retire
senior citizen
sibling
Social Security
stock
will

RELATED CAREER EDUCATION TERMS

career counselor
consultant
crossing guard
genealogist
geriatrics
    specialist
investment
    counselor
library aide
museum guide
nursing home aide
retirement home
program
    coordinator
sales clerk
security guard
social worker
teacher aide
therapist
travel agent
volunteer
    coordinator

Henry Hudson Sailed Up the Hudson River

THEMES AND THOUGHTS

Duty, Courage, Loyalty, Exploration

I slept and dreamt that life was Beauty;
I woke, and found that life was Duty.

—*Ellen S. Hooper*

America was discovered accidentally by a great seaman who was looking for something else; when discovered it was not wanted; and most of the exploration for the next fifty years was done in the hope of getting through or around it. America was named after a man who discovered no part of the New World. History is like that, very chancy.

—*Samuel Eliot Morison*

FASCINATING FACTS

A British sea captain and adventurer, Henry Hudson, explored what came to be called the Hudson River while trying to find a passage to the Far East around North America. Hudson, like Captain John Smith, thought there might be a passage to China somewhere north of what is now known as the state of Virginia.

Hudson made four voyages seeking a short route to China by way of the Arctic Ocean. His voyage up the river from New York Harbor on the ship *Half Moon* took him 150 miles north to the vicinity of Albany. He thought that a narrow isthmus was the only land at 40 degrees north latitude to separate the Atlantic and Pacific Oceans.

After Hudson explored the Hudson Bay in Canada on the ship *Discovery* in 1610, some of his crew turned against him. He, his young son,

and seven others on board were dismissed from the ship and put adrift in a small boat, never to be heard from again.

Most of the important discoveries made on Hudson's voyages were accidents. His routes were often determined by ice fields that caused him to turn south toward ice-free waters.

ACTIVITIES FOR STUDENTS

Geography Research

1. Trace Hudson's course on a map or globe.
2. Make a list of places named for Henry Hudson.

Art and Visual Aids

3. Construct a model of Hudson's ship from paper. Write a description of the ship's dimensions and speed.

Word Game

4. What was Hudson trying to accomplish when he was exploring the waterways of North America? Find the mystery phrase by researching the Henry Hudson story and then answering the following questions. Place each answer vertically under the appropriate number. The mystery phrase will be found on the first row of blanks from left to right.

1. Hudson was seeking the Northwest _____.
2. Another name for a mutineer.
3. The goal of Hudson's voyage.
4. The large body of water that Hudson explored.
5. Hudson sailed for the Dutch East _____ Company.
6. The direction of Hudson's early polar sailings.
7. Hudson explored the coast of _____ in the ship *Hopewell*.
8. _____ became a major product of Hudson Bay.
9. Hudson sailed the North American coastline along the Atlantic _____.
10. Hudson sailed up the _____ to Albany.
11. Hudson Strait is located in _____ .
12. The name of the ship that Hudson used in 1609 (two words).
13. Hudson's explorations were held back by winter _____ .
14. Hudson entered _____ _____ Harbor in the fall of 1609 (two words).
15. Hudson encountered some Indians where the city of _____ would later appear.

1	2	3	4	5	6	7	8	9	10	11	12	13	14	15

__ __ __ __ __ __ __ __ __ __ __ __ __ __ __

__ __ __ __ __ __ __ __ __ __ __ __ __ __ __

__ __ __ __ __ __ __ __ __ __ __ __ __ __ __

__ __ __ __ __ __ __ __ __ __ __ __ __ __ __

__ __ __ __ __ __ __ __

__ __ __

__ __

1	2	3	4	5	6	7	8	9	10	11	12	13	14	15
P	**R**	**O**	**B**	**I**	**N**	**G**	**F**	**O**	**R**	**C**	**H**	**I**	**N**	**A**
a	e	r	a	n	o	r	u	c	i	a	a	c	e	l
s	b	i	y	d	r	e	r	e	v	n	l	e	w	b
s	e	e		i	t	e	s	a	e	a	f		Y	a
a	l	n		a	h	n		n	r	d	M		o	n
g		t			l					a	o		r	y
e					a						o		k	
					n						n			
					d									

QUESTIONS FOR CLASS DISCUSSION

1. What might cause sailors to mutiny at sea?
2. Henry Hudson failed in his efforts to find a northwest passage to the Far East. Why do we remember him?
3. Are there professional explorers and adventurers who perform dangerous missions today? Can you identify them?
4. Why were mapmakers considered to be the most valuable crew members on board Hudson's ship?
5. It is not unusual to discover something by accident. Can you name other discoveries that came as a surprise?
6. How is Henry Hudson known and remembered today?
7. Hudson, an Englishman, explored for the Dutch. Why do some people lend their talents and skills in service to another country? Is it a duty to serve only your native country?
8. Why was Henry Hudson not appreciated by his crew?

KEY VOCABULARY

adventurer	pass
bow	passage
cartographer	port
chart	rigging
compass	river
discover	sail
explore	sextant
helm	starboard
isthmus	stern
log	strait
mate	telescope
mutiny	voyage

RELATED CAREER EDUCATION TERMS

cartographer	merchant marine
Coast Guard	navigator
explorer	sailor
longshoreman	

Francis Scott Key Wrote "The Star-Spangled Banner"

THEMES AND THOUGHTS

Pride, Creativity, Patriotism

A thoughtful mind, when it sees a nation's flag, sees not the flag only, but the Nation itself; and whatever may be its symbols, its insignia, reads chiefly in the flag the Government, the principles, the truths, the history which belongs to the Nation that sets it forth.
—*Henry Ward Beecher*

When Freedom from her mountain height,
Unfurled her standard to the air,
She tore the azure robe of night,
And set the stars of glory there.
—*Joseph Rodman Drake*

Yet, Freedom! yet thy banner, torn, but flying,
Streams like the thunderstorm against the wind.
—*Lord Byron*

FASCINATING FACTS

Francis Scott Key (1779–1843) was a Washington attorney who once wanted to be a clergyman. He wrote amateur verse, which was mostly religious. Key wrote the national anthem during the War of 1812 (which actually lasted until 1815) while he was interceding with the British for the release of a friend, William Beanes. He wrote his poem from a prisoner exchange ship in the Baltimore harbor after witnessing the bombardment of Fort McHenry. The flag that flew over Fort McHenry can be seen in the National Museum in Washington, D.C. The tune of the anthem is that of an English song, "To Anacreon in Heaven." "The Star-Spangled Banner" became the U.S. national anthem in 1931.

The word *spangled* means "to adorn with gleaming spots." A spangle is a clasp or glittering ornament.

ACTIVITIES FOR STUDENTS

Music

1. Learn "The Star-Spangled Banner" as a poem and as a song.
2. With your class, sing patriotic songs.
3. Write a "school anthem" or a patriotic song parody, using the melody of a popular tune. Try singing your song for the class.

Critical Thinking

4. With your class, discuss the meaning of

"The Star-Spangled Banner" today.

5. Discuss or write an essay about how Francis Scott Key might be honored today.

6. Select another patriotic song that might be suitable as our nation's anthem and defend your choice.

Dramatics and Role-Playing

7. Role-play the writing of "The Star-Spangled Banner."

Writing and Language Arts

8. Write a poem or song about our nation's flag.

9. Write an essay entitled "What the Flag Means to Me."

10. Write a composition entitled "I Was There," assuming the role of Francis Scott Key.

Information Gathering and Sharing

11. With your class, write a letter requesting information about Fort McHenry (Fort McHenry, National Park Service, Department of Interior, Washington, D.C. 20242). Display the information you learn on a bulletin board.

Art and Visual Aids

12. With your class, design and make a chalk mural of the scene that inspired Francis Scott Key to write his poem.

QUESTIONS FOR CLASS DISCUSSION

1. Why do you think "The Star-Spangled Banner" was selected as our nation's anthem? Do you think this was a wise selection? Explain.

2. Why do we need a national anthem?

3. Why do we usually play our national anthem at important occasions and public events? Why do we stand when it is played?

4. What special feelings do you have when you hear the national anthem being sung or played?

5. What kinds of feelings do you think inspired Francis Scott Key to write a poem after witnessing a battle?

6. How does the saying "The pen is mightier than the sword" apply to the story of "The Star-Spangled Banner"?

KEY VOCABULARY

allegiance	pledge
amateur	respect
attention	salute
banner	signal
colors	spangle
creative	SOS
display	staff
national anthem	symbol
patriotism	

RELATED CAREER EDUCATION TERMS

attorney	poet
cleric	reporter
flag designer	soldier
flagmaker	writer
musician	

First Day of Autumn

THEMES AND THOUGHTS

Beauty, Nature

The melancholy days are come,
the saddest of the year,
  Of wailing winds, and naked
woods,
  and meadows brown and sere.
    —*William C. Bryant*

Autumn is a second spring when
every life is a flower.
    —*Camus*

Take care of the minutes, and
the hours will take care of themselves.
    —*Lord Chesterfield*

Days decrease,
And autumn grows, autumn in
everything.
    —*Robert Browning*

FASCINATING FACTS

Although calendars show September 21 as the first day of autumn, the autumnal equinox is actually September 22 or 23. On this day, the sun's rays are directly over the earth at the equator.

Many people throughout the world celebrate the coming of the new year in autumn. It is then that they mark the expiration of summer vegetation (the old year) and the arrival of the new year. The new year is indicated by the completion of the harvest and by the leaves turning brilliant colors.

In Japan, the autumnal equinox is celebrated on September 23 with a religious service honoring departed ancestors. The Vietnamese and the Chinese celebrate in mid-autumn with foods, displays, legends, and customs about the moon.

ACTIVITIES FOR STUDENTS

Information Gathering and Sharing

1. As a class, go on a nature walk. Observe, record, and collect symbols of fall.
2. Study the constellations of the autumn sky. Identify these constellations and make drawings of them with white chalk on blue or black paper.
3. On the day of the autumnal equinox, determine the times of sunset and sunrise by consulting a newspaper or almanac. Compare the length of daylight and darkness hours to those at other times of the year. Several times during the year, measure and record the length and direction of the shadow of the flagpole (or any fixed pole) at the same time between noon and 1 P.M. Compare the length of the shadows

throughout the year. The length of the shadow is determined by the position of the sun on the horizon.

4. Make a study of the activities of people and animals during autumn.
5. List the ways life changes for most people when fall arrives.
6. Make a collection of common fall insects.
7. Present an oral report on what is meant by the term *harvest moon*.
8. Find out how an analemma works on a globe. Demonstrate its use to the class.

Gardening

9. Uproot and dry weeds and collect their seeds. Save them for a spring seed-growing project. Be sure to avoid poisonous plants.

Art and Visual Aids

10. Use a filmstrip projector or a flashlight and globe to demonstrate the seasonal changes of the position of the direct rays of the sun on the earth. Explain how these changes affect temperature and the length of daylight on various parts of the globe.
11. Make a picture of a fall scene showing things that you can hear, taste, feel, and smell. Set up a large display of all the pictures.
12. Make leaf spatter pictures with poster paint, small screens, brushes, and fall vegetation. Compile your pictures into a booklet and caption them with fall words and phrases.
13. Construct a shoebox diorama of a typical fall view, using construction paper, paste, poster paint, fall foliage, and odds and ends of materials.
14. As a class, hold a fall "garden club" exhibit. Create arrangements of fall flowers or floral decorations, using colored crepe or tissue paper.
15. Construct a globe out of papier-mâché over a balloon or ball. Paint it blue. Cut out outline maps of the continents and paste them on the globe. You might hang your globe from the ceiling as a mobile.
16. Draw a chart showing the earth's seasonal rotation and revolution around the moon.
17. Make a picture chart of the four seasons, showing changes in activities, sports, food, and clothing.
18. Collect leaves and paste them on a leaf identification chart.
19. Make a picture chart of late-blooming or fall flowers, such as chrysanthemums.

Writing and Language Arts

20. Compose an acrostic, using key words related to fall. For example:

    F—rost

    A—utumn

    L—eaves

    L—atitude

21. Write a four-line poem with a safety or health theme about aspects of the fall season, such as shorter days, fall weather, wet leaves, early frost, or fall clothing.
22. Make a picture glossary of fall vocabulary.

QUESTIONS FOR CLASS DISCUSSION

1. What health and safety precautions should people take during the fall?
2. Why have towns passed ordinances against the burning of leaves?
3. Why is fall considered to be the most desirable time of year to plant or sow seeds for a lawn?
4. What connection does the latitude of an area have to do with the length of the growing season?
5. What effect does the arrival of autumn have upon the habits and natural changes of the animal kingdom?
6. What decorations and colors are associated with autumn?
7. Why are the number of daylight and darkness hours fairly even during the fall?
8. When does autumn begin in the Southern Hemisphere? Explain why this is so.
9. Explain what each of the following terms has to do with fall: *Indian summer, harvest moon, autumn leaves.*
10. Why is a cornucopia an important symbol of autumn? Can you identify other appropriate signs of autumn?
11. How do the changes in the seasons affect

the kinds of clothing we wear, the sports we play, the foods we eat, and other habits and customs?

KEY VOCABULARY

adaptation
analemma
autumnal
axis
calendar
circle
clock
coloration
daylight
degree
earth
equator
equinox
frigid
fall
foliage
frost
globe
Greenwich Meridian
growing season
harvest
hemisphere
hibernation
inclination
international
    date line

latitude
longitude
meridian
migration
north
orbit
parallel
prime meridian
rays
resolve
rotate
season
solstice
south
spring
summer
temperature
tropic
Tropic of
    Cancer
Tropic of
    Capricorn
vernal
winter
zone

RELATED CAREER EDUCATION TERMS

agriculturist
anthropologist
astronomer
botanist
environmentalist
farmer
forest ranger
greenhouse or
    nursery worker

landscape
    contractor
meteorologist
naturalist
scientist
travel agent
weather forecaster

American Indian Day

THEMES AND THOUGHTS

Indebtedness, Nature, Understanding, Fairness, Tolerance

My people are few. They resemble the scattering trees of a storm-swept plain. . . . There was a time when our people covered the land as the waves of a wind-ruffled sea cover its shell-paved floor, but that time long since passed away with the greatness of tribes that are now but a mournful memory.

—*Seattle, chief of Puget Sound tribes (on surrendering tribal lands to governor of Washington Territory, 1855)*

Here lived and loved another race of beings. Beneath the same sun that rolls over your heads the Indian hunter pursued the panting deer.

—*Charles Sprague*

These lands are ours. No one has a right to remove us, because we were the first owners. The Great Spirit above has appointed this place for us, on which to light our fires, and here we will remain. As to boundaries, the Great Spirit knows no boundaries, nor will his red children acknowledge any.

—*Tecumseh (to President James Madison)*

A people without history is like the wind on the buffalo grass.

—*Sioux saying*

FASCINATING FACTS

The American Indians probably came to America from Asia by way of the Bering Strait 20,000–40,000 years ago. The name *Indian* was given to the first people in America by the first Europeans who came to the New World. Columbus called the natives *Indios* (Spanish for "Indians") because he thought he had reached the Indies, which was then the term for what is today China, Japan, India, and the East Indies. The Indians, however, referred to themselves only by the name of their particular tribe. They had no overall term that was the equivalent of the word *Indian*. Today, some American Indians prefer to call themselves Native Americans.

Most Native Americans in the United States were not legally recognized as citizens until 1924. There are about 1,500,000 Native Americans in the United States today, about half of whom still live on reservations. There are about 300,000 in Canada and about 20 million in Latin America.

Most of the Native Americans portrayed in early movies were horse-riding Plains Indians with feather headdresses and tepees, but there are hundreds of different tribes and "nations" throughout the Americas with different customs, languages, and histories.

One of the most important Native American contributions to the European settlers was different foods, such as corn, sweet potatoes, peppers, pineapples, tomatoes, vanilla, squash, and peanuts. Native Americans also invented the hammock, grew tobacco, and made chocolate and maple sugar. Many common words—such as *skunk, canoe,* and *toboggan*—are of Native American origin, and over half of the states in the United States have Native American names.

The Native Americans had explored and knew the whereabouts of most of the minerals, resources, and riches of the New World well before European explorers and scouts ventured out in quest of them. This knowledge made Native American guides especially important to the explorers.

ACTIVITIES FOR STUDENTS

Arts and Crafts

1. Study the steps in preparing wool for weaving. Construct a simple loom and weave a square with a simple Native American design.
2. Study the steps in making pottery. If possible, arrange a visit to a local pottery factory. Make a piece of clay pottery with Native American designs.
3. Construct a three-dimensional tepee, pueblo, hogan, or other American Indian dwelling from brown wrapping paper for a table display of books and literature dealing with Native Americans.
4. Demonstrate the way Native Americans used berries for color.
5. As a class, construct Native American instruments, such as drums and rattles, out of round boxes and gourds. Learn to play the instruments. Create Native American songs and dances. Make items to accompany these dances, such as prayer sticks and masks.
6. Native Americans used picture writing to record their legends and family and tribal

history. Some symbols had the same meaning from tribe to tribe, but each tribe also had its own symbols. The symbols were derived from the kind of life the tribe led, as well as its location. Native Americans carved their stories in rocks, totem poles, and bark and drew on skins. Some tribes also painted themselves and their horses before going into battle in order to frighten their enemies or to ensure their victory. When painting on skins, they painted from left to right or in a spiral, starting at the top and ending in the center. "Write" a short letter or a story, using picture writing. For example, a story might begin with symbols for the following words: *mother, saw, fire, in the hills*. Paint or draw your story on brown paper cut out to represent an animal skin.

7. Make a mosaic from dried corn and other dried seeds.
8. Construct a totem pole with spools and boxes. Paint it with tempera.
9. Make a Native American doll, such as a kachina doll, by decorating a base of cardboard with burlap, paper, paint, feathers, and beads. Dolls can also be made out of corn husks. Some Native American tribes did not put faces on their dolls. They believed that if they did, the dolls would come alive!
10. Sand painting was used in some North American Indian ceremonies. These tribes believed the paintings had magical powers and would chase evil spirits away. Often the sand painting was destroyed after the ceremony. Make a sand painting. This can be done in one of three ways:
    a. Draw a design with crayons on sandpaper.
    b. Draw a design with pencil on cardboard, go over the design with glue, and sprinkle colored aquarium sand over it.
    c. Make "colored sand" by shaking white cornmeal with food coloring. After drawing a design on cardboard and spreading glue on the design, sprinkle the sand over the glue.
11. Make Native American jewelry in one of three ways:

a. Use different shapes of macaroni that have each been colored with a different shade of food coloring. String the macaroni on yarn, heavy thread, or string. If you use heavy thread, tie the thread around the first bead. This keeps the other beads from slipping off the end.

b. Soak some corn kernels overnight in water to make them soft. You can add food coloring to the water if you wish. With a needle, string the corn on a heavy thread. You can also use dried pumpkin seeds to make a necklace.

c. Salt clay can make pretty necklaces and bracelets. Shape beads from the clay, making a hole in each one with a toothpick. After the beads dry, paint them with tempera paint and add designs. String the dried and painted beads on a heavy string. A drop of glue in the hole of each bead will hold the beads in place.

Salt Clay Recipe

Mix 1 cup of flour and 1 cup of salt. Add cool water and mix. Add only as much water as needed to roll the mixture into a ball without being too sticky. If it gets too sticky, add a little more flour. Store the clay in a plastic bag.

12. Some tribes used knotted cords or thongs to make belts and accessories for their clothing. Learn how to tie knots and make macramé designs.

13. Many Native American tribes wore masks for their ceremonies. Masks were a significant part of their customs. Research and report orally on Native American masks. Construct a mask from a paper bag, a paper plate, or papier-mâché.

14. Native American money was usually made of the white parts of shells or dark purple beads. The dark purple beads were considered to be more valuable than the white shells. Sometimes the beads were used to make belts. A belt was often given as a gesture of friendship. Dye some macaroni purple, using food coloring. On heavy string or yarn, string some undyed macaroni with the purple pieces in a design to make a belt.

15. Make a Native American wall hanging, using cloth, construction paper, or a large piece of cardboard as the backing.

16. Select a Native American name for yourself and write it, using symbols. You can write your Native American name on a headband or on a tunic made of paper or cloth.

Writing and Language Arts

17. Correspond with students in a Native American school by writing to the Education Branch, Bureau of Indian Affairs, Haskell Institute, Lawrence, Kansas 66044.

18. Write a legend, story, or poem in the style of a Native American tribe.

19. Make a glossary of Native American vocabulary. List words that we have adopted into the English language, such as *hickory, moose, raccoon,* and *squash.*

Information Gathering and Sharing

20. On a large outline map, locate the six main Native American groups in the United States. Divide the class into six tribes. Each "tribe" will gather and present information about itself to the class.

21. Divide your class into three groups to represent the Native Americans of the plains, the woodlands, and the desert. Each group researches and constructs a model village for its region. Pipe cleaner figures and a backdrop made out of a painted cardboard carton could be added.

22. Do a report on an outstanding Native American. Some famous North American Indians are

Black Hawk	Pocahontas	Sitting Bull
Joseph Brant	Pontiac	Squanto
Geronimo	Powhatan	Tecumseh
Philip King	Sacagawea	Jim Thorpe
Massasoit	Samoset	Uncas
Osceola	Sequoya	

23. Collect and display plants or pictures of plants that Native Americans used for food.

24. Compile a list of cities, states, and places that have Native American names.

Dramatics and Role-Playing

25. Dramatize a phase of Native American life, such as a powwow, hunting, or trading.

Special Projects

26. As a class, select a Native American holiday to celebrate. Design costumes from brown wrapping paper or large bags, learn Native American songs and dances, display Native American artifacts. Invite your parents and friends.
27. Have a Native American Fair to culminate your class' study. Invite other classes, parents, and friends. Set up displays of crafts and have the students in your class serve as guides. You might also make some Native American foods, such as corn-meal, to serve your guests. You can demonstrate a dance, games, or sand painting. You can also make a display of gifts Native Americans have given to the rest of us. These gifts include the following:

avocado	kayak	pumpkin
bean	maple sugar	quinine
cashew nut	moccasin	squash
chili pepper	parka	tapioca
cocoa	peanut	toboggan
corn (maize)	pineapple	tomato
gourd	pipe	wild rice
guinea pig	potato	

QUESTIONS FOR CLASS DISCUSSION

1. What are some things for which we are indebted to the Native Americans?
2. Name a number of foods Native Americans made from corn. What other things are produced from corn today?
3. Each Native American tribe has its own distinctive forms of arts and crafts. Can you provide some examples?
4. What wrong ideas have been conveyed about Native Americans by books, movies, and television? Why do you think these misconceptions appeared?
5. What well-known geographical names in the United States originated from Native American languages?
6. Give examples of religious beliefs of various tribes of Native Americans.

KEY VOCABULARY

adobe	medicine man
arrowhead	moccasin
ancestor	native
calumet	nomad
canoe	ornament
ceremony	papoose
chief	peace pipe
clan	pottery
concho belt	reservation
council meeting	scalp lock
custom	signal
dance	squaw
dugout	stockade
harpoon	tepee
headdress	totem pole
hogan	tribe
jewelry	weapon
long house	wigwam
maize	

RELATED CAREER EDUCATION TERMS

museum curator	cultural educator
language instructor	history professor

Balboa Sighted the Pacific Ocean

THEMES AND THOUGHTS

Opportunity, Discovery, Exploration

He star'd at the Pacific—and all his men
Look'd at each other with a wild surmise—
Silent, upon a peak in Darien.
—*John Keats*

. . . Come my friends,
'Tis not too late to seek a newer world.
Push off, and sitting well in order smite
The sounding furrows; for my purpose holds
To sail beyond the sunset, and the baths
Of all the western stars, until I die.
—*Alfred Lord Tennyson*

FASCINATING FACTS

Vasco Núñez de Balboa was born in Spain around 1475. At age 17, he wanted to go to the New World for gold, but his father would not give him permission. Balboa was being trained to become the head of the family, so his father did not want him leaving home. However, eight years later, in 1500, he joined Rodrigo de Bastida's expedition to the Caribbean as a swordsman. They sailed to the coast of what is now Colombia and then to the island of Hispaniola, which is now divided into the countries of Haiti and the Dominican Republic.

Balboa settled on the island as a farmer, but was neither happy nor very successful. To escape his creditors, he hid in a large cask and was carried on board a ship heading for South America. The colony in South America was not very successful either, so Balboa organized the colonists to resettle further west where the natives were less hostile.

An enemy of Balboa's had brought some serious charges against him in Spain. To redeem himself and to avoid returning to Spain to face these charges, Balboa decided to organize a special expedition. On September 1, 1513, he set sail with 190 Spaniards and 800 Indians, and on September 29 reached the narrowest part of the Isthmus of Panama. He and his band then crossed the isthmus on foot. He is credited with being the first Spaniard to sight the Pacific Ocean, which he called the South Sea.

Although Balboa is credited for first sighting the Pacific Ocean, it was named by Ferdinand Magellan seven years later. It is thought that Magellan chose the name *Pacific* because he was impressed with the ocean's peaceful, calm appearance. *Pacífico* is the word for "peaceful" in Portuguese and Spanish.

Balboa's superior, a man named Pedrarias, disliked Balboa and presented false charges of treason against him in 1519. After a hasty trial, Balboa was convicted and beheaded. A sad ending for the discoverer of the peaceful Pacific Ocean!

ACTIVITIES FOR STUDENTS

Art and Visual Aids

1. Using a wall map, chart Balboa's voyage.
2. With your class, make a mural of Balboa and his men sighting the Pacific Ocean for the first time.

Writing and Language Arts

3. Write a diary entry that might have been written by a member of Balboa's crew, Balboa himself, or a family member awaiting the ship's return.
4. Construct a replica of a ship's log, like one Balboa may have kept on one of his expeditions.
5. Write a story of life in Balboa's settlement in Colombia.

Information Gathering and Sharing

6. Research and compile a chart that compares ocean travel today with ocean travel in Balboa's day. Here's the beginning for your chart.

BALBOA	TODAY
• The food supply could not be refrigerated. Often, they would run out of food. • The men sailed by the stars.	

7. Make a list of unusual facts or a "Did You Know?" booklet about the Pacific Ocean.
8. Research the way the Incas lived during

Balboa's time. Construct a model of an Incan village.

Dramatics and Role-Playing

9. Role-play Balboa sighting the Pacific Ocean.
10. Compose a dialogue between Balboa and his friends regarding the charges of treason against him.
11. With some of your classmates, reenact Balboa's trial for treason.

QUESTIONS FOR CLASS DISCUSSION

1. About how long did it take Balboa to cross the Isthmus and find the "South Sea"? How long do you think the trip would take today? Why is there a difference in the time?
2. How did the Pacific Ocean get its name? Do you think that it was well chosen? Why? What might be a better name?
3. Why could you say that Balboa was a courageous man? Can you show ways that he was not courageous? Give examples.
4. The Pacific Ocean touches five U.S. states and one province of Canada. What major U.S. and Canadian cities are located on the Pacific Ocean?
5. In what ways is the Pacific Ocean similar to and in what ways is it different from the Atlantic Ocean?
6. What new kinds of land features are being formed, but are yet to be discovered in the Pacific Ocean region today?
7. Where are the new frontiers of discovery or exploration in the world today?

KEY VOCABULARY

adventurer	continental shelf
alliance	
Caribbean	coral
coastline	current
colonist	deep
conquistador	discover

equator	opportunity
expedition	Pacific Ocean
explorer	Panama
gulf	parallel
hurricane	peaceful
isthmus	reef
jungle	route
massacre	sea
New World	sextant

cartographer	meteorologist
Coast Guard	navigator
engineer	oceanographer
explorer	pilot
farmer	sailor
geologist	ship builder
land developer	

Johnny Appleseed Day

THEMES AND THOUGHTS

Generosity, Conservation,
Kindness, Charitableness

We plant upon the sunny lea,
A shadow for the noontime hour,
A shelter from the summer
shower
When we plant the apple tree.
—*William Cullen Bryant*

Kindness is the sunshine in
which virtue grows.
—*R. G. Ingersoll*

Remember Johnny Appleseed,
All ye who love the apple;
He served his kind by word and
deed,
In God's grand greenwood
chapel.
—*William Henry Venable*

FASCINATING FACTS

Johnny Appleseed was born John Chapman in Leominster, Massachusetts, on September 26, 1775. He has become an American folk hero, and many tales and legends are told about his wanderings among the early settlers, distributing and planting apple seeds from the Allegheny region in Pennsylvania to central Ohio. He is the "patron saint" of U.S. orcharding, floriculture, and conservation.

Johnny is often depicted as a tall, bearded, kindly looking man who wore castoff clothing, no shoes, and a tin pan for a hat. He was, according to the many legends about him, a lover of animals and a friend to both Indians and settlers. The Indians called him the "great medicine man" because he scattered seeds of healing herbs. Besides apple seeds, he planted plants of the mint family—pennyroyal, catnip, and horehound.

Johnny supposedly would not accept money for his gift of seeds, and if anyone paid him, he gave the money to the poor or bought religious books, or bought food for animals. He is credited with giving deerskin bags of seeds to families traveling westward.

Johnny Appleseed, after traveling for over 40 years planting orchards across the United States, died near Fort Wayne, Indiana, where a city park and other monuments honor his unmarked grave.

ACTIVITIES FOR STUDENTS

Information Gathering and Sharing

1. As a class, go to the library and research the history of apples and their appearance in the United States.
2. Ask the librarian to make a reading list

about Johnny Appleseed for your class. Read some of these books and report what you learn about Johnny Appleseed to the class.

3. With a small group, describe to the rest of the class various ways of eating and preparing apples. If possible, bring samples.

4. Collect stories and folktales featuring apples in the plot, such as the stories of William Tell and Snow White.

Writing and Language Arts

5. After learning as much as you can about Johnny Appleseed, write a jingle about him and his apple growing activities.

6. As a class, compile a book of apple recipes. Give it a catchy title. The book could be in the shape of an apple.

7. As a class, write letters to nearby apple orchards, asking for a speaker to tell you about apple growing, varieties of apples, and so on.

Field Trips

8. Research and list as many different varieties of apples as possible. Take a class trip to a local market or grocery store and identify the apples sold there. (Apple tasting might be fun, too.) As a follow-up activity, compile a list of words describing the various apples, including appearance and taste. Print these words on an apple chart.

9. As a class, compile a list of apple orchards within a 100-mile radius of your town. Take a family trip or a class field trip to one of the orchards in the autumn.

Art and Visual Aids

10. Illustrate the story of the apple from blossom to grocery store. The drawings can be done on a large roll of paper or on separate sheets. Indicate the numerical order of the pictures by adding an apple cutout, with a number in it, to each drawing.

QUESTIONS FOR CLASS DISCUSSION

1. The Indiana Horticultural Society erected a monument in Fort Wayne with the inscription "He lived for others." Why do you think this inscription was chosen to describe Johnny Appleseed?

2. Why do some people want to believe that all aspects of a legend or tale are true?

3. Why would a man like Johnny Appleseed not be too concerned about his clothing or appearance?

4. What do you think Johnny Appleseed could have learned from the Indians? What could the Indians have learned from him?

5. Johnny Appleseed would not accept money for his gifts of seeds. What kind of rewards did he receive?

6. What kind of burial site would be most fitting for the remembrance of Johnny Appleseed?

7. Why do you think Johnny Appleseed gave away many bags of seeds to families traveling westward?

8. Why do you think Johnny Appleseed always stayed close to nature in his wanderings?

9. Most frontiersmen carried guns with them. Can you explain why Johnny Appleseed did not?

KEY VOCABULARY

adventurer	horticulture
agriculture	humane
courage	itinerant
covered wagon	land seeker
deerskin	legend
eccentric	nursery
endurance	nurseryman
floriculture	orchard
folk hero	seedling
folklore	tale
frontiersman	tradition
generosity	woodsman

RELATED CAREER EDUCATION TERMS

agronomist

botanist

conservationist

county agent

farmer

fruit farmer

horticulturist

landscaper

nursery planter

zoologist

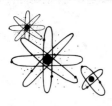

October

First Week:

Child Health Day (1st Monday)
* National Employ-the-Handicapped Week

1
First "Model T" Ford introduced, 1908
Agricultural Fair Day

2
Mohandas K. Gandhi, Indian pacifist, born, 1869
Wild and Scenic Rivers Act passed, 1968

3
Thurgood Marshall became the first black Supreme Court Justice, 1967
William Crawford Gorgas, who developed the cure for yellow fever, born, 1854

4
President Rutherford B. Hayes born, 1822
Sputnik (first satellite to orbit earth) launched, 1957

5
Universal Children's Day
President Chester A. Arthur born, 1830
President Harry S. Truman made first presidential address telecast from the White House, 1947

6
George Westinghouse, inventor and manufacturer, born, 1846
Thomas A. Edison, in West Orange, NJ, showed the first movie, 1889

7
James Whitcomb Riley, poet, born 1849

*A teaching unit is included on the following pages for each starred entry.

Second Week:

* Fire Prevention Week (week including October 8)
* National Newspaper Week
National Metric Week (week including October 10)

8 Great Chicago Fire began, 1871

9 Fingerprint Society founded, 1915
Leif Ericson Day

10 Metric Day
U.S. Naval Academy opened at Annapolis, 1845

11 General Casimir Pulaski Memorial Day
Eleanor Roosevelt born, 1884

12 * Columbus sighted America, 1492
Elmer A. Sperry, inventor of gyrocompass, born, 1860

13 White House cornerstone laid, 1792
Birthday of the U.S. Navy, 1775

14 President Dwight D. Eisenhower born, 1890
William Penn, founder of Pennsylvania colony, born, 1644
Chuck Yeager, flying the rocket-powered Bell X-1 airplane, was first human to break the sound barrier, 1947

15 World Poetry Day

Third Week:

National Forest Products Week (begins on 3rd Sunday)

16
Dictionary Day—Noah Webster, who wrote first American dictionary, born, 1758
National Bosses' Day

17
Bessemer steel process patented, 1855
Surrender of General Burgoyne at Saratoga, 1777
Black Poetry Day

18
Mason-Dixon Line completed, 1767

19
British surrendered at Yorktown, 1781
President John Adams born, 1735
Thomas A. Edison's first successful demonstration of electric light, 1879

20
John Dewey, educator, born, 1859

21
USS *Constitution,* or "Old Ironsides," launched, 1797
Magellan entered strait that bears his name, 1520

22
Sam Houston inaugurated as first president of the Republic of Texas, 1836

23
Swallows depart from San Juan Capistrano Mission

Every Day's a Holiday

Fourth Week:

National Cleaner Air Week (last full week of October)
National Red Ribbon Week, sponsored by National Federation of Parents for Drug-Free Youth

24

* United Nations Day

25

George Washington Bridge, between New York and New Jersey, opened, 1931

26

Erie Canal opened, 1825

27

Navy Day (observed since 1922)
* President Theodore Roosevelt born, 1858

28

* Statue of Liberty dedicated, 1886

29

Stock market crash, 1929
National Organization for Women (NOW) established, 1966

30

Mischief Night

31

* Halloween
Juliette Gordon Low, founder of the Girl Scouts, born, 1860
National Magic Day—Harry Houdini died, 1926
UNICEF Day—to aid UN International Children's Fund

National Employ-the-Handicapped Week

THEMES AND THOUGHTS

Perseverance, Compassion, Empathy, Fairness

Our dignity is not in what we do, but what we understand.
—*George Santayana*

And though hard be the task, keep a stiff upper lip.
—*Phoebe Cary*

Let me win. But if I cannot win, let me be brave in the attempt.
—*The Special Olympics Oath*

It is only with the heart that one can see rightly; what is essential is invisible to the eye.
—*Antoine de Saint-Exupéry*

FASCINATING FACTS

Imagine yourself blindfolded. Could you get through an entire day without someone's help? Suppose you had to go through a day without being able to hear a thing. Would this change how your day would go?

Handicapped people must deal with such conditions every day. A handicapped person is one who has a physical or mental disability. There are about 30 million people in the United States who are disabled, but most of them lead fulfilling, useful lives.

Handicapped people have not always been helped by society (some "physically challenged" or "differently abled" have many needs that are still unmet). In ancient times, it was believed that the safety of the tribe depended on the ability of each member to fight and work. People with problems were often considered a danger and driven away. During the Middle Ages, such people were ridiculed and looked upon with suspicion. Attitudes toward the handicapped began to change during the 1800s.

During World War I, doctors and others began to make artificial body parts, especially limbs. The art of replacing body parts with artificial substitutes is called *prosthetics*.

Many well-known people have had handicaps. They were able, with drive and determination, to overcome their handicaps and thus make important contributions to their communities and their nations. Although she became blind and deaf before the age of 2, Helen Keller learned to read, write, and speak. She eventually became a celebrated author and lecturer. Franklin Delano Roosevelt was crippled by polio, but he went on to become president of the United States. At the age of 8, Glenn Cunningham's legs were scarred to the bone in a fire, yet he became a track star. In the 1930s, he was known as the "world's fastest human." Beethoven composed his best-known classical music after he became deaf. Stephen Hawking, a brilliant astrophysicist, must use a wheelchair because of Lou Gehrig's disease. The list goes on and on. Handicapped people can learn how to use their abilities to overcome their disabilities.

At the 1987 International Summer Special Olympics Games in South Bend, Indiana, over 4,500 athletes from 72 countries competed in over 100 sports events. All the athletes were mentally retarded. The Special Olympics is an annual event.

Today many handicapped people hold responsible jobs. In fact, such people often have excellent attendance records. It is important that employers give worthwhile jobs to the handicapped.

ACTIVITIES FOR STUDENTS

Information Gathering and Sharing

1. Use reference books in the library to find information that will help students complete the following roster of people who have lived with handicaps. Add other names as well (see page 185 for additional names).
2. Invite a handicapped person to come speak to the class about special problems, programs, mechanical aids, and so on.
3. Invite the school nurse to demonstrate an audiometer to your class and to discuss hearing losses. Ask the nurse to explain how the audiometer works, since most students probably have been tested with it periodically.
4. Divide your class into two groups. As a way to "tune in" to hearing loss, ask half to watch a TV program without turning up the sound and then write a summary of what they were able to comprehend from just watching the program. The other half can watch and listen to the program. In class the next day, develop comparisons between the two groups.
5. Do some research about Louis Braille and his contributions to the blind.
6. Do some research about the training of seeing-eye dogs.
7. Research handicaps that have been conquered or are being successfully treated today.

Dramatics and Role-Playing

8. To help understand the special problems of the handicapped, take turns completing each of the following activities with a partner:

   a. Blindfold one partner and try to navigate around the room. The partner without the blindfold should make sure that no difficulties arise.
   b. Stuff your ears with cotton and try to identify what's happening around you.
   c. Remain in a chair and note what your limitations are when you cannot readily move about.

9. In a small group, create your own sign language and try to communicate with one another.

Name	Handicap	Accomplishment
Peter Stuyvesant		
Gouverneur Morris		
Isaac Mill		
John Wesley Powell		
Thomas A. Edison		
Joseph Pulitzer		
Al Capp		
James Thurber		
Wiley Post		
Stevie Wonder		

Also refer to the units on Thomas A. Edison (pages 183–186) and on Helen Keller (pages 303–305) for additional information and activities regarding the handicapped.

QUESTIONS FOR CLASS DISCUSSION

1. Do you think seriously handicapped children should attend regular schools? Why?
2. Is there any way that a ramp can be dangerous for a person in a wheelchair? How?
3. What are some of the most important problems that any handicapped person faces?
4. It is often said that everyone has some kind of handicap. Do you agree? Explain what this might mean.
5. What are some alternatives to the word *handicapped?* Which do you prefer?
6. It is claimed that the handicapped work twice as hard to be as productive as nonhandicapped persons. Why might that be so?
7. What does *compensate* mean? Why are some people who are at a disadvantage in one area of ability able to excel at another skill or talent?
8. Discuss the advantages and disadvantages of special parking places, ramps, and assigned seating for the handicapped.
9. How do inconsiderate people sometimes take advantage of the handicapped?
10. If you were a legislator, what laws would you introduce to aid and protect the handicapped?
11. What employment opportunities exist for handicapped people in your community?
12. "Every athlete at the Special Olympics excels at clearing hurdles." Explain the meaning of this statement.

KEY VOCABULARY

artificial limb
auditory training
barrier-free
blind
brace
braille
disability
exercise
guide dog
handicapped
hearing aid
hearing impaired
independent
invalid (noun)
limitation
lip reading

mentally retarded
mute
occupational therapy
overcome
paralyzed
partially sighted
physical therapy
prosthetics
sign language
special educational services
Special Olympics
specialized task
treatment

RELATED CAREER EDUCATION TERMS

doctor
employment agency counselor
Goodwill Industries
medical equipment salesperson
nurse
occupational therapist

physical therapist
special education teacher
special-needs counselor
speech therapist
teacher of the blind
teacher of the deaf

Fire Prevention Week

THEMES AND THOUGHTS

Volunteering, Safety, Caution,
Prevention, Cooperation

Fire is the best of servants; but
what a master!
—*Thomas Carlyle*

It is better to be safe than sorry.
—*Anonymous saying*

FASCINATING FACTS

North America's first recorded fire was in Jamestown, Virginia, in 1608. The colony's blockhouse caught fire and nearly every building was destroyed. The chief cause of fire during colonial times was fire in the mud-covered wood chimneys that each home needed for cooking and heating.

The colonists' first fire regulations were published in 1635 in Boston as a result of a fire. The Boston selectman ordered the following precautions:

1. Chimneys could not be built out of wood and roofs could not be covered with thatch.
2. Every home was to have a ladder and a 12-foot pole with a swab on the end.
3. An open fire could not be built within 3 rods of a building [1 rod = 5 1/2 yards or 16 1/2 feet].
4. No one could carry live coals in a open container.
5. A public cistern with fire buckets was to be built in the town square.
6. The meeting house was to have six ladders and four fire hooks to be used for fire.
7. A night watchman would patrol the streets looking for fires.
8. Death was to be the penalty for arson.

The colonies' first fire prevention act was issued in 1648 in New Amsterdam. Four fire wardens were appointed to inspect all chimneys and fine all offenders. The fines were used to buy ladders and other equipment. Citizens were also ordered to keep a bucket of water on their doorstep to use in case of a fire. In colonial times, it was everyone's responsibility to fight a fire. Firefighters often used leather buckets filled with water from the nearest stream.

A fire engine company formed in 1679 in Boston hired the first paid firefighter in the United States. A fire "engine" was ordered from London and a carpenter, Thomas Atkins, was hired to take care of it. The "engine" was a tublike wooden box 3 feet long and 18 inches wide, equipped with carrying handles and a pump for hoses. A bucket brigade was needed to keep the tub filled with water.

Benjamin Franklin organized the first volunteer fire company, the Union Fire Company, in 1736 in Philadelphia. As a newspaper publisher, he wrote articles to let his readers know about fire safety. The first city to have its own company of paid firefighters was Cincinnati, which set up a fire company in 1853.

The invention of the fire alarm box in 1852 in Boston by William F. Channing made firefighting easier because firefighters could quickly locate a fire.

There have been some very serious fires in the history of the United States. One of the most famous fires was the Great Chicago Fire of 1871, which burned much of the city. Legend has it that the fire was started by Mrs. O'Leary's cow kicking over a kerosene lantern. This legend has a grain of truth to it because the fire did start in the O'Leary barn, but it is not certain that the cow started it. The Great Chicago Fire caused nearly $200 million in damages and burned a third of the city's 17,450 buildings. It burned an area five miles long and one mile wide, killing 300 people and leaving 90,000 homeless.

Children in schools have fire drills for their protection. In 1908, the Lake View Elementary School in Collingswood, Ohio, burned, killing 178 children and adults. Another serious fire in a school occurred in 1958 at Our Lady of Angels Elementary School in Chicago, Illinois, where 92 children and three teachers died.

Despite fire prevention measures, there are around 300 fires per hour in the United States. The United States has over 1,200,000 firefighters. It is a dangerous but very necessary job. On the average, one firefighter is killed every three days on the job.

Although firefighting methods have changed over the years, the cut of the firefighter's clothes has not changed much except for materials used. The helmet today is almost the same as it was 200 years ago. The crown is shaped like an eagle's head. The hat is hard in order to protect the firefighter's head, while the broad brim keeps water and embers away from the firefighter's clothing.

The shield on the front brim of the fire helmet identifies the firefighter. It contains the fire company name and the firefighter's name and number.

A firefighter's badge is shaped like the Maltese cross worn by medieval knights. (The wide arms of the cross represent the spreading wings of a bird protecting its young.) The badge of each company shows the special equipment it uses. The chief's badge has an eagle, the ruler of the birds. The badge is worn on the left side of the coat or on the helmet.

Today many communities have volunteer firefighters, both men and women. Paid firefighters must have a high school diploma and pass a civil service examination. Some companies require a degree from a junior college. Candidates must pass a physical fitness test and study first aid, too.

ACTIVITIES FOR STUDENTS

Information Gathering and Sharing

1. Visit a local firehouse. Then, as a class, construct a firehouse and engine in the classroom, using wooden blocks and heavy red and brown paper.
2. Invite the local fire chief to give a demonstration to your class or to a school assembly.
3. With the rest of the class, pretend you are fire inspectors. Discuss what you would look for when inspecting a building. Make a fire safety check of your home or the school and report your findings.
4. With a committee of student reporters, interview a local firefighter or fire chief and report on your interview. You might want to tape the interview, too.
5. As a class, compile a fire safety handbook, listing and illustrating the rules of fire prevention and safety. Have your teacher duplicate the handbook and give one to each class member.
6. Form a committee to report on the history of firefighting.
7. As a class, make a scrapbook of news items about fires.
8. Report on a famous fire, such as the Great Chicago Fire of 1871.

9. Each year, forest fires cause a great loss of life and property. Make a cause-and-effect chart about forest fires.

Art and Visual Aids

10. As a class, discuss fire prevention rules and what to do when you see a fire. Make a poster listing the rules.
11. As a class, create a bulletin-board display of different ways to extinguish fires.
12. Construct a fire alarm box from a paper carton. Demonstrate the proper way to use an alarm box. Explain and demonstrate how fire alarm boxes direct firefighters to fires.
13. As a class, prepare a bulletin-board display about firefighters and firefighting equipment. Create a chart of firefighting apparatus.
14. Draw a scene showing a fire. Write a fire prevention caption for your drawing.
15. Design a fire prevention poster to be displayed in a local store.

Game

16. Divide the class into teams and play a game called "What Would You Do?" Each student describes a fire emergency situation on a slip of paper. To play the game, the members of each team take turns selecting an emergency and telling what should be done. The response should be given within a specific amount of time. One point is given for each acceptable step named. Be sure to include in your answers (when it's appropriate) the way a fire should be reported on the telephone.

Writing and Language Arts

17. Write a simple but meaningful poem about fire or fire safety. Here's an example.

> When blowing out candles,
> Don't get too close to the flame,
> For if you burn yourself,
> That would be a shame.

18. Write a composition or construct a pictogram about how to prevent fires in your community.

QUESTIONS FOR CLASS DISCUSSION

1. In what ways can fire be helpful? In what ways can it be harmful?
2. What special qualifications and training does a firefighter need?
3. How have firefighting techniques changed over the years?
4. How is the phrase "It is better to be safe than sorry" relevant to fire?
5. What are some general rules of first aid to remember in treating someone who has suffered burns or smoke inhalation? How would you put out a small fire to prevent it from spreading?
6. Is water the best way to fight all fires? Identify other kinds of extinguishers that are effective for various types of fires.
7. What conditions or essentials are required for burning things outdoors?
8. Why are dogs often seen in fire stations?
9. EDITH stands for Exit Drills in the Home. SDR reminds a person to Stop, Drop, and Roll when clothing catches fire. Why are these two rules good to practice and remember?
10. Why should you avoid using an elevator during a fire in a high-rise building?
11. Why are chemical fires especially dangerous?

KEY VOCABULARY

air mask	combustion
alert	company
apparatus	explosion
arson	extension ladder
asphyxiate	extinguish
axe	false alarm
battalion	fire door
boots	fire drill
bucket brigade	fire escape
buddy system	fire extinguisher
cherry picker	firefighter
chief	fire pole

KEY VOCABULARY CONTINUED

fireproof	oxygen tank
fire tower	prevention
fire truck	pumper
first aid	rescue
flammable	resuscitator
fuel	safety net
hazard	smoke
helmet	smoke detector
hook and ladder	"smoke eaters"
hooks	smoke mask
hose	spontaneous combustion
hydrant	suffocate
inflammable	temperate
inhalation	turn out
kindling	vaporize
life nets	ventilation
marshal	volunteer
oxidation	

RELATED CAREER EDUCATION TERMS

dispatcher	fire investigator
firefighter	fire marshal
fire inspector	forest ranger

National Newspaper Week

THEMES AND THOUGHTS

Education, Honesty, Impartiality, Knowledge

No government ought to be without censors, and where the press is free none ever will.
—*Thomas Jefferson*

Newspapers are the schoolmaster of the common people. That endless book, the newspaper, is our national glory.
—*Henry Ward Beecher*

FASCINATING FACTS

Credit for founding the first daily newspaper is given to Julius Caesar, who had a handwritten bulletin posted in the market square in ancient Rome each morning.

Long ago, a town crier rang bells to alert people to the public announcement of events. In medieval Venice, a newssheet called a *gazetta* was posted and read aloud to anyone who paid a coin to the reader.

In 1454, Johann Gutenberg built the first movable-type press in Germany, thus making printing possible. The movable metal type and the improvement in ink quality made it possible for large quantities of paper to be printed.

The first colonial newspaper in America was published in 1690 by John Harris. This four-page newspaper was called *Publick Occurrences Both Foreign and Domestick*. The last page was left blank for handwritten notes. Harris' newspaper was to be published monthly, but came out only once. He was not able to obtain a license, because he printed material critical of British policies.

Early newspapers included a sign at the top of the first page of each issue indicating the four points of the compass. This implied that the information printed came from the north, east, west, and south (N-E-W-S), or the four corners of the globe.

The landmark for establishing freedom of the press was the trial of a New York printer, John Peter Zenger, in 1735. Mr. Zenger was accused of printing material that offended the governor. The information was proven to be true, so Zenger was found not guilty. This trial established freedom of the press, or the right of newspapers to publish the truth, no matter who it offends.

A newspaper is not only a business, but also a public service. Newspapers are protected by the government in their right to publish news. They also receive reduced mailing rates.

There are about 500,000 newspapers in the world today, with a combined circulation of over 400 million. Twenty-five percent of the daily newspapers are published in the English language, with the next highest number being published in Chinese, followed by German and Spanish. The United States has over 1,600 daily newspapers with about 63 million readers. Britain has the highest percentage of newspaper readers in the world, followed by Norway, Denmark, Sweden, Japan, and the United States.

ACTIVITIES FOR STUDENTS

Writing and Language Arts

1. As a class, publish a class or school newspaper. Each student should select a specific job, such as editor-in-chief, reporter, copywriter, artist, cartoonist, columnist, or printer. The newspaper can be typed or printed on a duplicating master. Copies can be distributed to each class in the school.
2. Write a news story that answers these five basic questions: What? Where? When? Why? How? Read your story to your classmates and have them identify the answers to the five questions.
3. By yourself or with a small group, write headlines for articles that your teacher has cut out of various newspapers. Your headlines, as well as the original headlines for the articles, should be shared with the class. Select the best headline for each article, presenting the rationale for your choice.
4. By yourself or with the class, write a letter to the editor about a timely topic of interest.
5. Create a replica newspaper about the events of a past era.
6. Cut a picture out of a newspaper or news magazine. Before you read the caption or the story, write your own caption or story. Then compare it with the original caption or article.

Information Gathering and Sharing

7. Contact your local newspaper to invite an editor, reporter, photographer, or printer to come speak to your class about his or her role in publishing a newspaper. You might follow up with a field trip to the newspaper to see it being printed and to tour the newsroom.
8. Cut out examples of the different types of stories in a newspaper, such as a feature article, sports story, or news story. Name the types and classify the stories as local, state, national, or international. Cut out illustrations of some key newspaper terms, such as *masthead, byline, headline, advertisement, flag, caption, editorial,* and *cartoon.* Paste the clippings on colored construction paper, label them, and compile them into a newspaper booklet.
9. Select a story to follow for a specific period of time. Collect newspaper stories on the topic and present a current events "special feature bulletin" news report.
10. Describe the role that each of the following people plays in making or distributing a newspaper:

editor	plate maker
data processor	feature-story writer
reporter	printer
typesetter	librarian
photographer	delivery truck driver
composing room worker	obituary writer
	newsstand operator
classified advertisement manager	newspaper delivery person

Critical Thinking

11. Examine a newspaper for examples of facts and opinions. List the "news views" and the "news facts" on a two-column chart.
12. Compare the first page of two area newspapers on the same day. How are they alike? How are they different?

Interviewing

13. Pretend you are an inquiring reporter. Interview adults about their occupations. Prepare your questions in advance. Use the information from your interviews to compose a news feature article.
14. Select your favorite comic strip character. Compose ten questions you would like to ask the character.

Word Game

15. Words about newspapers are hidden in the block below. Find the following words: assign, computer, cover, darkroom, deliver, develop, editor, facts, headline, homes, page, paper, paste, photographer, pictures, press, print, reporter, rollers, newspaper, newsstands, read, story, write.

P	H	O	T	O	G	R	A	P	H	E	R	U	V	N
I	H	A	H	W	D	E	V	E	L	O	P	A	G	E
C	O	V	E	R	H	D	I	A	S	S	I	G	N	W
T	M	B	A	W	R	I	T	E	S	T	O	R	Y	S
U	E	C	D	B	F	T	D	E	L	I	V	E	R	P
R	S	D	L	G	R	O	L	L	E	R	S	F	T	A
E	P	R	I	N	T	R	J	K	L	R	E	A	D	P
S	M	N	N	R	E	P	O	R	T	E	R	C	X	E
O	P	R	E	S	S	Q	C	O	M	P	U	T	E	R
P	D	A	R	K	R	O	O	M	R	P	A	S	T	E
N	E	W	S	S	T	A	N	D	S	P	A	P	E	R

Art and Visual Aids

16. Prepare a collage of pictures, numbers, and words from newspapers to illustrate how newspapers influence your life. You might use clippings from the fashion pages, the sports section, the financial news, the science news, and the travel section.

Special Resources

17. Many newspapers provide learning packets with activities for using the newspaper. Ask your teacher to contact a local or regional newspaper for a month-long subscription and the accompanying learning packet. Your teacher might also subscribe to one of the monthly filmstrip news summaries produced by newspapers and filmstrip companies.

QUESTIONS FOR CLASS DISCUSSION

1. In what ways can newspapers be considered "teachers"?
2. Explain how a newspaper is each of the following: a reporter, an opinion maker, a record keeper, a salesperson, a personal shopper, a grocer, a meal planner, a community helper, an entertainer, a career adviser, a weather forecaster.
3. Why are newspapers of value in education?
4. How does newspaper reading relate to the expression "an informed person is an interesting person"?
5. Why is it important for newspaper readers to learn how to skim? How are news stories written to make skimming easier?
6. "I may not agree with what you say, but I will defend to the end your right to say (or print) it." What does this expression mean?

KEY VOCABULARY

advertisement
assignment
bank
beat (noun)
boldface
bulletin
byline
caption
cartoon
chain
circulation
classified ad
clipping
column
compose
computerized
    typesetting
copy
correspondent
cover story
credit line
crop
cut
cutline
daily
dateline
deadline
deck
dummy
editorial
editorialize
exclusive
fact
"fast-breaking"
    news
feature
flag
flash
galley

galley proof
headline
insert
interview
investigative
    reporting
issue
journalism
kill
layout
lead
libel
make-up
margin
masthead
morgue
negative
obituary
opinion
overline
photoengrave
plate
press
press sheet
proofread
publish
recruit
route
staff
stand
subhead
subscribe
tabloid
teletypewriter
type
typeface (or font)
underline
wire
yellow journalism

RELATED CAREER EDUCATION TERMS

advertising sales
    person
artist
carrier
cartoonist
columnist
copyeditor
copywriter
delivery person
editor
editor-in-chief
family life editor
librarian
mailer
make-up editor
managing editor
newscaster
news editor

photoengraver
photographer
press operator
printer
producer
proofreader
public relations
    manager
publisher
reporter
sportscaster
teletypist
TV anchor person
TV camera person
typesetter
typist
wire editor

Columbus Sighted America

THEMES AND THOUGHTS

Faith, Perseverance, Aspiration, Planning, Courage

He gained a world; he gave the world its grandest lesson: "On! Sail on!"

—*Cincinnatus Hein (Joaquin Miller)*

If at first you don't succeed, try, try again.

—*Anonymous saying*

Columbus found a world, and had no chart,
Save one that faith deciphered in the skies;
To trust the soul's invincible surmise
Was all his science and his only art.

—*George Santayana*

At two hours after midnight appeared the land, at a distance of 2 leagues. They handed all sails and set the *treo,* which is the mainsail without bonnets, and lay-to waiting for daylight Friday, when they arrived at an island of the Bahamas that was called in the Indians' tongue Guanahaní [San Salvador].

—*Bartolomé de Las Casas (abstract of Christopher Columbus' journal)*

He [Columbus] enjoyed long stretches of pure delight such as only a seaman may know, and moments of high, proud exultation that only a discoverer can experience.

—*Samuel Eliot Morison*

FASCINATING FACTS

Christopher Columbus (1451–1506) was an Italian navigator from Genoa. He planned his voyages with his two brothers, Diego, who helped rule Hispaniola (now Haiti and the Dominican Republic), and Bartholomew.

Columbus had little formal schooling, but taught himself Portuguese, Spanish, and Latin. He never learned to read or write Italian. As a boy, he was dreamy and sensitive. He was described as a "tall man and well built, ruddy, of a great creative talent and with a long face." He was trained in his father's trade of wool weaving, yet he was interested in the sea and spent time as a youth around Genoa's busy port.

Columbus was determined to make a transatlantic voyage. He was convinced he could sail west and reach the Indies (which in Columbus' time included China, Japan, and India) in a few weeks. He sought support unsuccessfully from England and Portugal, but was finally successful in being sponsored by Spain.

For his famous voyage, he received three ships fully equipped at the king and queen's expense (about $14,000), a large share in the trade, the governorship of any lands he might discover, the title of admiral, and noble rank. Columbus asked a great deal for himself in order to save his heirs from being as poor as he was. Thus, all of his rewards were to be inherited by his children.

The dimensions of Columbus' ships are not known. However, historians have been able to make estimates based on their studies of the times. The *Santa María,* the flagship, was the largest and was believed to weigh between 100 and 120 tons and to be 80–85 feet (24–25 meters) long. It was thought to carry about 40 of the three ships' total crew of 90 men. The *Niña* and the *Pinta* were believed to be 65–70 feet (20–21 meters) long. The ships were lightly armed and carried the usual cargo for trading: cloth, knives, glass beads, and trinkets.

Columbus made a total of four voyages to the New World. In the course of these trips, he discovered the northern coast of South America and further explored the western Caribbean. During these voyages, he learned the best way to make use of the North Atlantic wind system for transatlantic sailing.

It is known that other explorers, such as the Vikings, sailed to the Americas long before Columbus. But only after Columbus' voyages did significant numbers of Europeans settle in the New World, primarily in the West Indies.

ACTIVITIES FOR STUDENTS

Information Gathering and Sharing

1. Use an encyclopedia and other reference books as well as a container of water and a model ship to research how and why ships float.
2. Plot on a map or globe the probable routes that Columbus took. Have a class discussion of the wind belts of the earth and their influence on navigation.
3. Make a collection of false ideas that people had about the sea and the world at the time of Columbus' journeys.
4. Make a list of the provisions recorded in Columbus' ships' logs.

Art and Visual Aids

5. Investigate the types of navigational instruments and techniques Columbus used on his voyages. Construct one of the simpler types.
6. Make a three-dimensional model of one of Columbus' ships, the *Niña,* the *Pinta,* or the *Santa María,* using construction paper and a plastic bleach bottle or oatmeal box.
7. Design and make a montage of Columbus' life. (A montage is a composite of different pictures that blend into a single composition.)

Critical Thinking

8. As a class, discuss the use of spices and why they were so important in Columbus' day.
9. Compare Columbus' first voyage to Leif Ericson's voyage several hundred years before.
10. Compare one of Columbus' ships to a modern ocean liner.

Writing and Language Arts

11. Write a creative story about one of Columbus' voyages, using the "I Was There" approach.
12. Write an announcement of one of Columbus' voyages and deliver it as it might have been done in a town square during his time.
13. Research and write about Columbus' personality.

Dramatics and Role-Playing

14. With a small group, dramatize the departure, landing, or return of one of Columbus' voyages.
15. Pretend you are Columbus and prepare a five-minute talk in an effort to convince Queen Isabella of the merits of a voyage to find a new route to the Indies.
16. With a small group, enact a series of private conversations that might have taken place among the crew of one of Columbus' ships at different stages during the journey.

QUESTIONS FOR CLASS DISCUSSION

1. Columbus had a difficult time selling European rulers on his plan for the voyage to the Indies. Why was this so?
2. Some of Columbus' crew were worried about falling off the edge of the earth. What did Columbus think of the idea that the earth was flat? What evidence do we have that the earth is a sphere?
3. What did Columbus hope to find on his first journey?
4. Why was Columbus given the ships and crew for three additional voyages after his initial discovery?
5. What leadership characteristics did Columbus need to retain his crew's loyalty and to maintain discipline?
6. What lessons can we learn from Columbus' story?
7. How can Columbus be compared to today's astronauts? In what ways was he different?
8. Who do you think should be given credit for the discovery of America? Why do you think so?
9. Why is it wise to plan and check out your ideas with others before a major undertaking?
10. It is said that great explorers are great dreamers. Do you agree or disagree with this statement? Explain your response.
11. Columbus' voyages were motivated by the possibility of riches and glory. Do you think that this is still the main reason why people undertake risky adventures today? Explain your answer.
12. Why do you think the Vikings are not given more credit for their "discovery" of North America?
13. What kinds of daring missions being carried out today can be compared to Columbus' voyages of the past?
14. Why is Columbus honored as the discoverer of America?
15. Why were Columbus' expeditions sometimes called the "vanguard voyages"? What other phrases might also describe them?

KEY VOCABULARY

admiral	navigation
almanac	perseverance
cargo	port
coat of arms	prevailing westerlies
colonize	provisions
crew	route
current (noun)	seaman
diary	spice
discover	strait
doldrums	survivor
hourglass	trade wind
latitude	vessel
log	voyage
map	West Indies
mutiny	

RELATED CAREER EDUCATION TERMS

cartographer	sailor
designer	shipbuilder
helmsman	ship captain
navigator	

United Nations Day

THEMES AND THOUGHTS

Peace, Humanitarianism, Helpfulness, Caring

Buried was the bloody hatchet
Buried was the dreadful war-club
Buried were all warlike weapons,
And the war cry was forgotten
There was peace among the
nations.
—*Henry Wadsworth Longfellow*

They shall beat their swords into plowshares, and their shears into pruninghooks; nations shall not lift up sword against nation, neither shall they learn war any more.
—*Isaiah 2:4*

We must conquer war, or war will conquer us.

—*Ely Culbertson*

We, the peoples of the United Nations, determined to save succeeding generations from the scourge of war, which twice in our lifetime has brought untold sorrow… and to reaffirm faith in fundamental human rights, in the dignity and worth of the human person, in the equal right of men and women and of nations large and small . . .
And for these ends to practice tolerance and live together in peace with one another as good neighbors . . .
Have resolved to combine these efforts to accomplish our aims.
—*Charter of the United Nations*

FASCINATING FACTS

During World War II, in August 1941, the United States and Great Britain made an agreement known as the Atlantic Charter. It was designed to establish world security at the end of the war.

Five months later, on January 1, 1942, representatives of twenty-six nations allied in the war against the Axis powers met and signed the United Nations Declaration in Washington, D.C. The term *United Nations* was coined by Franklin D. Roosevelt to describe the Allies. By signing the declaration, the nations pledged their willingness to cooperate so that the world could be free of hunger and poverty.

The United Nations became a world organization as a result of a conference held in San Francisco in April of 1945. The number of member nations has grown from 51 in 1945 to 159 in 1988. The official languages of the United Nations are Arabic, Chinese, English, French, Russian, and Spanish.

Although the United Nations was the "child" of a war, it is considered a guardian of peace. The United Nations flag, which flies higher than all member nations' flags in front of the United Nations building in New York City, features the United Nations emblem—a map of the world as viewed from the North Pole, flanked by olive branches. The olive branches represent the United Nations' goal of world peace and security. It seeks to accomplish this goal by developing good relations and cooperation among nations.

The first United Nations meeting took place in London in January of 1946. Later, industrialist John D. Rockefeller donated $8.5 million to buy an 18-acre site on the East River in New York City. The buildings were designed by eleven architects from eleven different countries. Nowadays, the United Nations has extraterritorial status; that is, once you enter the United Nations gate, you have left the territory of the United States.

There are six main components of the United Nations: the General Assembly, the Security Council, the Trusteeship Council, the Economic and Social Council, the International Court of Justice, and the Secretariat. In addition to these divisions, the United Nations system includes specialized agencies, which were formed to provide international service in various economic, cultural, and technical fields.

ACTIVITIES FOR STUDENTS

Critical Thinking

1. Make a list of ideas entitled "How We Can Have Peace in the World."
2. As a class, list some other appropriate names for the United Nations.
3. Many students take an active part in helping to run their schools through student councils. Make a diagram that compares the organization of a student council to that of the United Nations, with its General Assembly, Secretariat, Security Council, Trusteeship Council, Economic and Social Council, and International Court of Justice.

Information Gathering and Sharing

4. As a class, make a diagrammatic chart of the United Nations. Briefly describe the functions of each organ and agency.
5. Write to the United Nations for classroom aids and information booklets (Office of Public Information, United Nations, New York, NY 10017).
6. In rotation with your classmates, serve as United Nations reporter and periodically present updates about United Nations activities. Ask your teacher to reserve a section of the current bulletin board for United Nations news items.
7. Learn a game or a song from another country.
8. Make a list of recognized United Nations accomplishments—for example, peacekeeping forces in Cyprus, Lebanon, and elsewhere; FAO; World Health Organization; UNESCO; and UNICEF.
9. Select a United Nations agency of interest to you. Report on its purpose, structure, and accomplishments.
10. Do a report on Wendell Willkie's "One World" concept.

Dramatics and Role-Playing

11. Serve as a guide for an imaginary trip through the United Nations building.
12. As a class, conduct a mock United Nations meeting or act out the sessions during which the United Nations Charter was framed in San Francisco in 1945.
13. Write and deliver a speech to commemorate United Nations Day.

Art and Visual Aids

14. As a class, make small flags from cloth or paper for each United Nations member. Attach each flag to a straight pin. Plot the flags on a world map.
15. Design and create your own "native" costume to represent one of the members of the United Nations.

Writing and Language Arts

16. Write to a foreign pen pal. In order to start a correspondence with a boy or girl living in another country, write to International Friendship League, Inc., 40 Mount Vernon Street, Boston, MA 02108. An application blank will be sent if you include a stamped, self-addressed envelope.

Special Projects

17. As a class, make a United Nations information booth and place it either in your room or in another location of the school. Students can staff the booth, answer questions, and provide oral and duplicated information about the United Nations. Be sure to provide information about UNICEF Day (write to UNICEF, 3 United Nations Plaza, New York, NY 10017).

Word Game

18. The names of 20 countries appear incognito, or disguised, in the following story, and none of the names are abbreviated. Can you locate them within the time set aside for your social studies period? Circle the name of each nation you discover. Finding 15 or more nations is considered good. If you have difficulty, refer to any current list of the nations of the world. When you have finished this puzzle, see if you can construct a similar article including various countries of the world.

PROGRESS IN THE SOUTH

Can a day elapse without a few thoughts about the South, famous as an agricultural region for over three hundred years? One must agree certainly that this great region has long offered much that was good to the nation. Today the South is changing. To go there today via gulf ports, the visitor will immediately see the beach in a rapidly changing profile. Ban on progress? Not in the new South, for it is becoming a manufacturing region as well as a farming area.

The landscape now is painted with oil derricks, mills, and refineries, wherein diamondback terrapin turtles once were found in abundance. Well before Columbus, native worshippers of fire landed their war canoes in the marshy coves where the presently productive continental shelf ran certainly and untouched into the sea. These days, people are busy, and there is no time for malice. Now, too, the manor way of life in the old South is fading into the past. Alteration has spread, as if a jinni ran from town to town with a magical torch of illumination. As for the people, many are eager, many are ready for progress.

It is high time to laud a homey, friendly region of America and sing to it a lyrical praise of accomplishment. The traditional South is blending and moving ahead hand in hand with a fine pal—progress. Like her native magnolia, a flower fit for the Garden of Eden, mark this nice land for continuing good growth, bloom, and performance. Whether you go to a minute little burgh, an alert town, or a bustling city, it will be obvious, as per usual, that the South is on the move.

ANSWER KEY

PROGRESS IN THE SOUTH

Can a day elapse without a few thoughts about the South, famous as an agricultural region for over three hundred years? One must **agree cer**tainly that this great region has long offered much that was good to the nation. Today the South is changing. **To go** there today via gulf ports, the visitor will immediately see the bea**ch in a** rapidly changing profi**le. Ban on** progress? Not in the new South, for it is becoming a manufacturing region as well as a farming area.

The landscape now i**s pain**ted with oil derricks, mills, and refineries, where**in dia**mondback terrapin turtles once were found in abundance. Well before Columbus, native worshippers of **fire land**ed their war canoes in the marshy coves where the presently productive continental shel**f ran c**ertainly and untouched into the sea. These days people are busy, and there is no time for malice. Now, too, the ma**nor way** of life in the old South is fading into the past. Alteration has spread, as if a jinn**i ran** from town to town with a magical torch of illumination. As for the people, many are ea**ger, many** are ready for progress.

It is high time to lau**d a homey**, friendly region of America and sing to **it a ly**rical praise of accomplishment. The traditional South is blending and moving ahead hand in hand with a fi**ne pal**—progress. Like her native magnolia, a flower fit for the Garden of E**den, mark** this n**ice land** for continuing good growth, bloom, and performance. Whether you go to a minute little bur**gh, an a**lert town, or a bustling city, it will be obvious, as **per u**sual, that the South is on the move.

QUESTIONS FOR CLASS DISCUSSION

1. What do we mean by "It's a small world, after all"?
2. Why is the United States interested in the affairs of the United Nations?
3. The United Nations is not a world government. Explain why not.
4. What can people in the United States do to improve the effectiveness of the United Nations?
5. Do you feel that New York is the best location for the United Nations building? What other locations might be suitable?
6. Why is the United Nations called the best friend of the world's children?

KEY VOCABULARY

agency	peace
assembly	pledge
buffer zone	political
charter	quorum
committee	representative
council	security
debate	social
delegate	teamwork
diplomat	tolerance
dissent	treaty
economic	truce
emerging nation	trustee
	united
health	veto
international	vote
majority	war
member	world
nation	
organization	

RELATED CAREER EDUCATION TERMS

agriculturist	guide
ambassador	judge
arbitrator	lawyer
armament (or munitions) expert	military attaché
	negotiator
diplomat	nurse
disarmament expert	political scientist
	scientist
doctor	teacher
economist	translator

President Theodore Roosevelt Born

THEMES AND THOUGHTS

Compassion, Conservation, Nature, Courage, Vision

I believe in honesty, sincerity, and the square deal, in making up one's mind what to do—and doing it.

I believe in fearing God and taking one's own part.

I believe in hitting the line hard when you are right.

I believe in hard work and honest sport.

I believe in a sane mind and in a sane body.

I believe we have room for but one sole loyalty, and that is loyalty to the American people.

—Theodore Roosevelt

To waste, to destroy our natural resources, to skin and exhaust the land instead of using it so as to increase its usefulness, will result in undermining in the days of our children the very prosperity which we ought by right to hand down to them amplified and developed.

—Theodore Roosevelt

FASCINATING FACTS

As a child, Teddy Roosevelt (1858–1919) suffered from asthma and poor eyesight. Due to his poor health, Teddy was tutored at home. In the hope of improving his health, Teddy's parents took him to Europe and the Middle East. His father had a gymnasium built in the family home to help build Teddy's physical strength.

As a young boy, Teddy was interested in books and nature. His room always contained a pet mouse or a collection of stuffed birds.

As an adult, Roosevelt bought two ranches in North Dakota, and he learned the rugged life of a cowboy. Later, as an officer in the Spanish-American War, he organized the Rough Riders, a cavalry regiment of cowboys, big-game hunters, engineers, and businessmen who wanted to fight for their country. Their charge up San Juan Hill in Cuba made the regiment famous.

Roosevelt became president after William McKinley's assassination in 1901. At 42 years of age, Teddy was the youngest U.S. President the United States had ever had. The six Roosevelt children, known as the "White House Gang," were allowed to bring their pets to the White House. As President, Roosevelt enjoyed many sports, such as tennis on the White House lawn, hiking, horseback riding, and even swimming across the Potomac in winter.

President Roosevelt was interested in the development of the nation's natural resources. His work in the field of conservation is regarded as a major achievement. Zoologists recognized him as one of the best field naturalists in the country, and he was an authority on the life histories of big game in North America.

President Roosevelt was also a writer. He wrote many books, including a four-volume historical work, *The Winning of the West* (1889–1896).

The teddy bear became a symbol associated with President Roosevelt as a result of a hunting trip. While bear hunting in the Little Sunflower River area in Mississippi, some members of the party caught a small brown cub. President Roosevelt refused to shoot the cub and set it free. The newspapers featured the bear cub story, including a cartoon, "Drawing the Line in Mississippi." In order to capitalize upon the newspaper coverage, toymakers designed a toy bear. The teddy bear was bought for adults as well as for children.

ACTIVITIES FOR STUDENTS

Outdoor Activities

1. With your class, make a nature trail in the woods or nearby fields (with permission), and mark names of natural features and habitats.
2. Learn how to make a shelter for hikes through the woods in the fall and during other seasons.

Word Game

3. Use the word *conservation* in an anagram exercise to form words related directly or indirectly to the topics of conservation and nature, such as *iron, tons, nest, save, rest*. Do the same with other related key words.

Information Gathering and Sharing

4. Research Theodore Roosevelt's contribution to the U.S. Navy. Why is it fitting that Navy Day and Roosevelt's birthday are celebrated on the same day?
5. Theodore Roosevelt, although always ready for war, was also a man of peace. Research the reasons for his winning the Nobel Peace Prize.
6. Find out details about the Mount Rushmore National Memorial, located in South Dakota.
7. Write to various state and federal government offices that make literature on conservation and natural resources available for students. Collect this material and display it in your classroom.
8. Keep a scientific record of observations over a period of time of a bird's or other animal's habits.

Art and Visual Aids

9. Draw a caricature or picture description of an event in the life of Theodore Roosevelt.
10. Make an illustrated timeline showing changes in the U.S. Navy during its history.
11. Make a cross-sectional diagram depicting the way the Panama Canal operates.

Critical Thinking

12. Make a list of reasons for the need to conserve resources, natural life, and the beauty of the land.
13. Make a list of things for which we can be grateful to Theodore Roosevelt. Think of an interesting title for your list.

Dramatics and Role-Playing

14. With a small group, write a dramatic script about some aspect of Theodore Roosevelt's life.

Writing and Language Arts

15. Write a composition about a camping experience.
16. Compose a glossary of naval terms, conservation terms, or naturalist terms.
17. Write a brief biography of Theodore Roosevelt.

QUESTIONS FOR CLASS DISCUSSION

1. Why is Theodore Roosevelt sometimes referred to as the "trust buster"?
2. Teddy Roosevelt was considered a sickly, yet happy child. Why was this so?
3. The Federal Food and Drug Act (1906) became law during the Roosevelt administration. Why do we need such a law?
4. What does the phrase "Speak softly and carry a big stick" mean?
5. Why did Theodore Roosevelt call one of his programs the "Square Deal"?
6. What were the factors and conditions in Theodore Roosevelt's early life that caused him to become an outdoorsman?
7. The Panama Canal Zone was obtained from Panama by treaty in 1903 during the Roosevelt era. How has the United States profited from this acquisition?
8. What are some appropriate adjectives to describe Theodore Roosevelt?
9. Why is it more important today than ever to have a program of conservation?
10. Though Teddy Roosevelt had poor eyesight, he was considered a "man of vision." Explain what that phrase means.

KEY VOCABULARY

assassination	monopoly
asthma	naturalist
cavalry	natural resource
conservation	nearsightedness
cub	officer
game	politics
graft	regiment
habitat	sportsman
handicap	statesman
hero	symbol
historian	teddy bear
immigration	treaty
inauguration	wildlife
legacy	zoologist

RELATED CAREER EDUCATION TERMS

adventurer	naturalist
conservationist	president
explorer	writer
forest ranger	zoologist
historian	

Statue of Liberty Dedicated

Freedom, Liberty, Affection, Opportunity

Doing what we please is not freedom, it is not liberty; rather, it is the abuse of true liberty and freedom.
—*Patrick Joseph Hayes*

The love of liberty is the love of others; the love of power is the love of ourselves.
—*William Hazlitt*

FASCINATING FACTS

The Statue of Liberty was France's gift to commemorate the birth of the United States of America and the friendship of the people of France and the United States. The right arm and hand were the first parts of the statue completed and were exhibited at the Centennial Exhibition in Philadelphia and in Madison Square Garden, New York, in 1875.

The statue, which was designed by Frédéric August Bartholdi, is a figure of a walking woman with a torch in her raised right hand. The height of the statue is 151 feet (46 meters); with the pedestal, it is 305 feet (93 meters). Its forefinger is 8 feet (2.44 meters) long. Each eye is 2.5 feet (0.8 meters) wide. The waist is 35 feet (11 meters) in diameter, and the right arm is 42 feet (13 meters) long. The statue covering consists of over 300 copper sheets, each 3/32 of an inch (2.34 millimeters) thick, over an iron and steel framework. In the statue's crown is an observation platform, which can be reached by a spiral staircase, 260 feet (79 meters) above the New York Harbor. By one foot of the statue is a chain with a broken shackle and a plaque with the date, July 4, 1776, in Roman numerals. The statue is officially entitled "Liberty Enlightening the World."

The pedestal foundation is 91 feet (27.7 meters) square and 66 feet 7 inches (20 meters) square at the top. There is a balcony on the pedestal. From one side you can see New York City, Brooklyn, Governor's Island, New Jersey, and the East River Bridge, and from the other side, Staten Island and the Bay. The pedestal was designed by R. M. Hunt, an American. School children in the United States helped raise funds to pay for the pedestal. On a bronze plaque inside the pedestal is an inscription of a sonnet, "The New Colossus," by Emma Lazarus. (See page 68.)

On July 4, 1884, the completed statue, which cost $250,000, was delivered to the U.S. ambassador in Paris. The statue was then disassembled and transported in pieces on one ship, *Isere,* from Rouen, France. President Grover Cleveland dedicated the statue on October 28,

1886. President Calvin Coolidge proclaimed the Statue of Liberty a national monument in 1924.

In 1956, Congress changed the name of the site of the statue from Bedloe's Island to Liberty Island. On the island, there is a museum dealing with the history of U.S. immigration. There is a ferry service to the island from Battery Park in Manhattan. A new state park, called Liberty Park, is located in Jersey City, a few hundred yards across the harbor from the statue.

In 1984, the statue was closed for restoration, and an immense scaffolding was built around it. During the July 4 weekend in 1986, a spectacular rededication celebration was held in New York Harbor in honor of the 100th anniversary of the Statue of Liberty. Millions of school children and others had helped raise funds to defray the cost of the restoration.

ACTIVITIES FOR STUDENTS

Reading Aloud

1. Read the sonnet "The New Colossus" by Emma Lazarus that is inscribed on the pedestal of the Statue of Liberty. Recite it in unison with the class.

THE NEW COLOSSUS

Not like the brazen giant of Greek fame,
With conquering limbs astride from land to land;
Here at our sea-washed, sunset gates shall stand
A mighty woman with a torch, whose flame
Is the imprisoned lightning, and her name
Mother of Exiles. From her beacon-hand
Glows world-wide welcome; her mild eyes command
The air-bridged harbor that twin cities frame.
"Keep ancient lands, your storied pomp!" cries she
With silent lips. "Give me your tired, your poor,
Your huddled masses yearning to breathe free,
The wretched refuse of your teeming shore.
Send these, the homeless, tempest-tost to me,
I lift my lamp beside the golden door!"

—Emma Lazarus

Writing and Language Arts

2. Write an original inscription for the Statue of Liberty.
3. Write your impressions of an imaginary field trip to the Statue of Liberty. If you live nearby, ask your teacher to arrange a real trip.
4. Make a list of synonyms and antonyms for the word *liberty*.
5. Write a brief script for the Statue of Liberty, revealing all her views and impressions of the past years.

Art and Visual Aids

6. With the class, build a model of the Statue of Liberty using papier-mâché.
7. With your class, draw an outline of the Statue of Liberty in chalk on the playground. Draw the statue to approximate scale. Include the famous inscription of Emma Lazarus. If the principal gives permission, paint the drawing and lettering.
8. Design an appropriate gift that the United States could have given to France at the time we received the Statue of Liberty.

Critical Thinking

9. Pretend you are the curator of the museum on Liberty Island. Draw up a list of the types of items that you would display.
10. Describe the things you would have put into a time capsule placed in the pedestal of the Statue of Liberty at its dedication in 1886 or its rededication in 1986.

Dramatics and Role-Playing

11. Role-play some U.S. soldiers on the deck of a troop ship returning home from an overseas war and seeing the Statue of Liberty for the first time in four years.

Information Gathering and Sharing

12. Make a report about the role of Ellis Island as a processing center for the U.S. Immigration Service.
13. Use an almanac to research the countries of origin of the immigrants to the United States and the numbers that arrived for the decades before and after the year 1880. Use several colors to make an immigration graph or a series of pie graphs based on the data you find.

14. Make a large class chart of other famous statues or monuments found throughout our country, listing name, person or event memorialized, artist or sculptor, location, description, inscription, and miscellaneous information.

QUESTIONS FOR CLASS DISCUSSION

1. In bygone days, most European immigrants passed through New York Harbor. How do immigrants arrive in the United States today?
2. What is the true meaning of nations giving gifts to or exchanging gifts with other countries?
3. What is the significance of the statue being a woman, having a chain with a broken shackle by one foot, and raising a torch?
4. What adjectives, words of appreciation, or emotions might have gone through the minds of immigrants viewing the Statue of Liberty for the first time?
5. Some monuments are better than others in keeping alive the memory of a person or event. Why is the Statue of Liberty such a successful monument?
6. What is your understanding of Emma Lazarus' great poem in terms of the past, present, and future?
7. Why do millions of people in the United States, young and old, find it easy to relate to the Statue of Liberty?
8. Why is the Statue of Liberty considered one of the United States' most popular monuments and tourist attractions?
9. Why is the location of the Statue of Liberty in New York Harbor, the "gateway" to the city, an ideal choice?

KEY VOCABULARY

balcony	monument
base	opportunity
dedicated	oppressed
design	pedestal
ferry	plaque
foreigner	shackle
gateway	sonnet
immigrant	statue
inscription	symbol
island	torch
liberty	

RELATED CAREER EDUCATION TERMS

architect	mason
construction worker	shipper
	souvenir vendor
designer	stonemason
ferryboat captain	U.S. Park Ranger
	U.S. Customs Service Officer
guide	

Halloween

Consideration, Creativity, Manners, Safety, Originality

HINTS FOR A HAPPY HALLOWEEN

- Eat treats in moderation.
- Wear white, reflectors, or something that will glow in the dark at night.
- Never go trick-or-treating alone.
- Do not enter a stranger's house.
- Do not venture too far away from your own neighborhood.
- Make sure you can easily breathe through and see out of your mask.
- Make sure your costume is made of flame-resistant or flame-retardant material.
- Report home at the expected hour.
- Dress according to the weather of the evening.
- Be aware of the dangers of lighted candles as a cause of house and costume fires.
- Do not destroy another person's property.
- Do not take things that have been given to other children.
- Remember "please" and "thank you."
- Check all treats before eating them.

FASCINATING FACTS

In A.D. 853, the Roman Catholic Church made November 1 a church holiday to honor all the saints. This holy day was called *All Saints' Day*, or *Hallowmas*, or *Allhallows*. People celebrated October 31 as All Hallow Even (*even* is an old-fashioned form of the word *evening*), and in time the name was shortened to Hallowe'en or Halloween. November 2 was a holy day called *All Souls' Day*, when all dead people were honored.

There are many superstitions and symbols associated with Halloween. Orange and black are "Halloween colors." Halloween was once a harvest festival. Orange is the color of ripened fruits and vegetables. Halloween was also the time for evil spirits. Black was the color associated with death and evil.

In England and Scotland, a traditional belief is that if a supper is not left for the hobgoblin (a mischievous sprite or fairy) on Halloween, it will upset all the cooking and scatter ashes all over the house.

The word *jack-o'-lantern* is from an old Irish story. Once there was a man named Jack who was very mean. When he died, he went to the Devil. The Devil threw Jack a hot coal and told him to put it inside the turnip he was eating. "This is your lantern," said the Devil. Jack is still walking with his lantern, looking for a place to stay.

At one time, Halloween was a celebration filled with fear. People wore costumes to ward off evil spirits and gathered together because they were afraid to be alone. This came to be known as *Witches' Night*, and since then, witches have become common symbols of Halloween.

The colonists brought their Halloween customs from England. Halloween changed over the years, from a time when the Devil did his evil work to a more fun-filled time. The colonists gathered at farmhouses and sang songs, told ghost stories, and bobbed for apples. They called this *Nutcrack Night* or *Snap Apple Night*.

Now it is customary for children dressed in costumes to participate in school parades, parties, and trick-or-treating in their neighborhoods on Halloween. Mischief Night, when tricks are played, is the night preceding Halloween. Children visiting the neighbors and asking for treats is a custom that may have originated in the 1800s in Ireland. Irish peasants went from door to door asking for money to buy food for a special feast for St. Columba.

Today, on Halloween many children go "trick-or-treating" for UNICEF, the abbreviation for the United Nations International Children's Emergency Fund, or the UN Children's Fund, for short. This custom was started in 1950 by children from a small Sunday school near Philadelphia who decided to send the money from their trick-or-treating to UNICEF. The money was used to buy food and medicine for children in poor countries. A presidential proclamation in 1967 made October 31 National UNICEF Day in the United States.

ACTIVITIES FOR STUDENTS

Dramatics and Role-Playing

1. With your class, collect and save historical masks and masks of public figures for special dramatic use at other times of the year.
2. Read the tale of Ichabod Crane. Illustrate the story or dramatize it with a group.
3. With your class, give a ghost play, using Halloween handkerchief puppets.

Arts and Crafts

4. Make a Halloween mobile, using wire coat hangers and colored paper cutouts.
5. Make a mask from a paper bag or a paper plate decorated with colored paper and yarn.
6. Make a crazy ghost or a silly spook. Draw a ghost on paper and give it a plaid or polka-dot robe, using crayons or fabric. Add a hat and other accessories.
7. Have your teacher carve a jack-o'lantern. After every student has sketched a jack-o'-lantern face on paper, the class can decide which one they want carved. The student who makes the drawing can sketch the features on the pumpkin. The other students can help in other ways, such as scooping out the seeds, planning where to display the pumpkin, and planning display accessories.
8. More accidents, vandalism, and child abuse occur on Halloween than on any other day of the year. Make a Halloween safety poster.
9. Draw a ghost picture on black paper with wet white chalk.
10. Make a ghost from facial tissues. Roll one piece of tissue into a ball for the head. Cover it with another piece of tissue. Tie a string around the "neck." Make the face by pasting on cutout colored paper eyes and a mouth.
11. Decorate a brown paper bag to make your own trick-or-treat sack.
12. Make a paper bag owl. Stuff the bag with paper. Cut the edges for a feathery effect. Add eyes and color the owl.
13. Cut out big letters to make the title "Halloween Parade" or "Boo." Put the letters on a bulletin board or wall. Draw yourself or a friend in a costume. Arrange the class' drawings in a line—like a parade—under the title.

Writing and Language Arts

14. With a small group, write a ghost story.
15. Write a story, using these or other Halloween words: *rattles, noises, scare, spooky, mischief, laugh.* The stories can be compiled into a book. The book could be made in the shape of a witch or a pumpkin.

Special Projects

16. With the class, plan a Halloween fashion show. Students can "model" their costumes. Select a moderator to describe the costumes as students "model." Write a creative description of your costume for the moderator to read. Invite another class to attend the fashion show.
17. Have your teacher construct a three-dimensional cutout of a witch stirring a brew in a big pot. "What Can You Brew?" can be the caption. Each student can then pull a slip of paper from the pot with an activity to do for Halloween, such as "Write a story or poem using special words" or "Draw a witch."

Information Gathering and Sharing

18. Research the significance of Halloween colors and symbols. For example, orange and gold signify ripe fruit and grains; black signifies magic and mystery.
19. Write to UNICEF (3 United Nations Plaza, New York, NY 10017) for information about the UNICEF program and UNICEF Halloween activities.

Critical Thinking

20. Read about the origin of Halloween. With the class, discuss the differences between superstition and facts.

QUESTIONS FOR CLASS DISCUSSION

1. In what ways can Halloween be either sad or glad?
2. How is each of the "Hints for a Happy Halloween" (page 70) an important safety or good conduct rule for Halloween?
3. Even though Halloween has lost its original religious significance, why do you suppose that we continue to celebrate this holiday?
4. Why is Halloween a time to be careful as well as carefree?
5. What are some different categories of Halloween costumes?
6. Why do people enjoy wearing a costume on Halloween?
7. What are the popular symbols of Halloween?

KEY VOCABULARY

cemetery	parade
collect	polite
considerate	pranks
costume	pumpkin
disguise	respect
eerie	scared
fact	skeleton
fantasy	spook
ghost	superstition
goblin	treat
hallow	trick
inspect	vandalism
make-up	vision
mask	weird
mischief	witch
mystery	

RELATED CAREER EDUCATION TERMS

candy manufacturer	magician
cosmetician	make-up artist
costume designer	mask maker
costume distributor	police officer
entertainment consultant	special-effects technician

November

First Week:

* Election Day (the 1st Tuesday after the 1st Monday in November)

1

Author's Day

2

President James Polk born, 1795
President Warren Harding born, 1865
First regular radio broadcasting—over station KDKA in Pittsburgh, 1920
Daniel Boone, the trailblazer of Kentucky, born, 1734

3

World Community Day

4

* Will Rogers, humorist, born, 1879
Erie Canal formally opened, 1825

5

First transcontinental flight completed, 1911
Crossword puzzles first published in book form, 1924

6

John Philip Sousa, the march king, born, 1854
James Naismith, inventor of basketball, born, 1861
* First intercollegiate football game in the U.S., 1869

7

* Lewis and Clark expedition reached the Pacific Ocean, 1805
Last spike driven in Canadian Pacific Railway, 1885

*A teaching unit is included on the following pages for each starred entry.

Second Week:

National Stamp Collecting Week
World Fellowship Week
Sadie Hawkins Day (1st Saturday after November 11)

8

Montana became the 41st state, 1889
First circulating library established by Ben Franklin in Philadelphia, 1731
Edmund Halley, British astronomer, born, 1656

9

* Benjamin Banneker, engineer, inventor, mathematician, and gazetteer, born, 1731

10

* U.S. Marine Corps founded, 1775

11

* Veterans Day
Massachusetts passed first compulsory school law, 1647
Indian summer begins
Remembrance Day (Canada)

12

Elizabeth Cady Stanton, suffragist, born, 1815

13

Robert Louis Stevenson, Scottish poet and novelist, born, 1850
Holland Tunnel opened in New York City, 1927

14

Robert Fulton, inventor of the steamboat, born, 1765

15

Articles of Confederation approved by Congress, 1777
Pikes Peak discovered by Zebulon Pike, 1806

Third Week:

Geography Awareness Week (November 15–21)
National Arts Week (November 15–21)
National Children's Book Week
American Education Week

16

Oklahoma became a state, 1907

17

Suez Canal opened, 1869

18

Mickey Mouse first appeared on the screen in *Steamboat Willie*, 1928
National Smoke-Out Day
* Standard time began in the U.S., 1883
Louis Daguerre, father of photography, born, 1789
Asa Gray, botanist and taxonomist, born, 1810
Panama Canal Zone created, 1903

19

Abraham Lincoln delivered Gettysburg Address, 1863
President James A. Garfield born, 1831
George Rogers Clark, frontiersman, born, 1752

20

Robert F. Kennedy born, 1925

21

Thomas A. Edison invented phonograph, 1877
Mayflower Compact signed, 1620

22

President John F. Kennedy assassinated, 1963
Robert Cavelier, sieur de La Salle, French explorer, born, 1643
SOS adopted as a signal of distress, 1906

23

President Franklin Pierce born, 1804

Fourth Week:

* Thanksgiving (the 4th Thursday in November; 1st national Thanksgiving Day, November 26, 1789)

24
President Zachary Taylor born, 1784
Carlo Lorenzini, author of *Pinocchio*, born, 1826

25
Andrew Carnegie, steel magnate and friend of libraries, born, 1835
Joe DiMaggio, baseball star, born, 1914

26
First street railway in the U.S. began, 1832
Charles Schulz, creator of "Peanuts," born, 1922

27
Magellan entered the Pacific Ocean, 1520
Army War College established, 1901

28
First U.S. post office opened, in New York City, 1785

29
Admiral Byrd flew over the South Pole, 1929
Louisa May Alcott, author of young people's classics, born, 1832

30
Samuel Clemens (Mark Twain), born, 1835
Jonathan Swift, author of *Gulliver's Travels*, born, 1667

Election Day

THEMES AND THOUGHTS

Democracy, Obligation, Rights,
Freedom, Trust

Government is a trust, and the
officers of the government are
trustees; and both the trust and the
trustees are created for the benefit
of the people.

—*Henry Clay*

FASCINATING FACTS

In 1845, Congress set Election Day as the first Tuesday after the first Monday of November. Before this legislation, each state could choose its presidential electors on any day within thirty-four days before the date in December when the Electoral College convened.

The Constitution of the United States arranges for the election of the President and Vice President through the Electoral College. The Electoral College is the group of electors, nominated by political parties within the states and popularly elected, who meet after the votes are counted. They vote for the two top national officers. In our history, three men have been elected President by the Electoral College, although they received fewer popular votes than their opponents. These presidents were John Quincy Adams, Rutherford B. Hayes, and Benjamin Harrison.

Until 1868, only white men could vote. The Fourteenth Amendment gave black men the right to vote. Women were not given the right to vote until the Nineteenth Amendment was adopted in 1920.

The word *vote* originally meant a solemn pledge.

In the United States different kinds of elections are held. In addition to elections for national leaders, elections are also held for governors, state legislators, county and local officials, and members of boards of education. There are also primary elections to select candidates to run for office in general elections, run-off elections if no candidate wins a clear majority in the general elections, and special elections to replace public officials who die or leave office before the end of their terms.

The initiative procedure allows citizens to vote on a proposed law or public question. The referendum procedure refers measures passed or proposed by a legislative body to the electorate for approval or rejection. The recall procedure allows citizens to vote to remove a public official from office.

Information Gathering and Sharing

1. Invite a lawyer or a member of the local board of elections to come speak to the class about election procedures.
2. If a voting machine is installed in a school building prior to an election, have your teacher ask if the class can visit the poll and be briefed on the operation of a voting machine. For this briefing, bring in the sample ballot sent to your home.
3. As a class, conduct a class, school, or community pre-election survey or poll on referendum issues, as well as candidate preference.
4. Report on unusual, humorous, and fascinating events of past elections.
5. With a few classmates, choose a candidate to follow "on the stump." Keep a daily bulletin board (or one for each party), displaying highlights of speeches, campaign literature, reports of polls, and other pertinent campaign news items.
6. Compare voter turnout in the United States to that in other countries by charting the differences.
7. Make a "Fascinating Facts" booklet about voting.

Art and Visual Aids

8. Collect photos, literature, and campaign items for a bulletin board or a table display about an upcoming election.
9. Develop some campaign slogans for a current campaign or a mock election, and make a poster using them.

Writing and Language Arts

10. Write a newspaper article about current elections or a class mock election.

Critical Thinking

11. Compose a checklist of information to find out about a candidate's background, stands on issues, and qualifications.
12. Read and discuss provisions in the U.S. and state constitutions regarding voting laws.

Dramatics and Role-Playing

13. With a small group, role-play a women's suffrage episode, a campaign debate, a political discussion on TV, polling-place procedures, TV and radio coverage of an election night, or concession and victory speeches by the candidates.

Special Projects

14. A mock convention and election is an effective way of developing skills in candidate selection, platforms, campaign procedures, and the voting process. With your class, make and wear simple paper campaign buttons. Culminate the activity with an election day, using real voting machines if possible and having the "elected officials" serve for a day.
15. With your class, produce a movie or videotape about the history of women voting in the United States. The script may be narrated and synchronized to the film by using a tape recorder. After presenting the film to the class, prepared questions about it may be distributed.

QUESTIONS FOR CLASS DISCUSSION

1. What problems might be caused by not having a standard national election day?
2. In what ways can you as a student make people aware of their responsibility to vote?
3. Voter participation in national elections in the United States (under 60% of the voting-age population) is not as great as that in Australia, Israel, Italy, and other European nations (90%). Why do you think this is so?
4. In what ways have election practices changed in the United States within the past 25 years?
5. What are the advantages and disadvantages of the Electoral College? Why was this system established? What is a primary election?
6. Which election practices and customs in the United States should be changed? Which should be retained?
7. Is the two-party system working well in the United States, or would it be appropriate to

have a larger number of political parties?

8. Some people think that voting is more of an obligation (requirement) than a right (option to vote or not to vote). What is your opinion?

9. Some people feel that voters who are displeased with all the candidates should have the chance to vote "none of the above," thereby protesting the selections on the ballot. How do you feel about this?

RELATED CAREER EDUCATION TERMS

campaign manager	journalist
civil service employee	lawyer
county clerk	opinion pollster
election clerk	political scientist
historian	politician
	researcher

KEY VOCABULARY

absentee voting	poll
ballot	popular vote
campaign	primary election
candidate	primary vote
convene	qualification
dark horse	recall
Democrat	referendum
election	register
Electoral College	registration
electoral vote	representation
electorate	Republican
eligible	run-off election
franchise	secret ballot
funds	special election
government	straw vote
independent	suffrage
initiative	vote
nomination	voter
platform	voting district
plurality	voting machine
political party	write-in vote

Will Rogers Born

THEMES AND THOUGHTS

Humility, Humor,
Broad-Mindedness, Affection,
Cheerfulness

Your best buy is real estate—
they're not making any more.
—*Will Rogers*

All I know is just what I read in
the papers.
—*Will Rogers*

I am just an old country boy in a
big town trying to get along.
—*Will Rogers*

FASCINATING FACTS

Will Rogers, who gained worldwide fame as a humorist and homespun philosopher, was born on a ranch near Oolagah in the Indian Territory (now Oklahoma) in 1879. He was part Cherokee Indian—and proud of it. He often said, "My ancestors may not have come over on the Mayflower, but they met 'em at the boat."

Rogers began his career as a cowhand in Texas and Oklahoma, but he didn't like the lifestyle. So he went to Argentina and then to South Africa in 1902 to seek adventure. He ended up joining a "Wild West" show and then a circus as a trick roper. He toured Australia and New Zealand before returning to the United States. Rogers used ropes from 7 feet to 90 feet long to perform his tricks.

He began a vaudeville career as a trick roper and a humorist. People laughed at his jokes and remarks about U.S. society. He opposed greed, hypocrisy, and smugness.

Soon he was in demand in Hollywood—first for silent films and later for "talkies." With his slow drawl and his sharp wit, he became a popular radio personality and lecturer. Rogers also wrote a column that appeared in over 350 newspapers, numerous magazine articles for the *Saturday Evening Post,* and six books.

Rogers gathered a number of nicknames during his colorful and varied career, including "Cherokee Kid," "Poet Lariat," "Cowboy Philosopher," and "America's Goodwill Ambassador." In 1935, he died in a plane crash near Point Barrow, Alaska, while flying with the pioneer aviator Wiley Post. The Will Rogers Memorial is in Claremore, Oklahoma, and a statue of Rogers stands in the U.S. Capitol in Washington, D.C.

ACTIVITIES FOR STUDENTS

Information Gathering and Sharing

1. Ask your teacher to locate and play for the class an old phonograph record of some of Will Rogers' famous performances or clever sayings.

2. As a class, make a collection of some of Will Rogers' sayings. Discuss their significance and meaning.
3. On an outline map of the United States, locate all the places associated with Will Rogers. Label these places on the map.
4. Read about Will Rogers and report your findings to the class.
5. Make a timeline of major U.S. and world events during Will Rogers' lifetime (1879–1935).
6. The world that Will Rogers grew up in was very different from the one he lived in after he became a famous humorist. Make a chart comparing life in the Indian Territory in the 1890s and life in New York or Hollywood in the 1920s.

Writing and Language Arts

7. Write a newspaper review of your impressions of one of Will Rogers' stage or motion picture performances.
8. Make a word list of Will Rogers' outstanding characteristics.

Special Activities

9. Attempt some rope tricks.
10. With your class, establish a "Humorous Thought for the Day" project. Collect quotable sayings and communicate them to the student body either by an intercom announcement each morning or by posting them in a prominent place in your school.

QUESTIONS FOR CLASS DISCUSSION

1. What topics in modern life might Will Rogers talk about?
2. Why do you think Will Rogers saw the bright side of every problem?
3. What is there about life on the range that might make a cowboy a wise philosopher?
4. Why do you think Will Rogers was not spoiled by fame or fortune?
5. It was said that Will Rogers was a "self-made man." What does this mean?
6. Which present-day humorist do you enjoy most? Why?

7. Why is humor especially important to a country during trying times, such as wars and economic depressions?

KEY VOCABULARY

adventurer	repertoire
cowboy	rodeo
entertainer	roper
folk story	satire
frontier	shrewd
homespun	spoof
humility	spurs
humorist	star performer
kerchief	ten-gallon hat
lariat	wit
philosophy	yarn
punch line	

RELATED CAREER EDUCATION TERMS

author	humorist
cowhand	philosopher
entertainer	

First Intercollegiate Football Game in the U.S.

Sportsmanship, Teamwork, Cooperation, Winning

And if I should lose, let me stand by the road and cheer as the winners go by!
—*Berton Braley*

The game isn't over till it's over.
—*Yogi Berra*

In life, as in a football game, the principle to follow is: Hit the line hard.
—*Theodore Roosevelt*

FASCINATING FACTS

Many ancient civilizations, including the Egyptians, the Greeks, the Chinese, the Mayas, and the Aztecs, played games in which a spherical object was kicked or carried forward. The game we know today in North America as football may have originated from a game the Roman legions brought to Britain in the first century A.D. There were no rules for playing, and the teams had any number of players. The ball was made of the inflated bladder of an animal, usually a pig. That is perhaps where we get the term *pigskin* for a football.

Football was brought to North America by the colonists and was played on village greens. In the mid-1800s, it became a popular sport on school campuses. This game resembled soccer, however, because the ball could only be kicked, not carried or thrown. Princeton and Rutgers played the first college football game in New Brunswick, New Jersey, on November 6, 1869, using soccer rules and a round ball. There were 25 players on each team. Rutgers won, 6–4.

Rugby, which allows players to run with the ball and to tackle each other, originated as a variation of soccer at Rugby School in England

in 1823. Rugby was brought to Canada soon after that. In 1874, a team from McGill University in Montreal, Canada, introduced rugby to Harvard University's team. The Harvard team liked this version of "football" so much that it introduced the game to teams from other East Coast colleges.

By 1900, football had become a very rough game. It consisted mainly of running, blocking, and tackling. And the players did not wear helmets or padded uniforms. President Theodore Roosevelt, a football fan, met with representatives of Harvard, Yale, and Princeton in 1905 to urge them to make the game less violent. As a result, the Intercollegiate Athletic Association was formed to establish standard rules for the game.

Today, the basic principle of North American football is to kick, throw, or carry the ball into the scoring area marked at the end of the playing field. A regulation football weighs 14–15 ounces (397–425 grams) and is 11–11 1/2 inches (28–29.2 centimeters) long. It is an elongated sphere made of a rubber bladder inflated to 13 pounds (5.9 kilograms) of pressure and covered with leather, rubber, or plastic.

In U.S. football, there are 11 players on a team. A game for high school and college teams is 48 minutes clock time (60 minutes for professional teams). Each team has to move the ball 10 yards in four downs or relinquish the ball. The team scoring the most points wins. The field is 100 yards (91.4 meters) long by 53 yards (48.5 meters) wide.

Canadian football is slightly different. A team consists of 12 players. Only three downs are allowed. And the field is slightly larger than that in U.S. football—110 yards (100.6 meters) by 65 yards (59.4 meters).

In most countries, except the United States and Canada, the word *football* describes the game that North Americans call *soccer*. This kind of "football" is played in at least 140 countries and is by far the most popular international sport.

ACTIVITIES FOR STUDENTS

Information Gathering and Sharing

1. Report on a famous football hero, such as Amos Alonzo Stagg, Knute Rockne, Pop Warner, Jim Thorpe, Jim Brown, Johnny Unitas, Joe Namath, George Blanda, Roger Staubach, Dan Marino, or Lawrence Taylor.
2. Report on the first intercollegiate football game, held in New Brunswick, New Jersey, 1869.
3. With your class, make a list of outstanding leaders who were sports participants, such as Theodore Roosevelt (football), Gerald Ford (golf and football), Dwight Eisenhower (golf), Ronald Reagan (football), Bill Bradley (basketball), Jack Kemp (football), and George Bush (baseball).
4. Write to the Professional Football Hall of Fame (Canton, Ohio 44700) for information on the origin of football.
5. Write to the sports editor of your local newspaper for the names of outstanding regional football players. Make a local "Hall of Fame."

Critical Thinking

6. Make up a football rules quiz for use in a class chalkboard football game.
7. Make a list of good sportsmanship qualities. For example: be a good loser, accept the decision of the referee, respect a good play.

Writing and Language Arts

8. As a class, develop and duplicate a glossary of important football signals and terms for spectators to take to games.

Public Speaking

9. Have a class debate of the proposition "Winning supersedes all else" or "Try to win at any cost."

Art and Visual Aids

10. Draw illustrations of sports equipment designed for the safety of the opponent as well as the wearer, such as a helmet (unbreakable plastic with a face mask and webbing to lessen shock), pads (to protect shoulders, ribs, thighs, hips, knees), shoes (with cleats for traction to avoid slipping), and a mouth guard (to protect lips and teeth).

QUESTIONS FOR CLASS DISCUSSION

1. Why is a football field sometimes referred to as a gridiron?
2. Why is it important to train and prepare before playing in a football game?
3. What are the major purposes of football rules?
4. In what ways would you try to improve the game of football as played in our country today?
5. Why did early football players suffer serious injuries?
6. Why do football teams have team names?
7. What makes football so popular today?
8. How is football similar to soccer and rugby?

9. Why are so many officials needed at a football game?
10. In what ways do cheerleaders help a football team?
11. List what it takes to be a good football player.

KEY VOCABULARY

backfield	league
block	marker
captain	offense
cheer	official
cheerleader	pass
coach	penalty
defense	pigskin
field goal	play
first down	punt
fumble	rugby
game plan	safety
gear	shoulder pads
goal posts	soccer
gridiron	spectator
helmet	substitute
huddle	tackle
intercollegiate	touchdown
jersey	yard stripes
kickoff	

RELATED CAREER EDUCATION TERMS

cheerleader	public relations person
coach	quarterback
head linesman	referee
judge	scout
legal consultant	sportscaster
official	sports doctor
physical education teacher	trainer
player	umpire

Lewis and Clark Expedition Reached the Pacific Ocean

THEMES AND THOUGHTS

Imagination, Exploration, Discovery, Friendship

Beyond the East the sunrise,
beyond the West the sea,
And East and West the wander-thirst
that will not let me be.
—*Gerald Gould*

If the mountain will not come to Mahomet, Mahomet must go to the mountain.
—*Proverb, adapted from Francis Bacon*

FASCINATING FACTS

Meriwether Lewis and William Clark blazed a trail to the Pacific Ocean, which strengthened U.S. claims to the Oregon territory, stimulated fur trading in the West, and provided valuable information about Native American tribes and lands. Lewis and Clark were selected by President Jefferson to head the expedition. Their party was composed of about forty soldiers, nine Kentucky frontiersmen, and two French boatmen, as well as Clark's slave, York, and Sacagawea, a female American Indian guide and translator. They were gone for two years, four months, and nine days and traveled approximately 7,700 miles (12,400 kilometers).

The outward journey across the Louisiana Territory took them up the Missouri River, over the Continental Divide atop the Rocky Mountains, and down the Columbia River. Much of the river travel was done in a large keelboat and two smaller vessels. The expedition was laden with many kinds of supplies and gifts for the Native American tribes the explorers would encounter.

The journals kept by Lewis and Clark, both young army officers, told about sighting grizzly bears, encounters with unfriendly tribes, and other dangerous incidents. Included also was information about the region's geography and climate, with maps for additional trails to the West.

Lewis and Clark are remembered as two important pathfinders.

ACTIVITIES FOR STUDENTS

Writing and Language Arts

1. Pretend you are a member of the Lewis and Clark expedition and write a diary for part of the trip.
2. Write an article about the expedition that might have appeared in a newspaper of the time.
3. Write an original television or radio program covering the expedition.

4. Make an alphabetized list of words that describe Lewis and Clark's characters and contribution to history. Try to think of at least one adjective or noun for each letter of the alphabet.

Critical Thinking

5. Make a list of the items the expedition might take if they were traveling the same route today. Compare this list with the equipment Lewis and Clark expedition's probably did travel with.
6. Compile a list of the kinds of topography, fauna, and flora the expedition probably happened upon.

Role-Playing and Public Speaking

7. Compose and deliver a speech that President Jefferson might have made about the expedition.
8. Have two students assume the roles of Lewis and Clark. The rest of the class can be journalists interviewing the team upon their arrival in St. Louis.

Information Gathering and Reporting

9. With a committee, report on the routes and demonstrate the ways the Lewis and Clark expedition was able to find its way across uncharted wilderness.
10. Make a flip story of the expedition.
11. As a class, collect and discuss types of navigation instruments and their uses.
12. Divide the class into three groups. Each group will choose one of the following topics to read about in *The Journals of Lewis and Clark* (Mentor, 1964) and then report on their readings to the class: (a) animals seen on the expedition, (b) meetings with Native Americans, and (c) traveling around the Great Falls.

Map Skills

13. Define the Continental Divide. Trace it on a map of the United States.
14. Retrace the Lewis and Clark expedition on a map. What cities are now located along the route they took?

Art and Visual Aids

15. Design a Lewis and Clark Expedition Medal to be awarded to modern-day explorers.

QUESTIONS FOR CLASS DISCUSSION

1. Often the preparation for a task is almost as difficult and as trying as completing the task itself. What preparations did Lewis and Clark have to make in order to undertake the expedition?
2. What qualities of leadership did President Jefferson seek that persuaded him to select Lewis and Clark for this expedition?
3. Why did the expedition party include frontiersmen?
4. What hardships did the members of the expedition experience?
5. If you had been a member of the expedition, what information and specimens would you have brought back with you?
6. What area of the world would be an exciting place in which to conduct an expedition today?
7. How did the Lewis and Clark expedition differ from Columbus' voyage?
8. What kind of equipment do you think these trailblazers had to take with them? What did they need to provide for themselves along the way?
9. What kind of character and personality do you think Lewis, Clark, and each member of their party needed to have in order to make the expedition?
10. What is the difference between the terms "up river" and "down river"?
11. Who are the Lewises and Clarks of our present era?
12. In what manner and forms are Lewis and Clark remembered today?

KEY VOCABULARY

camp
chronicle
Continental
   Divide
equipment
expedition
explore
frontiersman
guide
journal
journey

keelboat
log
map
portage
precaution
scout
territory
trail
traverse
uncharted

RELATED CAREER EDUCATION TERMS

adventurer
cartographer
engineer
explorer
geographer
geologist
guide
military officer

naturalist
navigator
negotiator
ranger
researcher
supplier
trader (business
   person)

Benjamin Banneker Born

THEMES AND THOUGHTS

Perseverance, Fairness, Recognition, Imagination, Planning

One universal Father hath given to us all. . . . Endowed us with the same faculties. . . . We are all of the same family.
—Benjamin Banneker, in a letter dated August 19, 1791, to Thomas Jefferson

Great works are performed not only by strength, but by perseverance.
—Samuel Johnson

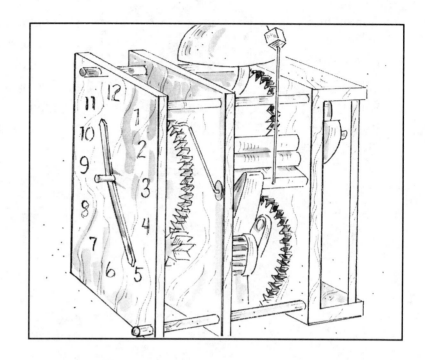

FASCINATING FACTS

Benjamin Banneker was one of the most exceptional men in the United States during the eighteenth century. Born in 1731 in Ellicott's Mills, Maryland (near Baltimore), to a free mother and a slave father, Banneker received much of his early education from his grandmother, who used the Bible to teach him how to read. Later he attended a one-room schoolhouse, where he completed the eighth grade. But he never stopped learning. He continued to educate himself until he died at the age of 75.

The most important lesson to be learned from Banneker's life is that a thirst for knowledge is not limited to youth and that the process of learning does not distinguish between color, race, or creed.

In his youth, Banneker spent most of his time working on the farm close to his home and family. Although a free black man, he still could not easily travel about. Perhaps this is why he began to develop a deep interest in observing all living things around him. Growing up on a farm helped him develop a special interest in beekeeping and locusts. He kept scientific records about them and wrote about his observations.

Throughout his youth, Banneker showed an unusual ability in mathematics and mechanical things. All his life, he loved to work on mathematical puzzles. In 1753, he completed a "striking" clock, which was probably the first wooden timepiece of this kind to be made in America. His clock continued to operate until his death in 1806.

At age 32, an important event in Banneker's life was the purchase of his first book—the *Holy Bible*. He began to read more and became very curious about the skies and the visible heavens around him. He started to teach himself astronomy. He also learned about the science of surveying. In his lonely hours after work, Banneker turned to music. He owned a flute and violin and learned to play both reasonably well. He received much pleasure from the sounds that his music produced.

As the years went on, Banneker became known in his region as a man of learning. He continued to work and study. Usually only the wealthy landowners knew how to read and write, so many of Benjamin Banneker's neighbors came to him for advice and help. Many also came to see his famous clock. Everyone liked him for his modesty, dignity, and gentlemanly conduct.

He wrote an almanac, which was published in 1792—the first scientific book published by a black American. In his lifetime, he contributed important scientific articles to several almanacs. Banneker also actively campaigned against slavery.

Benjamin Banneker was greatly influenced by Major Andrew Ellicott, a professional surveyor, and his family. He often worked with Ellicott and used his surveying instruments on special projects. Early in 1791, Banneker became involved in the greatest adventure of his life—the survey and planning of a federal city (Washington, D.C.) that was to serve as the capital of the new republic, the United States of America. After Thomas Jefferson commissioned Major Ellicott to survey the District of Columbia, Ellicott asked Banneker to assist him in surveying the ten-square mile area and in establishing lines for some of the major points in the city.

ACTIVITIES FOR STUDENTS

Information Gathering and Sharing

1. Invite a surveyor to come speak to your class. Municipal governments, construction companies, and engineering companies employ surveyors. Or one of your classmates' parents may be a surveyor. With your classmates, prepare in advance a list of questions that you would like the surveyor to discuss. For example:

   • What kind of work does a surveyor do?

   • What do you like about your work?

   • What do you not like about surveying?

   • What skills should a surveyor have?

   • What is the salary range for surveyors?

   • How do you use special surveyors' instruments, such as a plane table and an alidade?

   • Are there many women in this field? If not, why?

2. Write to the Superintendent of Documents, U.S. Government Printing Office, Washington, DC 20402, for a list of free and inexpensive materials about our nation's capital, its important government buildings, and Benjamin Banneker.

3. Banneker's wooden "striking" clock reportedly worked for over 50 years, from 1753 to 1806. Many things can happen in 50 years. Use the library as a source of information to compile a list of the major events in the United States during the 50 years that Banneker's clock worked—for example, the Boston Tea Party (1773), the First Continental Congress (1774), the American Revolution (1775–1783), and the Declaration of Independence (signed July 4, 1775). With a small group, create a pictorial timeline or chart listing these highlights. Or create a monologue spoken by the clock to describe what it saw and heard during those 50 years.

Map Making and Reading

4. Obtain and study building blueprints, street maps, civil engineering construction site maps, topographic sheets, and other maps of nearby places.

5. With your class, undertake a simple surveying or field mapping project. Make a map of the classroom, the school, the playground, or a nearby park.

   Materials needed:
   Fiber board, clipboard, or lightweight folding tray table to be used as a plane table

   Large piece of paper on which to draw the map

   Straight pins (or small nails) to be used to make an alidade

   Ruler (or straight edge) to be used to make an alidade

   Compass to be used to determine direction

   Procedure:
   Identify a section of the playground or

your neighborhood that you will field map. Assemble your instruments. An alidade can be made by placing a straight pin in each end of the ruler. The pins are used to align and sight reference, or fixed, points to be mapped.

Steps:

    a. Fix paper on board of hard, flat surface. Orient paper to compass direction by making a compass rose (N, S, E, W) and aligning paper with corresponding compass directions.

    b. Sight marker in line with alidade pins (makeshift telescope).

    c. Draw ray line (a straight line of sight extending from a point on baseline) along ruler.

    d. Proceed to next marker and sight from that location. Follow procedure from point to point to complete map.

    e. Measure distance by counting paces from point to point. Convert each pace to feet while moving about during mapping.

    f. Indicate estimated distances and plot buildings and landscape features on map. Include a key or legend.

6. Create a "Community of Tomorrow." Develop a map showing natural and cultural features.

7. Obtain a map of your city or town. Offer ideas that might improve the area. Give reasons for your ideas.

Art and Visual Aids

8. With your class, discuss the reasons for making a model when one is either planning to build something or trying to understand how something was built. A model is a miniature likeness or representation. Use sugar cubes, styrofoam, and glue to construct a model of a historical building, such as the White House, the Capitol, or a government building in your community or state. Make a list of the scales used for the model, such as 1 cube = 100 feet.

Critical Thinking

9. Civil rights laws help us live up to our nation's guiding principles of freedom and democracy. These laws were enacted because, throughout our nation's history, people have stood up for the principle of equality for all Americans. Brainstorm with your classmates about what life would have been like had particular African-Americans never lived or had particular events in black history not occurred. Select one person or event for a class research project, and then decide on subtopics for small groups to research. Use an outline. Plan a "division of labor" together: choose the members of each subtopic committee, decide on a timeline for the completion of each group's work, and plan daily work periods, clearing time for library use with the librarian. When the research is completed, work out a way of presenting it to another class in the school.

For additional activities about black history, see "Emancipation Proclamation Issued" (pages 146-148), "Martin Luther King, Jr." (pages 155–157), "Frederick Douglass" (pages 174–177), "Crispus Attucks" (pages 210–212), "Harriet Tubman" (pages 216–218), and "Booker T. Washington" (pages 247–249).

QUESTIONS FOR CLASS DISCUSSION

1. In what ways were the two Bens—Benjamin Banneker and Benjamin Franklin—similar? How did they differ?

2. What problems do you think Benjamin Banneker faced? How did he make the most of his opportunities?

3. If Benjamin Banneker were alive today, what projects do you think he would be interested in exploring? Why?

4. How did young Benjamin Banneker's fondness for arithmetic help in his work in later life? Give some examples.

5. Can you think of some ways Benjamin Banneker earned recognition for his "famous firsts"?

6. What personal characteristics do you think Benjamin Banneker had? Explain your selections.

7. What is your interpretation of the quotation from the letter Banneker sent to Jefferson? How did his own life prove his point?
8. How do you think Benjamin Banneker might have used his almanac to help him survey the Territory of Columbia, which later became the city of Washington, D.C.?
9. Benjamin Banneker made important contributions to three separate fields of scholarship—the history of science, black studies, and U.S. history. What other credits should he receive?

RELATED CAREER EDUCATION TERMS

architect	engineer
astronomer	journalist
author	mathematician
city planner	surveyor
draftsman	

KEY VOCABULARY

almanac	linear
altitude	mathematician
angular	measurement
aptitude	pace
astronomer	planet
blueprint	prejudice
boundary	publish
capital	scale
capitol	sextant
celestial	sighting
crosshairs	survey
design	surveyor
eclipse	surveyor's chair
elevation	
instrument	telescope
land	tract

U.S. Marine Corps Founded

THEMES AND THOUGHTS

Loyalty, Responsibility, Courage

From the Halls of Montezuma
To the shores of Tripoli,
We fight our country's battles
In the air, on land and sea.
—*Marines' Hymn*

I am myself the guardian of my honor.

—*Nicholas Rowe*

FASCINATING FACTS

The Marine is a sea soldier specially trained for landing operations. Marines are called upon to serve their country quickly in special emergencies by combining the skills of soldiers and sailors. They are trained to fight anywhere in the world.

The U.S. Marine Corps was established by the Continental Congress on November 10, 1775, to fight in the Revolutionary War and was re-created in 1798. Marines have fought in almost every major war in which the United States has been involved.

The Marine Corps motto is "Semper Fidelis—Always Faithful." The official colors are scarlet and gold. The emblem adorning the Marine uniform consists of an eagle, which is a symbol of the United States, the globe, which represents worldwide service, and the anchor, which recalls the Marine Corps' origin as a naval organization. The Marine Corps band is called the "President's Own" because it plays at state affairs.

Marines are often called "leathernecks" because they once wore leather bands around their throats. "Devil Dogs," a nickname given to the Marines in the twentieth century, is a translation of the epithet "Teufelhunden," said to have been coined by enemy German soldiers during World War I.

Marines are on duty at more than 500 stations around the globe, guarding and protecting U.S. interests 24 hours each day of the year.

ACTIVITIES FOR STUDENTS

Information Gathering and Sharing

1. Learn and sing the three verses of the "Marines' Hymn."
2. Write a report on the training of a Marine.
3. Investigate and report on a Marine's day.
4. Make a timeline of outstanding events in the history of the Marine Corps.

5. Find out what happened on the "shores of Tripoli" on April 27, 1805, and in the "halls of Montezuma" in Mexico City, September 14, 1847.

6. Make an illustrated fact book about the U.S. Marine Corps. Give your book an appropriate title.

7. Find out the nicknames of some famous Marine Corps fighting units, past and present.

8. Make a list of the pieces of equipment a Marine must usually carry into a battle zone.

9. With your class, visit a Marine recruiting station to obtain information about the Marine Corps.

10. The Iwo Jima campaign was one of the most significant and costly battles of World War II. As a class, make a special report about that encounter and the famous statue showing the raising of the U.S. flag on Mt. Suribachi on February 23, 1945. Discuss this symbol of courage and valor. Class artists may want to reproduce the dramatic memorial.

11. Research and report on the role Marines played in one of the following military operations:

Bahamas (1776)
The Tripolitan War and the War of 1812
Creek and Seminole Wars (1836–42)
Mexican War (1846–48)
Civil War (1861–65)
China, Japan, Korea (19th century)
Panama, South America, Haiti, Nicaragua during Spanish-American War (1898)
Philippine Islands, Cuba (20th century)
Vera Cruz, Mexico (1914)
China (1905–41)
Panama (1903–14)
Nicaragua (1910–13 and 1926–33)
Haiti (1915–34)
Dominican Republic (1916–24)
World War I (1917–18)
Guadalcanal (1942)
South Pacific during World War II (1942–46)
Korea (1950–53)
Inchon (1950)
Vietnam (1965–73)
Beirut, Lebanon (1958 and 1983–84)

Writing and Language Arts

12. Write a song or poem in tribute to the U.S. Marine Corps.

13. With your class, or by yourself, write a letter to a "leatherneck" serving in the Marine Corps.

14. Pretend you are a Marine stationed overseas. Write to a loved one at home telling about your experiences.

15. Make a glossary of Marine Corps terms, such as ashore, aye-aye sir, boondocks, chit, CO, gung ho, hunker-down, liberty, PX, grunt, quarters, reveille, scuttlebutt, and swab.

Art and Visual Aids

16. Collect and display pictures showing the various Marine Corps uniforms.

17. Draw and report on the Marine Corps officers' and enlisted men's grade insignias.

18. Contribute to a bulletin-board display of clippings from newspapers about Marines throughout the world.

19. Contribute to a montage of Marine Corps drawings in an ongoing display on the bulletin board.

QUESTIONS FOR CLASS DISCUSSION

1. Why are the Marines so proud of their uniform and history?

2. Why does a Marine live by the motto "Semper Fidelis," or "Always Faithful"?

3. Why must a Marine undergo very difficult training before he is ready for combat?

4. How has the Marine Corps changed since 1775?

5. Why are Marines called upon to guard U.S. embassies, legations, and consulates in other countries?

6. What is the relationship between the root word *mar* and the word *marine*?

7. The Marine Corps sometimes advertises or puts out a call for "A Few Good Men and Women." Some other Marine Corps slogans are "First to Fight" and "Esprit de Corps."

What do you think each saying is intended to mean?

8. What does it take to be a Marine? Why is it so difficult to become a Marine recruit?
9. Why are Marines especially useful in today's new kinds of global trouble spots?
10. What do you think the expression "Once a Marine, always a Marine" implies?
11. Women Marines are usually not allowed to participate in hostile combat encounters. Is this policy a good or bad idea? Why?
12. Why do the U.S. Marines try to recruit only "A Few Good Men and Women"?
13. Why does the Marine Corps training at boot camp need to be vigorous and challenging?
14. Why are Marines often called "grunts"?

KEY VOCABULARY

amphibious	honor guard
assault	infantry
barracks	insignia
base	inspection
bivouac	leatherneck
boot camp	mail call
casualty	Marine
combat	Pentagon
commandant	platoon
corps	pride
deployment	rank
dress blues	readiness
drill instructor	recruit
embassy	sea soldier
enlist	Semper Fidelis
fitness	strategy
fox hole	tradition
guerrilla warfare	vigil

RELATED CAREER EDUCATION TERMS

boat or aircraft mechanic	medical assistant
career officer or soldier	military attaché
communications operations and repair technician	munitions expert
computer technician	navigator
cook and food management worker	park ranger
embassy official	personnel manager
mechanical technician	pilot
	sailor
	transportation expert
	weapons expert

Veterans Day

THEMES AND THOUGHTS

Service, Duty, Loyalty,
Patriotism, Honor

And they who for their country die
    Shall fill an honored grave,
    For glory lights the soldier's tomb,
    And beauty weeps the brave.
        —*Joseph Rodman Drake*

And we'll all feel gay when
Johnny comes marching home.
        —*Patrick Sarsfield*

I pledge allegiance to the flag of
the United States of America, and to
the Republic for which it stands,
indivisible, with liberty and justice
for all.
        —*Francis Bellamy (Congress
added "one Nation under God" in 1954)*

If I lose my honor, I lose myself.
        —*William Shakespeare*

FASCINATING FACTS

The courage and patriotism of all the women and men who have served in the armed services of the United States are honored on Veterans Day. In 1919, President Woodrow Wilson proclaimed November 11 Armistice Day, but the day did not become a national holiday until 1938. Its name was changed to Veterans Day by Congress in 1954. President Dwight D. Eisenhower signed the bill into law for this day "to honor veterans . . . a day dedicated to world peace."

Observances are held throughout the country on this federal holiday in the form of prayer services, rallies, assembly programs, parades, patriotic speeches, and grave-side flag displays. The Tomb of the Unknown Soldier at Arlington National Cemetery outside Washing-

ton, D.C., where thousands of service personnel are buried, is the focus of the nation's tribute on Veterans Day.

A number of veteran organizations (perhaps 700) exist in the United States. Many, like the American Legion, the Veterans of Foreign Wars, and the Disabled American Veterans, are chartered by the U.S. Congress. They are primarily organized to help veterans and their families in time of need, to support measures to promote the welfare and security of the country, and to support patriotic and moral values through special school, hospital, and civic programs. Their special concerns are to see that veterans' rights are protected, that hospitalization and service-connected medical care are provided, and that the men and women who wore the uniforms of their nation's armed forces are remembered.

Critical Thinking

1. Review the meaning of the "Pledge of Allegiance."
2. With the class, discuss why "Taps" is played at memorial services.

Information Gathering and Sharing

3. Make a class or school survey of relatives who were veterans and their branch of service.
4. Invite a local veteran to come speak to the class about his or her military experiences.
5. With your class, sponsor a flag display and tell about the history, rules for use, and meaning of the design and colors. Emphasize proper use and display of the American flag.
6. Find out which Veterans Day parades, programs, and other patriotic activities are scheduled to be held in your community.
7. With a committee, report on a branch of the armed services.
8. List some of the organizations founded by veterans in the United States.
9. Do a report on the U.S. Military, Naval, or Air Force Academy.
10. Report on the work of the USO.
11. Report on the famous people buried in the Arlington National Cemetery (Virginia) and the following shrines located there: Arlington House, the Robert E. Lee Memorial; the Confederate Memorial; the grave of President John F. Kennedy; the Marine Corps War Memorial; and the Tomb of the Unknown Soldier, commemorating soldiers of past wars.
12. Make a military service chart listing various service specialties (obtained from recruiting stations) for each of the five branches of the armed forces.
13. Report on the Vietnam War Memorial in Washington, D.C.
14. Make a list of monuments, buildings, stadiums, and other sites that honor veterans.

Music

15. With your class, sing patriotic and popular war songs, such as "The Battle Hymn of the Republic" or "America, the Beautiful." Learn the words to the national anthem.

Special Projects

16. Have a parade within your class or school to commemorate Veterans Day.
17. Participate in a civic or hospital drive for veterans.

Arts and Crafts

18. Make a placemat, bookmark, or other appropriate gift for distribution at a veterans hospital.
19. With your class, make a mural of a Veterans Day parade.

Writing and Language Arts

20. Write to someone on active duty at a distant base or to a veteran confined in a hospital or retirement home.
21. Look in poetry anthologies for poems about flags, national service, and service personnel. Then compose your own poem about one of these topics.
22. Write a patriotic speech for a Veterans Day celebration.

1. Why is a country's flag so important?
2. How might a soldier feel when called to defend his or her country? Why do many citizens volunteer for the armed services in peacetime?
3. Why does our country need the Veterans Administration, which aids former military personnel?
4. Why is it important to have a parade or other type of patriotic program on Veterans Day?
5. What are some of the advantages a young

man or woman might gain by joining a branch of the armed forces?

6. Why does the United States need a modern and strong Army, Air Force, Navy, Marine Corps, and Coast Guard?

7. Why does the nation owe veterans a debt of gratitude? What should be done for them upon return to civilian life?

8. How can a member of the armed forces be considered a "community helper"?

9. In what ways are our armed services called upon to guard and serve citizens on a daily basis, as well as in emergency situations?

10. Why are service academies needed for each of the armed forces?

RELATED CAREER EDUCATION TERMS

armed forces personnel	electronics specialist
business administrator	lawyer
computer specialist	manager
consultant	mechanic
cook	paramedic
doctor	pilot
	technician
	trainer

KEY VOCABULARY

allegiance	Occupational Specialty)
armed forces	National Guard
armistice	officer
armored division	overseas
basic training	paratrooper
benefit	patriot
campaign	Pentagon
combat	pledge
command	private
commando	rank
commemorate	remembrance
courage	ROTC
disability	salute
duty	serviceman
enlist	strategy
furlough	theater of operations
G.I.	Veterans Administration
helmet	volunteer
honorable discharge	WAC
loyalty	WAVES
medal	
MOS (Military	

Standard Time Began in the U.S.

THEMES AND THOUGHTS

Orderliness, Organization, Accuracy

Time goes, you say? Ah no! Alas, time stays, we go.
—*Austin Dobson*

Be ruled by time, the wisest counselor of all.
—*Pericles*

Nothing is ours except time.
—*Seneca*

There's a time for some things, and a time for all things; a time for great things, and a time for small things.
—*Cervantes*

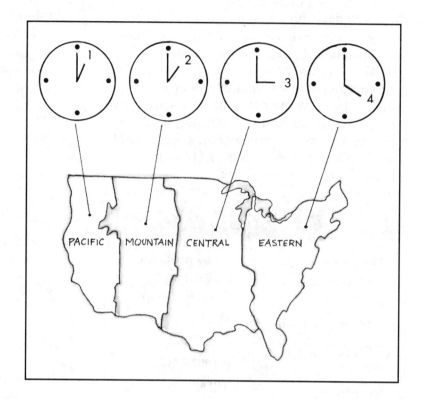

FASCINATING FACTS

Until late in the nineteenth century, there was no regional, national, or international standard time. People would set their timepieces according to the position of the sun. If local time were correct within a quarter of an hour, most people were satisfied. Until the telegraph and the railroad enabled people to communicate and travel long distances quickly, no one cared whether their local time was synchronized with the local time of a town one hundred miles away.

One of the first attempts to standardize time nationwide came in about 1865, when the U.S. Naval Observatory began sending time signals by telegraph. Large cities that chose to use this system set up a "time-ball" in a central location. This was a hollow 3-inch red ball that could travel up and down a mast. Each day at 3 minutes before noon, the ball was elevated to the top of the mast and dropped as soon as the time signal for noon arrived. People within view of

the time-ball could use this signal to set their watches.

The time-ball was a beginning, but there were still a number of local times in each state. For example, there were 27 local times in Minnesota, 38 in Wisconsin, and 23 in Indiana. For the convenience of travelers and shippers, railroad companies set up schedules for the trains on their lines. To make its schedule simpler, each railroad company developed its own system of time zones along its routes. But each of the dozens of railroad companies served only a small portion of the country. By the early 1870s, over 50 different railroad times were used across the United States, and the number continued to grow. Confusion abounded. A railroad station served by five railroad lines, each with its own time, would probably have five clocks, each showing a different time. A train passenger going from Maine to California would have to reset his or her watch at least 20 times during the trip in order not to miss connections between railway lines.

In 1883, U.S. railroad companies adopted a system of four time zones for their use: Eastern, Central, Mountain, and Pacific. Not until March 1918, however, did Congress instruct the Interstate Commerce Commission to determine the actual boundaries between the different zones.

In 1884, an international conference established a system of worldwide time zones. There are now twenty-four time zones around the world. The centers of the zones are 15° of longitude apart. In some land areas, the boundaries zigzag in order to avoid a change of time in the middle of a population center. Clock time changes exactly one hour from one zone to the next.

The United States and Canada stretch across eight time zones from the Eastern Zone along Canada's east coast to the Bering Zone along western Alaska.

ACTIVITIES FOR STUDENTS

Experiments

1. Even though we now have standardized time, all the watches and clocks in any one place do not necessarily show exactly the same time. Try this experiment in your school (or elsewhere in the community). Have everyone in your class synchronize their watches. Then spread out. Each of you should ask ten different people exactly what time it is. Record each answer. Compare the times recorded. Does everyone have the same time?

2. As a class, set your watches with a time-ball. Have one student go to the school office shortly before noon and at exactly noon, call or signal the classroom. Have someone in the classroom release the time-ball (constructed in advance). Everyone with a watch will set it to noon. Do this the next day to see if the correct time was kept by all the watches. (Note: Instead of using the office clock, you might check the time with the telephone operator.)

3. How close to high noon ("sun noon") is your "clock noon"? Go outdoors with your class a few minutes before noon on a sunny day and pair off. One member of each pair will stand tall while the other member checks his or her diminishing shadow. The shadow checker must check the shadow often until it seems to be at its shortest. That's high noon. Then check the clock time. Is it noon? (Note: You can also tell high noon by watching the shadow of the flagpole.)

4. Go outdoors with your class on a sunny day at 9:00 a.m., noon, and 3:00 p.m. Observe the position of your shadows. Point to the sun each time and identify the direction of the sun. Confirm the direction with a compass.

5. Construct a shadow clock. Draw a chalk circle on the schoolyard blacktop. When you stand in the center of the circle (or stand a large stick there), your shadow can be used to indicate the time. At the most northerly point of the circle, make a mark for noon. To find this point, use a compass, or see where your shadow is pointing when it is at its shortest. Mark the point for 6:00 p.m. 180° south of the "high noon" position. Use your shadow to find intermediate points between these two fixed settings. For example, mark where your shadow is pointing at 9:00 a.m. and at 3:00 p.m.

Information Gathering and Sharing

6. Investigate and report on the meaning of a.m. and p.m. as the terms relate to the 24-hour system of telling time (a.m. = ante meridiem, or before noon; p.m. = post meridiem, or after noon).

7. Report on the significance of the Royal Greenwich Observatory.

8. With your class, make a table display of various kinds of transportation time schedules. Show how one of the schedules works by explaining examples of routes and times between various locations.

9. Report on the history of systems for telling and recording time.

10. Make a list of expressions or sayings that use the words *hour, minute,* or *second.*

Art and Visual Aids

11. Construct an illustrated timeline of your daily activities.

12. With your class, construct twenty-four paper-plate clocks, each aligned to a world time zone.

13. With your class, collect twenty-four watches and small clocks. Place a large world map on a table. Put one watch or clock on each world time zone. Set the watches and clocks for the time at each zone. Refer to the timepieces on the map and talk about what people may be doing now in various parts of the world.

14. Make a "one-minute" hourglass. Fill a narrow-necked jar (such as a salad dressing bottle) with coarse salt or sand. Tape the mouth of an identical jar to the mouth of the jar with the salt or sand in it. Invert the hourglass and see how long it takes for the salt or sand to flow into the bottom jar.

15. Make a time zone wheel. Cut two circles out of index cards or heavy paper. One circle should be about two inches in diameter and the other about four inches in diameter. Put the smaller circle on top of the larger one. Put a paper fastener through the center of both circles so that the top circle can rotate. Divide the circumference of the smaller wheel into twenty-four equal units. Label each unit with an hour, 1 through 12 a.m. and 1 through 12 p.m. (or use the 24-hour military time sequence). Divide the circumference of the larger wheel into twenty-four equal units. Letter each unit, starting with "A." Label each time zone on a desk map with the letters A through X.

16. Refer to quotations about time (p. 98). Illustrate one of these quotations (or another saying about time) in a cartoon format. If appropriate, make your cartoon humorous.

QUESTIONS FOR CLASS DISCUSSION

1. Explain the notion that as life becomes more complex, the organization and accuracy of timekeeping becomes more important and more innovative.

2. Until the four time zones were established in the United States, railroads had been coursing through a maze of at least 50 regional times. Each town along their routes set its clocks according to the position of the sun; for example, noon was when the sun was at its zenith. How was this lack of standard time a disadvantage to trade, travel, and progress?

3. It has been said that by the year 2025, distances will be reported in hours rather than in miles. What is meant by this prediction?

4. The time in a particular location relates to its longitudinal position, but the number of daylight hours it has depends upon its latitude. Explain this phenomenon.

5. What is the purpose of Daylight Savings Time? Some people think it should be abandoned. What do you think about the idea?

6. What are some of the problems and inconveniences caused by having different time zones in the United States?

7. Some watches and clocks have special faces and functions. What are some special kinds of timepieces and what special features do they have?

8. List a number of definitions for the words *hour* and *minute*.

9. What problems may be caused by the boundary of a time zone running between two nearby towns or cities?

KEY VOCABULARY

accuracy	minute
calculation	observatory
digital screen	revolution
Greenwich	rotation
hourglass	salt timer
international date line	second
local time	standard
longitude	sundial
meridian	timepiece
	time zone

RELATED CAREER EDUCATION TERMS

calendar maker	jeweler
cartographer	sports timekeeper
engineer	watchmaker

Thanksgiving

THEMES AND THOUGHTS

Gratitude, Thankfulness, Compassion, Sharing, Religion

Heap high the board with plenteous cheer,
   and gather to the feast,
And toast the sturdy Pilgrim band whose
   courage never ceased.
              —*Alice W. Brotherton*

It is better to give than to receive.
              —*Proverb*

Harvest comes not every day, though it comes every year.
              —*Thomas Fuller*

When corn is ripe, 'tis time to reap.
              —*Martin Parker*

FASCINATING FACTS

Thanksgiving is now celebrated as a legal holiday on the fourth Thursday of November in the United States and in the Commonwealth of Puerto Rico. It is a time to express one's thanks for good fortune throughout the year.

The first Thanksgiving Day in the United States is thought to have been held on August 9, 1607, by colonists of the Popham Colony, which is now Phippsburg, Maine. The first big Thanksgiving celebration, however, is said to have taken place in 1621 in Plymouth, Massachusetts. The Pilgrims and Indians feasted for three days to celebrate their rich harvest after suffering a severe winter following the Pilgrims' long, harsh journey to America.

In 1789, George Washington proclaimed November 26 as Thanksgiving Day in honor of the adoption of the United States Constitution. Through the efforts of Sarah Josepha Hale, the editor of *Ladies' Magazine* in Boston, Thanksgiving became a national holiday observed on the same day every year. She proposed the fourth Thursday of November because November 26, the day George Washington had originally selected, had been the fourth Thursday. In 1863, President Lincoln acted on Hale's suggestion and proclaimed the fourth Thursday of November as Thanksgiving Day. It has, since 1863, been celebrated on that day—with a few exceptions. In 1865, President Andrew Johnson changed Thanksgiving to the first Thursday in December. In 1869, President Ulysses S. Grant selected the third Thursday in November. In 1939, President Franklin D. Roosevelt set November 23 as Thanksgiving Day. In 1941, he proclaimed the fourth Thursday as Thanksgiving Day in all the states and U.S. possessions. We have continued to celebrate Thanksgiving on this day ever since.

Thanksgiving Day is associated with certain symbols and foods. Turkey is part of the traditional Thanksgiving dinner, since it is believed that the Pilgrims and Native Americans had turkey at their feast. Cranberries are also part of Thanksgiving dinner, probably because the Pilgrims had cranberries, which they found in bogs around Plymouth. The "craneberry," as it was called, was used for dye, as well as for food.

The horn of plenty, or the cornucopia, is a familiar Thanksgiving symbol. It is a symbol of earth's bounty, and reminds us how much of our food comes from the earth.

Indian corn is used as a decoration. The American Indians taught the Pilgrims how to plant corn, which the Pilgrims used to survive their first winter. To keep hostile tribes from knowing how many Pilgrims had died, the Pilgrims planted corn over graves.

Today, Thanksgiving is the unofficial beginning of the Christmas season, and in many cities and communities, Thanksgiving marks the arrival of Santa Claus. Gimbel Brothers started this tradition with a parade of toys in Philadelphia in 1920. The famous Macy's Thanksgiving Day parade in New York City is part of the traditional celebration. It is viewed on television by millions of people each year.

ACTIVITIES FOR STUDENTS

Information Gathering and Sharing

1. Make a study comparing life today with the life of a Pilgrim. You could compare one or more of the following categories: occupations, daily routines, food, food sources, family life, transportation, the role of women, the role of men, and leisure or recreational activities.

Dramatics and Role-Playing

2. Dramatize the landing at Plymouth Rock with a "You Are There" or "I Was There" program. With your classmates, role-play the Indians and the Pilgrims.
3. With the class, make paper Pilgrim costumes for a class play dramatizing the first Thanksgiving. Make hats and caps out of black and white construction paper.
4. With your classmates, act out the occupations and activities of the Pilgrims and American Indians, such as weaving, hunting, candlemaking, salt fetching, farming, and timber clearing.
5. Discuss and list creatures that are protected by feathers. With your class, collect feathers from various kinds of fowl and display them on a feather chart.

Critical Thinking

6. Discuss the hardships of the Mayflower voyage. With your class, measure and plot the size of the Mayflower on the playground or in a multipurpose room. (The boat was approximately 25 feet wide and 90 feet long.) Figure out how one hundred passengers could have fit in the ship.
7. Plan a Thanksgiving Day menu.
8. With your class, discuss the things we can be grateful for in our own lives. After the discussion, make a thank-you book full of poems, paragraphs, and pictures.

Art and Visual Aids

9. With your classmates, make a bulletin-board display of the Mayflower story with appropriate cutouts to illustrate the Thanksgiving table or the first harvest festival.
10. With your classmates, construct a bulletin-board display illustrating the voyage of the Mayflower. Attach the ship to a fine wire (concealed by ocean waves cut out of paper). Move the ship a little closer to Plymouth Rock each day.
11. With the class, design and draw a mural depicting the history of Thanksgiving Day, or a present-day celebration.
12. Make a turkey out of a potato or paper bag.
13. Draw what you are thankful for. Arrange the drawings of all the class members in a giant cornucopia over the caption "We are thankful for many things."
14. Make a Pilgrim man or woman, using various sizes of triangles of black and white construction paper. Make a turkey out of a pinecone or an apple, decorated with toothpicks or pipe cleaners and a marsh-

mallow for the head.

15. Make a Thanksgiving favor (nut- or mint-holder), using a cardboard tube. Cover the tube with brightly colored paper. Fill the tube with nuts or mints. Then tie a ribbon around each end of the tube and add fringe. Decorate with a turkey made from a paper baking cup.

16. Draw, color, and cut out a turkey. Do some research to find an unusual or surprising fact about turkeys.

Writing and Language Arts

17. Compose an acrostic poem (by yourself or with the class), using words related to Thanksgiving. For example:

> T—urkey
> H—arbor
> A—ppreciation
> N—ew World
> K—indness
> S—ettlement
> G—overnor
> I—ndians
> V—enison
> I—nvitation
> N—uts
> G—obble-gobble

6. What do you think was mostly on the minds of the colonists who celebrated the first Thanksgiving?
7. Would the Pilgrims be pleased with the religious freedom practiced in America today? Why or why not?
8. Why is Thanksgiving a time of giving and caring for the poor, the homeless, and the hospitalized?

QUESTIONS FOR CLASS DISCUSSION

1. Why is it good to pause one day each year to take an account of yourself and your surroundings?
2. Thanksgiving has always been celebrated as a family day in the United States. Why do you think this is so?
3. What is the real message we can all learn from Thanksgiving?
4. Why is it a tradition to eat certain foods during the Thanksgiving meal?
5. Do you think the Thanksgiving celebration has changed much over the years? What do you think Thanksgiving will be like in the year 2025?

Every Day's a Holiday

December

First Week:

---

1 Hernán Cortés Day, the conqueror of Mexico, died, 1547

---

2 Monroe Doctrine proclaimed, 1823
Pan-American Health Day

---

3 Illinois admitted to the Union, 1818
Ellen Henrietta Richards, founder of home economics movement, born, 1842
First heart transplant—performed by Dr. Christiaan Barnard in South Africa, 1967

---

4 * Know Your State Capital Day

---

5 Walt Disney, producer of animated cartoons, born, 1901
President Martin Van Buren born, 1782

---

6 Joyce Kilmer, poet, born, 1886

---

7 Pearl Harbor attacked, 1941
First concert of Philharmonic Symphony Society of New York, 1842

---

*A teaching unit is included on the following pages for each starred entry.

Second Week:

Human Rights Week (December 10–16)

8 Eli Whitney, inventor of cotton gin, born, 1765

9 Emmett Kelly, circus clown, born, 1898

10 Nobel Peace Prize presentations
Human Rights Day—UN General Assembly adopted Universal Declaration of Human Rights, 1948
Emily Dickinson, poet, born, 1830

11 Robert Koch, German physician and bacteriologist, born, 1843

12 * Washington, D.C., became official capital of the U.S., 1800
Marconi sent first radio message across the ocean, from England to Newfoundland, 1901
Poinsettia Day—death of Dr. J. R. Poinsett, who introduced poinsettia to U.S. from Mexico, 1851

13 Winter Safety Day

14 Roald Amundsen, Norwegian explorer, became first person to reach South Pole, 1911
John Mercer Langston, one of first blacks to be elected to public office in the U.S., born, 1829

15 * Bill of Rights Day—Bill of Rights went into effect, 1791

Third Week:

16 Boston Tea Party, 1773

17 *Wright Brothers Day—first successful airplane flight, 1903

18 13th Amendment to the U.S. Constitution, which ended slavery, ratified, 1865

19 * Continental Army encamped at Valley Forge, 1777

20 Louisiana Purchase, 1803

21 Forefathers' Day—Pilgrims landed at Plymouth, 1620
Winter begins (traditional date)
* Apollo 8, carrying first humans to orbit the moon, launched, 1968

22 International Arbor Day
Lincoln Tunnel opened, linking New York to New Jersey, 1937

23 U.S. Federal Reserve System established, 1913

Fourth Week:

Hanukkah, 8-day Festival of Lights, beginning on 25th of Kislev, the 3rd month of Jewish year

24

Kit Carson, frontiersman, scout, and soldier, born, 1809

25

* Christmas
Washington crossed Delaware River, 1776
Clara Barton, founder of the American Red Cross, born, 1821

26

Battle of Trenton, 1776

27

Louis Pasteur, French biochemist, born, 1822

28

W. F. Semple received the first patent for chewing gum, 1869

29

President Woodrow Wilson born, 1856
President Andrew Johnson born, 1808
First YMCA in the U.S. founded, 1851

30

Rudyard Kipling, English poet, born, 1865

31

Ellis Island opened as a U.S. port of entry for immigrants, 1890
New Year's Eve—time to make New Year's resolutions!

Every Day's a Holiday

Know Your State Capital Day

THEMES AND THOUGHTS

Pride, Heritage, Democracy,
Participation, Service

The law is for the protection of
the weak more than the strong.
—*Sir William Erle*

The Constitution, in all its provi-
sion, looks to an indestructible
Union composed of indestructible
States.
—*Salmon Portland Chase*

The powers not delegated to the
United States by the Constitution,
nor prohibited by it to the States,
are reserved to the States respec-
tively, or to the people.
—*U.S. Constitution*
(10th Amendment)

FASCINATING FACTS

The word *capital* comes from the Latin word
for "head." Thus, a capital is where the head of
the government is located.

In the United States, each state is responsible for the organization of its state and local
governments. It is responsible for the collection
of state taxes, the enactment of state laws, and
the election of state officials. Each state must
write its own constitution. The place where all of
these responsibilities are carried out and administered is the state capital.

There is no uniform structure for state
governments in the United States. Each of the
states, except Nebraska, has a bicameral, or a
two-chambered, legislature. Each also has a
separate executive, or governor, and a judiciary.

No formal change may be made in the
Constitution of the United States without the
approval of three-fourths of the states, as sanc-
tioned through their state legislatures or

through conventions held in three-fourths of the
states.

The states have the power to make and
change their own institutions of state and local
government, to levy and collect taxes, to make
and enforce police regulations, and to regulate
education, public health, agriculture, and the
conservation of natural resources. They can
control certain human relationships dealing with
private law, the family, and private property.
They can also create corporations and trusts
and regulate other aspects of society.

The first state capitol was the statehouse on
Duke of Gloucester Street in Williamsburg,
Virginia, in which the General Assembly met.
The building was put up in 1698 by Governor
Francis Nicholson, who is credited with being
the first person to refer to the building housing
a legislative body as a capitol.

Art and Visual Aids

1. Have your teacher obtain a map of the state capital and enlarge it with an opaque projector or draw it to scale on an alphabetical-numerical grid system (1-inch coordinates on the original map should be increased to 3- or 4-inch squares on the enlarged map). With your class, locate and highlight important buildings and places in your state capital.

2. With your class, plan and paint a mural depicting the state capital.

3. Make a picture presentation of the history of your state's capitol. Draw a picture of the capitol, making its steps large enough to write in. Or add large steps below a picture of the building. Write a brief history of the capitol in the "steps." Be sure to include a description of the architecture and the building materials used.

4. Design a bumper sticker to advertise your state capital.

5. Draw the state flag. Investigate and report on the meaning of the symbolism used in it. Do the same for the state seal.

6. With your class, set up a replica of the state museum. Feature artifacts and historical treasures similar to those found in the state museum. Or set up a state art center. Draw state theme pictures for display.

7. Design a state motto banner.

Information Gathering and Sharing

8. On a state road map, locate the state capital and your school. Mark and plot the best route to travel to the capital. Measure the distances from various cities to the capital, and construct a distance chart.

9. Make a chart that highlights basic facts about your state, such as important bodies of water, dams, weather data, population, political divisions, cities, counties, state events, products, transportation, education, recreation, government agencies, communication, law enforcement, environmental protection, and historical information.

10. If distance allows, take a class trip to the state capital—or hear from some visitors who have been there.

11. With your class, research and report on interesting facts about the capital. Your report could take the form of a booklet, an assembly program, or a school hall display.

12. With your class, arrange a display of newspaper clippings, pictures, and pamphlets about the state capital. Write to various state bureaus for information.

13. Make a list of all the nicknames given to the state capital. Do the same for your city and other cities within the state.

14. Make an in-depth report about outstanding governors of the past and about the history of the official governor's residence.

15. Construct a timeline about the state capital and its development.

16. Invite your district's representative to the state legislature to come before your class and speak about activities and governmental functions in the capital.

17. Make a flow chart of the structure of the state government or of how a bill becomes a law in the state.

Critical Thinking

18. Obtain a copy of the state constitution for analysis and discuss it in class.

19. As a class, prepare a directory of outstanding tourist attractions for your state capital. Call it "The Capital Guidebook." With your classmates, take turns role-playing a capital guide.

Writing and Language Arts

20. Write a description of a trip (either real or imaginary) to the state capital.

21. Compile a list of new words that you have discovered in your study of the state capital.

22. Write a poem or song about your state capital.

23. Compose an original slogan for your state capital.

24. List all the state capitals. Then underline all the hidden words you can find in the various names.

Dramatics and Role-Playing

25. As a class, construct a "time machine" by decorating a large carton with paint and colored paper. Take turns coming out of the machine to tell about your state capital and life there in the past, in the present, or in the future.

Music

26. Learn and sing your state song.

Special Events

27. Divide the class into committees representing various state promotional departments. Have the committees plan and organize a "state fair." Invite students from another class or the entire school to the event.

Games

28. Learn the names of the capitals of other states. Plot them on a blank outline map. Divide your class into teams and play the game "Capital Spin." Each player in turn, with eyes closed or blindfolded, points to a state on a wall map. He or she must name the capital of that state to get another turn. If he or she misses, a player from the other team tries to name the capital. Keep score.
29. Find the names of the states and the state capitals in the following puzzle grids.

STATES

The names of all 50 states can be found among these letters. Some names read right to left, others read left to right, and still others read up, down, or diagonally. Draw a circle around the name of each state that you locate.

```
S  T  T  E  S  U  H  C  A  S  S  A  M  T  R  S  V  E  M  A  A  S
A  N  O  Z  I  R  A  I  N  I  G  R  I  V  T  S  E  W  I  D  N  Y
A  I  N  R  O  F  I  L  A  C  A  Z  X  Y  S  S  R  G  N  I  A  K
N  O  T  G  N  I  H  S  A  W  L  N  A  B  S  T  M  E  N  R  I  C
S  O  U  T  H  D  A  K  O  T  A  N  E  E  R  M  O  O  E  O  S  U
M  A  R  Y  L  A  N  D  L  M  I  L  N  W  N  O  N  R  S  L  I  T
O  P  U  T  A  H  R  E  T  L  N  N  A  E  J  W  T  G  O  F  U  N
A  K  W  X  H  O  A  W  O  I  E  Y  Z  S  V  E  R  I  T  S  O  E
K  R  L  S  B  C  D  R  E  T  F  G  I  J  K  A  R  A  A  X  L  K
S  O  M  A  I  N  A  V  L  Y  S  N  N  E  P  A  D  S  N  O  P  E
A  Y  R  X  H  C  S  R  N  A  G  I  H  C  I  M  N  A  E  T  U  R
R  W  V  E  H  O  W  Y  O  M  I  N  G  V  S  A  R  Y  S  Y  O  H
B  E  B  T  C  E  M  F  I  L  G  R  T  I  K  L  I  M  I  E  D  O
E  N  U  I  I  A  W  A  H  M  I  H  E  R  C  A  R  T  N  H  A  D
N  O  R  T  H  D  A  K  O  T  A  N  A  G  L  B  N  I  D  U  R  E
S  R  I  R  U  O  S  S  I  M  O  T  A  I  S  A  A  S  I  N  O  I
N  E  W  H  A  M  P  S  H  I  R  E  B  N  O  M  E  R  A  E  L  S
X  G  I  P  P  I  S  S  I  S  S  I  M  I  V  A  V  W  N  S  O  L
Y  O  C  I  X  E  M  W  E  N  D  E  L  A  W  A  R  E  A  F  C  A
X  N  I  S  N  O  C  S  I  W  R  T  S  A  N  A  T  N  O  M  L  N
T  T  U  C  I  T  C  E  N  N  O  C  S  I  O  N  I  L  L  I  E  D
```

STATE CAPITALS

Find the names of the 50 state capitals in this grid. The names appear right to left, left to right, up, down, or diagonally.

```
Q A N O T S E L R A H C S A C R A M E N T O
A R E B T R O F K N A R F B Z U N A A A K X
I B P A C O L U M B I A A V J A R P L L S O
P I J R A L E I G H G T R S E A T L A N T A
M S E N N E Y E H C O L S A B E A H N O P U
Y M A D I S O N D N R K Z U E H O A S T A G
L A D E N J N R R C E C M P A M I R I S U U
O R N D O A O O O A S O L S A O O R N O L S
T C O I T C U S D R N R S C R N V I G B X T
P K M E N G M R N S I E I J R T G S P M U A
R W H O E P O S O O E T N A T G R B Z Y A M
O K C S R F L U D N Y T D C A O E U D T E L
V P I P T U M B U C C I I K E M I R Q I N D
I A R R O M L M E I K L A S E E L G E C U O
D A A I I O E U Y T I C N O S R E F F E J V
E H O N O L U L U Y T L N N I Y P U A K M E
N E I G F T I O A S Y O A L O N T P T A P R
C V D F V V R C K S T C P D B A N S N L I E
E L L I V H S A N N S R O E O B O L A T E V
X I N E O H P C U A P S L W K L M X S L R N
A H E L E N A N L O C N I L V A R Z T A R E
B I N D I A N A P O L I S S E N I O M S E D
M A L I T T L E R O C K L E S T C E N T S E
```

ANSWER KEY: STATES AND STATE CAPITALS

Alabama _____ Montgomery	Florida _____ Tallahassee
Alaska _____ Juneau	Georgia _____ Atlanta
Arizona _____ Phoenix	Hawaii _____ Honolulu
Arkansas _____ Little Rock	Idaho _____ Boise
California _____ Sacramento	Illinois _____ Springfield
Colorado _____ Denver	Indiana _____ Indianapolis
Connecticut _____ Hartford	Iowa _____ Des Moines
Delaware _____ Dover	Kansas _____ Topeka

Kentucky _____ Frankfort

Louisiana _____ Baton Rouge

Maine _____ Augusta

Maryland _____ Annapolis

Massachusetts _____ Boston

Michigan _____ Lansing

Minnesota _____ St. Paul

Mississippi _____ Jackson

Missouri _____ Jefferson City

Montana _____ Helena

Nebraska _____ Lincoln

Nevada _____ Carson City

New Hampshire _____ Concord

New Jersey _____ Trenton

New Mexico _____ Santa Fe

New York _____ Albany

North Carolina _____ Raleigh

North Dakota_____ Bismarck

Ohio_____ Columbus

Oklahoma _____ Oklahoma City

Oregon _____ Salem

Pennsylvania _____ Harrisburg

Rhode Island _____ Providence

South Carolina _____ Columbia

South Dakota_____ Pierre

Tennessee _____ Nashville

Texas _____ Austin

Utah_____ Salt Lake City

Vermont_____ Montpelier

Virginia _____ Richmond

Washington _____ Olympia

West Virginia _____ Charleston

Wisconsin _____ Madison

Wyoming_____ Cheyenne

1. In what ways is a state capitol the living symbol of the state?
2. Do you think your state capital is located advantageously? If so, tell why. If not, select another capital site and state your reasons for this choice.
3. How does a bill become a law in your state?
4. How does the state police or highway patrol differ from local police agencies?
5. How does state government differ from local government?
6. Who are some of the famous heroes of your state? How are they honored in your state?
7. Have other cities in your state ever served as state capitals? Which ones were they?
8. Is it better for a state capital to be located in a large, small, or medium-sized city? Why?
9. What is meant by the expressions "All roads lead to the capital" and "Capitals are nerve centers"?
10. How many state senators and representatives are sent to the capital from your district? Who are they? What is the total representation in your state's legislative body?
11. When does your state legislature hold its meetings?
12. What institutions and services in your state are paid for with state taxes?
13. What sights, events, and products does your state have that are special enough to publicize throughout the United States? Why does every state have a bureau devoted to promoting tourism within the state?
14. What do you think is the biggest state problem that your leaders and representatives have to be concerned about? What is being done about these problems?
15. What street names and parks in the state capital represent other places in your state?
16. How do various designs and artworks located in your state's capitol show the state's history or geography?
17. How many state officials are elected in your state? Who are they?

18. Who is the present governor of your state? Did any former governor of your state ever become President of the United States? Who?

Key Vocabulary

agency	institution
archives	judicial
Assembly	legislative
assemblyman	legislature
assemblywoman	library
attorney general	lieutenant governor
auditor	lobby
authority	monument
bicameral	motto
budget	museum
bureau	official
cabinet	power
capital	roll call
capitol	seal
caucus	seat
commissioner	secretary
comptroller	Senate
debate	senator
department	speaker
dome	statehouse
executive	statue
governmental	suffrage
governor	superintendent
House of Representatives	Supreme Court
	taxes

Related Career Education Terms

archivist	legislator
attorney	librarian
auditor	lobbyist
business executive	politician
clerk	public health official
commissioner	secretary
comptroller	state department official
curator	tax collector
governor	treasurer
law enforcement agent	

Washington, D.C., Became the Official Capital of the U.S.

THEMES AND THOUGHTS

Pride, Beauty, Heritage,
Citizenship

The surest test of the civilization of a people . . . is to be found in their architecture, which presents so noble a field for the display of the grand and the beautiful, and which, at the same time, is so intimately connected with the essential comforts of life.
—*William Hickling Prescott*

A great city is that which has the greatest men and women.
—*Walt Whitman*

FASCINATING FACTS

Washington, D. C., is one of few national capitals in the world founded uniquely as a seat of government. Named for George Washington and Christopher Columbus, Washington, D.C., is the only city in the United States that is not located within one of the fifty states.

Plans began in 1790 for a permanent center of government for this country, but there was disagreement about its location. The leaders of the Southern states were in favor of an area on the Potomac River between Maryland and Virginia, but the leaders of the Northern states wanted the capital to be closer to New York and Philadelphia, the young nation's financial and communications centers. Finally, Secretary of Treasury Alexander Hamilton persuaded the Northern leaders to vote for the Potomac site in exchange for the Southerners' support for policies favored by the North. In 1791, a 10-mile-square Federal District was proposed.

George Washington appointed Major Pierre L'Enfant, a French engineer, to plan the city. He designed the eye-appealing core of the city—diagonal avenues and gridded streets, squares

with statues and fountains, the Capitol on its hill, and the "Presidential palace" on Pennsylvania Avenue about a mile away. An aerial view shows how the Capitol was planned as the focal point, with the streets and avenues radiating out from it. The plan was well thought-out and anticipated the city's growth. Certain disputes, however, caused the project to be turned over to Andrew Ellicott, assisted by a talented, free African-American, Benjamin Banneker.

Washington, D.C., officially replaced Philadelphia as the nation's capital in 1800. The Capitol, however, was not completed until around 1825. The White House, whose foundation was laid in 1792, has been the home of every President, with the exception of George Washington, and is the oldest public building in Washington, D.C. President John Adams and his wife, Abigail, were the first occupants of the White House.

Other buildings of note in Washington, D.C., include the National Archives Building, one of a group of buildings known as the Federal Triangle. This is the depository of our most important federal documents—the Declaration of Independence, the Constitution, and the Bill of Rights. These documents are on permanent display there. The Smithsonian Institution, our "nation's attic," houses approximately 100 million objects of artistic, cultural, and historical interest. The National Air and Space Museum, the National Gallery of Art, and the National Museum of Natural History are all part of the Smithsonian. The Library of Congress is the world's largest library, containing over 70 million items. It receives and stores copies of all works printed in the United States. Many famous memorials are also located in Washington, D.C., including the Jefferson Memorial, the Washington Monument, the Lincoln Memorial, and the Vietnam Veterans Memorial.

In addition to government and diplomatic activity, tourism is a major industry in Washington, D.C. Although tourists visit year-round, the peak season is early spring, when the Japanese cherry trees are in bloom around the Tidal Basin.

Washington, D.C., is one of the most important and beautiful cities in the world.

ACTIVITIES FOR STUDENTS

Art and Visual Aids

1. With your classmates, refer to a map of Washington, D.C., and make a basic "blueprint" of it that includes key national buildings, monuments, and parks. Transfer this blueprint onto a 4-foot square of wafer board. Add three-dimensional cardboard models of the buildings. Rivers and streets can be drawn in and then painted on.
2. Select a site of interest in Washington, D.C., and design and produce a brochure about it. Write for information to the National Park Service (1100 Ohio Drive SW, Washington, DC 20242), or do your research using local sources, such as the library or a tour book.
3. As a class, collect or draw pictures of main attractions in Washington, D.C. Connect each picture to a map with yarn, or use corresponding numbers to show the locations.

Critical Thinking

4. With your class, read the Declaration of Independence, the Constitution, and the Bill of Rights. Discuss the purpose of each document and what it means to us today.
5. Read through the Declaration of Independence with the class, especially noting the complaints against King George. Compose some responses to these complaints from the King's point of view.
6. Make a list of some of the things to be considered in planning a national capital.
7. With your class, plan a week's sightseeing tour of the major places and points of interest in the Washington, D.C., area. Plot the itinerary on a map.

Writing and Language Arts

8. Write your own "Declaration of Independence" from parental rules, from school, from music lessons, or from whatever else you'd like to write about.
9. Interview a person who has visited the capital and write a news article about their impressions.
10. Construct an illustrated "Did You Know" booklet about Washington, D.C.
11. Construct a "Fascinating Facts" booklet about the White House.
12. Write a short composition entitled "Why I Am Proud of Our Nation's Capital."

Information Gathering and Sharing

13. For information about visiting Washington, D.C., write to your representative in Congress, to the Public Information Officer, National Park Service (1100 Ohio Drive SW, Washington, DC 20242), or to the Visitor Information Center (Great Hall, U.S. Department of Commerce, 14th Street and Pennsylvania Avenue NW, Washington, DC 20004).
14. Use the phrase "Washington, our nation's capital" as the first letters of an acrostic poem formed with appropriate words relating to the city.

QUESTIONS FOR CLASS DISCUSSION

1. Why is it necessary to have a national capital?
2. Would it have made a difference if our national capital were New York or Philadelphia instead of Washington, D.C.? Explain.
3. What is the difference between the words capital and capitol?
4. Is it important to plan a city before settlement? Why?
5. If you were visiting Washington, D.C., what sites would you like to see? Why?
6. If our nation's capital were to be relocated, where would you place it? Explain your reasons.
7. What new building, museum, park, or memorial would you like to see added to the attractions of Washington, D.C.?
8. What changes would you suggest for improving Washington, D.C.?
9. Why is it important for Americans to visit their nation's capital and other historical sites?
10. Why is the Smithsonian Institution sometimes referred to as our "nation's attic"? Can you think of other appropriate names for some of Washington's other famous buildings?
11. Why do you think the Vietnam War Memorial has become such a popular tourist attraction?

KEY VOCABULARY

agency
anticipate
archive
bureau
capital
capitol
cemetery
Columbia
Congress
core
depository
diagonal
diplomatic
district
document
federal

focal
foundation
grid
House of Representatives
institute
library
memorial
monument
peak
Potomac River
Senate
site
tourism
White House

RELATED CAREER EDUCATION TERMS

architect
builder
bus driver
city planner
civil service worker
diplomat
engineer
hotel manager

hotel worker
law enforcement officer
lawyer
politician
surveyor
taxi driver
tour guide

Bill of Rights Day

THEMES AND THOUGHTS

Equality, Basic Rights, Liberty, Freedom, Law

I myself am a part of democracy—I myself must accept responsibilities. Democracy is not merely a privilege to be enjoyed—it is a trust to keep and maintain.
—*Stephen Vincent Benét*

The greatest glory of a free-born people is to transmit that freedom to their children.
—*William Havard*

Those who deny freedom to others deserve it not for themselves.
—*Abraham Lincoln*

We look forward to a world founded upon four essential freedoms. The first is freedom of speech and expression everywhere in the world. The second is freedom of every person to worship God in his [or her] own way—everywhere in the world. The third is freedom from want . . . everywhere in the world. The fourth is freedom from fear . . . anywhere in the world.
—*Franklin D. Roosevelt*

Congress shall make no law respecting an establishment of religion, or prohibiting the free exercise thereof; or abridging the freedom of speech, or of the press; or the right of the people peaceably to assemble, and to petition the government for a redress of grievances.
—*First Amendment to the U.S. Constitution*

The welfare of the people is the chief law.
—*Cicero*

FASCINATING FACTS

Our government's philosophy is predicated on the dignity and freedom of the individual citizen. Equality, freedom of speech, press, and religion, and sovereignty of the people are fundamentally guaranteed by the Constitution, the Bill of Rights, and the courts. The Declaration of Independence, the Constitution, and the Bill of Rights are considered sacred documents of the United States. They are on display at the National Archives Building in Washington, D.C.

The concept of individual liberties developed slowly over thousands of years. The development of such liberties can be traced from the records of the ancient Greeks and Jews to the spread of Christianity, to England and France, and finally to the American colonists.

The Constitution of the United States, written in 1787, is to this day the basic law of the land. The Bill of Rights is the first ten amendments to the U.S. Constitution. The term *bill of rights* was first used for a declaration that the English Parliament presented to the Prince and Princess of Orange in 1689.

There were several reasons why a bill of rights was not a part of the original Constitution. Many of the men who wrote the Constitution thought that individual rights were already protected by state constitutions. Others thought that making a list of people's rights was not a good idea because they might inadvertently leave some important rights out.

After the Constitution was written, however, many leaders, such as George Mason of Virginia, Thomas Jefferson, and James Madison, still felt that specific guarantees of personal rights and protections for the states should be added to the basic document. Their view prevailed, and ten amendments were added to assure our fundamental freedoms of religion, speech, and press, of due process of law, and other protections. New Jersey was the first state to ratify the Bill of Rights. The signing took place in Perth Amboy on November 20, 1789. Other states then ratified the document, and the document went into effect on December 15, 1791.

The First Amendment of the Constitution is the best known amendment. In the First Amendment, "freedom of religion" means that Congress cannot pass a law setting up a religion that everyone must follow. We are free to worship as we please. "Freedom of speech" means we are free to speak out and give our side of an issue and that others are free to listen. "Freedom of the press" means members of the press (media) do not need governmental approval to present their views or a news story, as long as they do not lie. "Freedom of assembly" means we are free to meet peacefully. "Freedom to petition" means we are free to ask the government to correct things we think are wrong.

December 15 was proclaimed Bill of Rights Day by President John F. Kennedy in 1962. Also, since the United Nations adopted the Universal Declaration of Human Rights in 1948, December 10 has been observed as Human Rights Day. The public has been encouraged to celebrate the week that embraces both anniversaries as Human Rights Week, commemorating these two landmark stands for freedom. It is important that each generation cares enough about our freedoms to understand them, to defend them, and to appreciate their priceless value.

ACTIVITIES FOR STUDENTS

Critical Thinking

1. Compare the purposes of Bill of Rights Day with those of Loyalty Day (May 1) and Flag Day (June 14).
2. With your class, discuss your rights and ways to show your loyalty to your classmates and to your school, for example, by having respect for one another, being cooperative, obeying rules, and taking pride in one's appearance and the appearance of the school.
3. Make a comparative chart of democratic ways in the United States and life in autocratic nations.
4. With your class, discuss additional proposals, if any, for amending the Constitution.
5. Compile a list of ways in which some people disregard the Bill of Rights.
6. Write a present-day Bill of Rights. Write a "Bill of Rights" for your class or school.
7. As a class, draw up a "Bill of Wrongs," or practices opposed to the Bill of Rights.

Dramatics and Role-Playing

8. With your class, enact a colonial town meeting discussing the ratification of the Constitution. A town crier may be the announcer, and other class members can serve as the town council members and other public officials.

Information Gathering and Sharing

9. Learn a little about *Roberts' Rules of Order*. During the class meeting period, practice some parliamentary procedures.
10. Contribute prose, poetry, news items, charts, and pictures to a class scrapbook on the rights and responsibilities of citizenship.
11. Write to the National Park Service in Philadelphia (143 South 3rd Street, Philadelphia, PA 19106) and request brochures and other literature about the famous freedom shrines located there.
12. As a class, make a collection of quotations about democracy to post on the chalkboard or bulletin board. Play "Who Said?" with

the quotations. The game can be expanded by adding "Where?" and "Why?" as well.

13. Formally invite a local lawyer, a member of the local chapter of the American Civil Liberties Union, or a magistrate to address your class or the entire school on the Bill of Rights.

14. Research and report on the proceedings and celebrations in Philadelphia and elsewhere of the bicentennial (200th) anniversary of the signing of our Constitution.

Art and Visual Aids

15. List and illustrate the rights guaranteed by the Bill of Rights. The class' lists may be compiled into a booklet or displayed on a bulletin board.

16. Add an ending to the phrase "Loyalty is…" or "Good citizenship is…" or "The Bill of Rights is… ." Draw a picture to illustrate the completed phrase. Compile everyone's illustrated phrases into a class book.

17. As a class, set up a school showcase or lobby display table with photocopied documents, citations, plaques, slogans, quotations, and other items relating to the Bill of Rights.

Writing and Language Arts

18. Write a theme on the meaning and importance of loyalty, civil rights, and freedoms.

19. Compose an unfinished story, centered on an incident involving loyalty or the Bill of Rights. Read your story to the class. Discuss probable outcomes for the story.

20. Draw up a list of key words related to the Bill of Rights (such as loyalty, citizenship, democracy). Construct a simple crossword puzzle with the words, using large block graph paper.

21. Write a brief essay on the type of society the United States might have had if the Bill of Rights had not been added to the Constitution.

QUESTIONS FOR CLASS DISCUSSION

1. What were the origins of the U.S. Bill of Rights?

2. Why was the Bill of Rights needed after the Constitution was ratified?

3. Which of the first ten amendments do you think is the most important for citizens today? Explain why. How would you rank the others in order of importance?

4. Who was John Peter Zenger? How did his case have an impact on the Bill of Rights?

5. What is meant by the phrase "The Constitution is a living document"?

6. What are the major principles underlying the Constitution?

7. Can there ever be too much freedom? Explain your position. Where do rights stop?

8. What makes the interpretation of a law by the courts change over the years?

9. Why do trials and other processes of the judicial system often take such a long time? Is this a good feature of democracy?

KEY VOCABULARY

amendment	indictment
anarchy	interpretation
appeal	jury
bill	law
civil	liberty
civilization	obligation
Constitution	press
contempt of court	principle
counsel	ratify
democracy	responsibility
federal	restriction
freedom	right (noun)
government	society
guarantee	sovereignty
humanity	testify
ignorance	violation

RELATED CAREER EDUCATION TERMS

American Civil
  Liberties Union

consumer
  advocate

judge

lawyer

legislator

paralegal

politician

prosecutor

public defender

researcher

Wright Brothers Day

THEMES AND THOUGHTS

Imagination, Courage, Initiative, Aspiration, Perseverance

That action is best which procures the greatest happiness for the greatest numbers.
—*Francis Hutcheson*

Nothing is achieved before it is thoroughly attempted.
—*Philip Sidney*

The chilly December day
  two shivering bicycle mechanics
from Dayton, Ohio,
  first felt their homemade contraption
  whittled out of hickory sticks,
  gummed together with
Arnstein's bicycle cement,
  stretched with muslin they'd
sewn on their
  sister's sewing machine in their
own
  backyard on Hawthorn Street in
Dayton, Ohio,
  soar into the air
  above the dunes and the wide
beach at Kitty Hawk.
—*John Dos Passos*

FASCINATING FACTS

Working with their father in his hobby shop in Dayton, Ohio, Orville and Wilbur Wright developed an interest in inventing. Dayton is now known as the "Birthplace of Aviation," and the Wright-Patterson Air Force Base there is named after the Wright brothers.

Orville and Wilbur Wright chose to try out their glider at Kitty Hawk, North Carolina, because the U.S. Weather Bureau recommended it as a location with a steady, strong wind. It was also secluded, so they could be away from the jeers of onlookers. Most people thought the Wright brothers were crazy to think they could fly.

Orville won the toss of a coin and piloted the first plane. (His birthday, August 19, is now observed as National Aviation Day.) Five people witnessed that first flight on December 17, 1903. The plane went 120 feet in 12 seconds. The brothers made four flights. The longest one was 852 feet, and the air time was 59 seconds.

The plane, named *The Flyer*, was launched from a monorail against a 21 mph wind. The plane's average speed was about 10 miles an hour. It measured 16 feet from wing tip to wing tip, weighed 745 pounds, and had a four-cylinder engine. The aircraft cost $15 to build.

The brothers later formed the American Wright Company and manufactured airplanes.

The site of their famous flights at Kitty Hawk is now the Wright Brothers National Memorial. A visitor center and a replica of their hangar and living quarters are located there. Their original plane is in Washington, D.C., in the National Air and Space Museum.

In 1963, Congress proclaimed December 17 Wright Brothers Day. On this day every year, special ceremonies are held near Kitty Hawk. Armed forces planes fly over the area at 10:35 a.m.—the time of Orville's first flight.

Only 58 years after the Wright brothers' flights, the first man, a Russian named Yuri Gagarin, orbited the earth in a spacecraft. In 1962, John H. Glenn became the first American to orbit the earth. Later in the 1960s, U.S. astronauts ventured to the moon. Now there are satellites, space stations, and other types of vehicles that can be launched into space.

In 1987, a U.S. airplane flew around the world without having to refuel.

ACTIVITIES FOR STUDENTS

Writing and Language Arts

1. Write a feature news story about NASA, space-age flight, satellites, space stations, flying saucers, jumbo jets, rockets, balloon flights, war planes, or some other aspect of flight.
2. Write a newspaper-style account of the flights made by the Wright brothers.
3. Compose a glossary of important and interesting aeronautical terms—past and present.

Information Gathering and Sharing

4. Study the interrelationships of the various kinds of workers who make flying a cooperative endeavor. Make a chart of all the kinds of workers needed to complete a successful airline flight today.
5. With your class, visit a nearby airport for an on-site study of air travel.
6. Make a chart of the different types of aircraft. Compare their size, purpose, and speed.
7. With your class, write to major and smaller airline companies for literature about their services. Display the information on a resource table.
8. Report on the ways the Wright brothers are memorialized at Kitty Hawk, North Carolina, and elsewhere in the United States.
9. Report on the Air and Space Museum in Washington, D.C.; the Wright Brothers Museum in Kitty Hawk, North Carolina; Wright-Patterson Field in Dayton, Ohio; the Goddard Space Flight Center in Greenbelt, Maryland; the Lyndon B. Johnson Space Center in Houston, Texas; and the John F. Kennedy Space Center in Cape Canaveral, Florida.
10. Report on Leonardo Da Vinci's sketch of an experimental flying machine.

Art and Visual Aids

11. Discuss the evolution of flight from hot-air balloon to spaceship. Draw an illustrated timeline of the history of flight. Include predictions of aircraft in the future.
12. With your class, organize an "airplane museum" with models, pictures, and reports of famous airplanes and aviation leaders.
13. Make an illustrated "Famous Firsts" booklet showing various aspects of the history of aviation.
14. Build a paper airplane or glider to sail into the air. Construct a paper rocket that can be blasted aloft by releasing the air in an attached balloon. These paper aircraft can be used to demonstrate the principles of flight.
15. Design an appropriate monument as a tribute to the Wright brothers. You can carve it from a soft material, such as soap, styrofoam, or balsa wood.
16. With your class, draw or cut out pictures of various types of aircraft and paste them on cardboard backing with identical dimensions. Suspend all the planes from the ceiling like mobiles.
17. Make a model of the interior and the instrumentation of a space shuttle.

Critical Thinking

18. Compare and contrast modern-day airplanes with the craft flown at Kitty Hawk.
19. As a class, compile a list of questions about the first flight, such as choice of location, description of the first airplane, and attitudes of the bystanders. Choose a few students to investigate the questions and make an oral or written report to the class.

Dramatics and Role-Playing

20. Have two students in your class assume the roles of the Wright brothers while the rest of you interview them.
21. With your class, role-play flight crew members, service personnel, weather observers, air traffic controllers, and other key airline staff members before and during a flight.

QUESTIONS FOR CLASS DISCUSSION

1. In what ways has the airplane changed our way of life?
2. Name a number of ways in which present-day aircraft serve people. In what ways do airplanes cause problems?
3. What are the steps involved in the construction of an airplane—from the idea to completion? How long does it take to construct an airplane?
4. What might have happened to the aviation industry if the Wright brothers had failed in their early flights?
5. What will planes be like by the year 2025?
6. How might our way of life change if inexpensive helicopters became plentiful?
7. What should be done about the increased congestion of air traffic, especially over large city airports?
8. How does aviation affect the life of every person?
9. What principles did the Wright brothers employ in order to get a heavier-than-air machine to fly?
10. Who were some of the other early experimenters and contributors to aviation?
11. Why do you think Charles A. Lindbergh is considered the most famous of all pilots?

Who are some other famous pioneers of flight?
12. What features besides speed do airplane designers have to take into consideration?
13. In what ways have wars advanced the aviation industry?
14. Why were California and the Southwest so important to the early aviation industry?
15. What is meant by the saying "It's a 12-hour world"? What is an SST airplane?
16. Vertical takeoff and landing (VTOL) planes have been designed by engineers. What are their advantages and disadvantages?
17. Why are the polar routes often the shortest distance to fly between two points?
18. How much does a giant airliner cost to manufacture today? How many passengers can it hold? What is its travel speed?
19. What further measures need to be taken to improve air travel safety?
20. Why are meteorologists important to aviation?

KEY VOCABULARY

aeronaut	fuselage
aeronautics	glider
aileron	hangar
airplane	helicopter
airport	instrument
altimeter	instrument panel
altitude	jet engine
astronaut	landing
balloon	launch
biplane	missile
cabin	monorail
cockpit	National Aeronautical Space Agency (NASA)
compass	
controls	
control tower	patent
dirigible	pilot
Federal Aviation Agency (FAA)	pressurized
	propeller
flight	radar
flight engineer	radio

KEY VOCABULARY CONTINUED

rudder
runway
satellite
seaplane
spacecraft
supersonic
  transport
tail

tailspin
takeoff
terminal
tower
vehicle
wheel
wind tunnel
wing

RELATED CAREER EDUCATION TERMS

aircraft designer
airport
  administrator
air traffic
  controller
astronaut
balloonist
communications
  officer
computer
  programmer
engineer
flight attendant

flight engineer
inventor
mechanic
meteorologist
NASA scientist
  or technician
navigator
pilot
radar specialist
reservation
  clerk
service crew
  member

Continental Army Encamped at Valley Forge

THEMES AND THOUGHTS

Duty, Patriotism, Loyalty, Commitment, Contribution, Sacrifice

And here in this place of sacrifice
In this vale of humiliation
In this valley of the shadow of the
death out of which the life of
America rose
Regenerate and free
Let us believe
With an abiding faith
That to them
Union will seem as dear
And liberty as sweet and progress
as glorious
As they were to our fathers
And are to you and me
And that the institutions
Which have made us happy
Preserved by the virtue of our
children
Shall bless the remotest generation
of the time to come.
—*Henry Armitt Brown*

It is always darkest just before
the day dawneth.
—*Thomas Fuller*

FASCINATING FACTS

General Washington arrived at Valley Forge, Pennsylvania, in December 1777 with 11,089 men. More than 3,000 soldiers died at Valley Forge during the "winter of despair" of 1777–1778. This was one-third the number of men who were killed in all the battles of the Revolutionary War. Almost another 3,000 men were unfit for duty because they were barefoot or had too little clothing to protect them against the winter cold. Many others were stricken by a smallpox epidemic.

General Howe, the British commander opposing Washington, and his army spent the very bitter winter in the comfort of Philadelphia,

making no attempt to attack or destroy the camp at Valley Forge. Howe thought that nature alone would overcome the American forces. Meanwhile, Washington's barefoot sentries had to stand on their hats during guard duty to keep their feet from freezing.

Nevertheless, most of the troops remained loyal to Washington and to the Revolution. Baron von Steuben and General Washington drilled the troops despite the harsh conditions and produced the army that, along with the French fleet, defeated the British troops under General Cornwallis at Yorktown. This was the battle that marked the end of the American

Revolution. The extreme hardship and suffering at Valley Forge made the fruit of victory taste even sweeter.

The Valley Forge State Park was the first state park established in Pennsylvania. It encompasses 2,103 acres. Reproductions of the huts and buildings of the Continental Army can be found in the park.

ACTIVITIES FOR STUDENTS

Information Gathering and Sharing

1. Plan a trip, real or imaginary, to Valley Forge State Park, Pennsylvania. Write what one should expect to do or see there.
2. As a class, write to the Freedoms Foundation (Valley Forge, PA 18481) for pictures, photographs, and a map of Valley Forge. Make a bulletin-board display of the items. The display title might be "Find Out About Me—Valley Forge, 1777–1778."
3. Report orally on Baron Frederick von Steuben.
4. Investigate and report orally on General Washington's reasons for selecting Valley Forge for encampment.
5. Investigate and report orally on why General Howe did not attack the Continental Army at Valley Forge.
6. With your class, discuss what our modern armies do to combat disease, harsh weather, and hunger.
7. Do some research about other historic military camps around the world.
8. Make a chart comparing the military situation in Valley Forge to that in nearby Gettysburg.

Art and Visual Aids

9. Locate Valley Forge on a map of Pennsylvania. Draw pictorial scenes of the campsite.
10. With your class, make a table display of the Valley Forge camp, using log cabins made from milk cartons or popsicle sticks, and soldiers made from stand-up cardboard cutouts.
11. Draw a pictorial map (using picture symbols of trees, river, campsite, and so on) of Valley Forge as it may have looked in 1778.

Dramatics and Role-Playing

12. With a small group, dramatize a discussion between General Washington and some of his men at Valley Forge.
13. With a classmate, role-play a conversation between two soldiers, one contemplating desertion and the other advocating loyalty.

Writing and Language Arts

14. Pretend you are a member of the Continental Army at Valley Forge and write a letter home describing the conditions at the encampment.
15. Write and deliver a speech General Washington might have made to his army at Valley Forge.
16. Write a diary recounting the experiences of one of Washington's men at Valley Forge, of one of General Howe's soldiers, or of the wife of a soldier in one of the armies.
17. Pretend to be a British spy who has infiltrated Washington's encampment. Write a report describing what you see. You might also include a spy map.
18. Write a poem in tribute to those who suffered and died at Valley Forge.

QUESTIONS FOR CLASS DISCUSSION

1. In what ways was Valley Forge a testing ground for a good soldier?
2. How do you think General Washington felt at Valley Forge?
3. Many people criticized Washington for his position at Valley Forge. Why did he stay there? What could he have done to avoid the tragedy of Valley Forge?
4. In what ways do we remember Valley Forge?
5. Why do you think the Boy Scouts of America frequently choose this state park for the site of their national jamborees and encampments?
6. Over 2,000 of Washington's men deserted his ranks. Why did some soldiers remain loyal while others deserted?
7. How do you think General Washington kept up his men's morale?
8. General Washington lived in a tent and did

not move into his rented house at Valley Forge until most of his men had shelter. Why do you suppose he did that?

9. What are some basic requirements for the location of any fortification? Which of these did Valley Forge possess?

10. What do you think a typical day was like for General Washington while he waited out the winter at Valley Forge?

11. Markers, memorials, and a museum help make Valley Forge a fine site for history-oriented hikers. What other features are located nearby for other historical excursions?

12. How does climate play an important role in warfare?

13. What is the difference between a "summer soldier" and "winter patriot"?

RELATED CAREER EDUCATION TERMS

dietitian	nurse
doctor	paramedic
engineer	soldier
military personnel	strategist
munitions manufacturer	weapons expert

KEY VOCABULARY

artillery	humiliation
bitter	independence
cabin	infantry
camp	morale
campfire	musket
commitment	patriot
Continental Army	perseverance
defeated	retreat
defense	sacrifice
desert (verb)	sentry
despair	shrine
disease	starvation
drill	suffering
encampment	tent
epidemic	trench
fleet	valley
fortification	wounded
headquarters	

Apollo 8 Launched

FASCINATING FACTS

The U.S. program to land a person on the moon was called the Apollo program. Several spacecraft without people on board were sent into orbit around the moon. The Apollo 8 mission sent the first spacecraft with astronauts to orbit the moon. This historic flight was launched on December 21, 1968.

The formal countdown began four days before the launch. During those four days, computers were used to check that the systems were ready and that each one was performing the important function it was programmed to carry out. Even before that, many indoor tests were carried out on the rockets and the modules.

The 28-story Saturn V rocket thrust the 100,000-pound spacecraft into space from a launch pad at the Kennedy Space Center in Florida. The spacecraft had three main parts: the command module, which housed the three astronauts, the service module, which was the propulsion system, and the lunar module, which was later used in the Apollo 11 flight to transfer two astronauts from the command module to the surface of the moon and back again.

The greatest view of Earth was seen not only by the three astronauts aboard, Col. Frank Borman, Capt. James A. Lovell, Jr., and Major William A. Anders, but also by millions of television viewers. Live broadcasts were made during the flight, as well as during the orbits around the moon.

Apollo 8 orbited the moon ten times on December 24 and 25. Then the engines were refired, and the command module re-entered earth's atmosphere at 24,695 mph on December 27, 1968. The three astronauts traveled a total distance of over 500,000 miles during the 147-hour flight. The moon had become a stepping-stone for future space explorations.

ACTIVITIES FOR STUDENTS

Experiments

1. Rockets are used to propel spacecrafts out

of the earth's gravitational pull. Experiment with the effect of gravity on objects of different weights. Write the results of the following three activities. Discuss the results of the experiment with the class. Does the weight of an object affect the speed with which it falls? Research Galileo's experiments with gravity. How do his findings compare with yours?

    a. Stand on a chair. Hold a pencil and a shoe in the air at the same height. Let go of both at the same time. What happens?

    b. Stand on a chair. Drop a marble and a ball from the same height. What happens?

    c. Stand on a chair. Drop a book and an eraser from the same height. What happens?

2. Experiment with the effects of gravity. Make a simple parachute, using a piece of paper or an old handkerchief, some string, and two washers. Make another parachute weighted with only one washer. Drop the two parachutes from the same height. What do you observe?

3. In order to further understand the pull of gravity, work with a magnet and a piece of iron or a nail. Can you "see" what pulls the iron to the magnet? Research the topics of magnetism and gravity.

Information Gathering and Sharing

4. Illustrate and explain how gravity helps space flights and other forms of air travel.

5. Construct a space-weight chart or table based on ten different earth weights. For example, if something weighs 60 pounds on earth, what will it weigh on various planets?

6. Compose a "Did You Know" booklet with illustrations of surprising, unusual, or little-known facts about space flights.

7. If you have visited a NASA space center, such as Cape Canaveral, Houston, or Goddard, report on your impressions.

8. Report on Robert Hutchings Goddard, the father of U.S. rocketry.

9. Research and report on one of the following topics: (a) spacecraft, (b) space science, or (c) manned space flights, space applications, and international space activities since the Apollo 8 flight. You can do an individual report or work with a group.

10. As a class, make a timeline tracing the history of U.S.-sponsored space flights.

11. Make a timeline or chart comparing the space programs of the United States and the Soviet Union.

Art and Visual Aids

12. Using various sources in the library as your guide, create a model of the surface of the moon. Either clay or papier-mâché would be a good substance to use.

13. With your class, create a mobile that includes the planets, the sun, and a spaceship orbiting the moon.

QUESTIONS FOR CLASS DISCUSSION

1. Why are some governments interested in space exploration?

2. Can governments without a space program conduct experiments and projects in space? How?

3. To be an astronaut, what knowledge and background should you have?

4. Do astronauts encounter problems more complex than the first venturers across oceans, deserts, and arctic ice? Why or why not?

5. What does the word *astronaut* mean? What do the Russians call their astronauts?

6. Who was the first American in space? When did this occur?

7. Do you think that you might one day be able to travel in space? Would you want to? Why or why not?

8. Are there any preparations being made today for commercial flights into space?

9. What does it take to be an astronaut, a space-vehicle engineer, or an astrophysicist? What subjects are especially important?

10. Do you believe that there is life on other planets? Give reasons for your answers.

KEY VOCABULARY

acceleration
apogee
Apollo
astronaut
atmosphere
calculation
capsule
commander
command module
control center
debriefing
deceleration
docking
experiment
flight pattern
flight plan
gravity
hydrogen
interplanetary
ionosphere
launching pad

lunar
orbit
outer space
oxygen
perigee
pitch
propellant
re-entry
retro-rocket
risk
satellite
space
spacecraft
spaceship
staging
thrust
tracking station
trajectory
weightlessness
yaw

RELATED CAREER EDUCATION TERMS

aerospace
  technician
armed forces
  personnel
astronaut
astronomer
cartographer
communications
  specialist
computer opera-
  tor/technician
draftsperson
electrician
engineer

laboratory
  technician
mechanic
meteorologist
physicist
pilot
scientist
space medicine
  specialist
technical writer/
  illustrator
tool designer
welder

December 25	# Christmas

THEMES AND THOUGHTS

Tradition, Religion, Faith,
Diversity, Family

I love the Christmas-tide, and yet
I notice this, each year I live;
I always like the gifts I get,
But how I love the gifts I give!
—*Carolyn Wells*

I will honor Christmas in my
heart, and try to keep it all the year.
—*Charles Dickens*

You give but little when you give
of your possessions. It is when you
give of yourself that you truly give.
—*Kahlil Gibran*

I have often thought . . . it
happens very well that Christmas
should fall out in the Middle of
Winter.

—*Joseph Addison*

FASCINATING FACTS

The word *Christmas* originated from the Old English Cristesmaesse, or Christ's Mass. Sometimes, especially in Christmas carols, Christmas is also referred to as Noël or Yule. Noël is a French word that comes from the Latin word for "born." Yule comes from an Old English word that was the name of a heathen festival at the winter solstice.

The custom of holiday gift-giving goes back to the ancient Romans, who exchanged gifts during their midwinter festival. This custom also reflects the Wise Men's bringing of gifts to the Christ Child.

Outdoor caroling dates back to the Middle Ages, when groups of people carrying torches went from home to home singing. Most of the

carols we sing today, however, were written in the 1800s.

"Santa Claus" is an Americanization of *Sinterklaas*, the Dutch name for St. Nicholas, the patron saint of children, whose feast day is December 6. The Dutch settlers in New York carried on the tradition of St. Nicholas bringing gifts to children on St. Nicholas Eve. Most English settlers soon adopted the custom. The Puritans of the Massachusetts Bay Colony, however, disapproved of the nonreligious aspects of the celebration of Christmas and forbade their observance.

The tradition of Santa coming down the chimney probably originates with an old Norse legend about the goddess Hertha, a symbol of good luck, who appeared at the fireplace.

The original St. Nicholas was a priest in what is now known as Turkey. St. Nicholas was first depicted as a tall, stately man wearing a bishop's miter and robes. In 1809, author Washington Irving began to transform St. Nicholas into the jolly Santa we are familiar with. His version of St. Nicholas was a stout, jolly man wearing a broad-brimmed hat and huge breeches and smoking a pipe. In 1823, Clement C. Moore made this vision of a jolly Santa popular in his poem "A Visit from St. Nicholas" (which begins with the line "'Twas the night before Christmas"). In the 1860s, cartoonist Thomas Nast completed the transformation with a series of cartoons for Harper's Weekly magazine in which he gave Santa his white beard.

The custom of decorating a Christmas tree comes from Germany. It dates back to medieval mystery plays in which the Paradiesbaum (tree of Paradise) decorated with apples symbolized the Garden of Eden.

Sending Christmas cards is a relatively new custom. The first Christmas card is believed to have been designed in England in 1843 by John Calcott Horsley, an illustrator. Christmas cards were introduced to the United States in 1875 by a German emigrant printer, Louis Prang. About two billion cards are mailed annually in the United States.

Christmas is celebrated in different ways in different lands. The following are some of the various Christmas customs around the world.

✢ MEXICO

Christmas festivities begin December 16 with the *posadas* (the Spanish word for inn or lodging). On each of the nine nights before Christmas, two children carry statues of Mary and Joseph and lead a procession to a different house in search of a room. At each house, there is feasting and celebrating. On the ninth night, Christmas Eve, the house has a miniature stable erected in it, and the two children put the figures of Mary and Joseph in the stable. Afterward, everyone attends midnight mass.

Mexican children receive their gifts by breaking the piñata, a brightly decorated figure made of papier-mâché or clay and filled with treats. The piñata is hung from a high place, and each child is blindfolded before taking a turn to try to break the piñata with a stick.

✢ GREAT BRITAIN

On Christmas Eve, British children hang their stockings for Father Christmas to fill. On Boxing Day, the day after Christmas, families remember the people who work for them by giving them a gift.

✢ DENMARK

On Christmas Eve, the children put out a bowl of porridge and some milk for Jul Nisse, the mischievous little man of the attic who brings the Christmas gifts. Danish families remember the birds on Christmas Day by decorating doorways, barns, and gables with grain.

✢ SWEDEN

Holiday celebrations start on December 13, which is Luciadagen, or St. Lucia's Day. St. Lucia is the Queen of Lights. Her holiday brings hope at the darkest time of the year. In Sweden, the daylight hours are few in December because it is so far north. According to tradition, the oldest daughter in each family dresses as St. Lucia—in a white robe and red sash—and wears a crown of candles. She brings coffee and saffron buns to all the adults in the family.

✢ NORWAY

"Christmas for a month" with special treats for children and birds mark this season in Norway. Children wearing festive costumes visit neighbors to share cakes and cookies. The birds are remembered with sheaves of grain tied to high poles.

✢ THE NETHERLANDS

On the last Saturday of November, St. Nicholas, accompanied by his servant, Black Peter, arrives by steamer in Amsterdam. As he rides down the street on his white horse, he distributes gifts to the people, who chant "St. Nicholas is coming!" Formal dinners and church services mark Christmas Day celebrations.

✤ FRANCE

On Christmas Eve, the children leave their shoes on the doorstep for le petit Noël (the Christ Child) or his helper Père Noël (Father Christmas) to fill with gifts. Many French homes are decorated with mistletoe, a good luck symbol.

Food is an important part of Christmas celebrations in France. Each region boasts its own specialties. In Paris, special treats include oysters, pâté de foie gras, blood sausage, crêpes, and many varieties of sweets. Goose is a favorite in many regions, as are snails, mullet, pike, roast chestnuts, chard, celery, figs, dates, and fruits. In Brittany, buckwheat crêpes and sour cream are traditionally served on Christmas Eve. Strasbourg pie (liver) and black pudding are traditional dishes in Alsace.

✤ SWITZERLAND

On Christmas Eve, young people visit nine fountains, taking three sips from each on their way to midnight church services. A legend says that after they do this, they will see their future wife or husband at the church door.

In Lucerne, a girl in white, wearing a crown, impersonates Christkindli (the Christ Child). A group of young girls carrying baskets of food and lighted lanterns accompany her to visit homes, singing carols and giving out presents.

Father Christmas delivers gifts to the boys, while his wife, Lucy (representing St. Lucy, whose feast day is December 13), distributes gifts to the girls.

✤ CZECHOSLOVAKIA

Children go to bed early on Christmas Eve to await St. Nicholas. According to Czech legend, he descends from a golden cord, aided by an angel. Throughout the Christmas season, carolers visit homes, dressed as the Three Kings and angels and carrying a miniature Bethlehem scene.

✤ SPAIN

Christmas Eve, or Nochebuena, is marked by a festive atmosphere of dancing in the streets, which includes a traditional Christmas dance called the *jota*. Children receive small gifts in the streets on Christmas Eve. But they put their shoes out on the balcony or near a window for the Three Wise Men to fill on January 6, or Epiphany Eve.

✤ ITALY

Each home displays a manger scene. Olive trees are trimmed with fresh apples and oranges, which may not be eaten before Christmas night. On Epiphany Eve, January 6, children receive gifts from La Befana, a kindly old witch.

✤ YUGOSLAVIA

It is the custom to spread straw on the floor on Christmas Eve and place a clean tablecloth over it. Candles and incense are lighted, and the members of the household kneel in prayer.

The day before Christmas (which Yugoslavians observe 13 days after December 25, according to the Julian calendar), the men cut the Yule log and offer a prayer and wish it a Happy Bandnji Dan (Christmas Eve). In the evening, the family gathers by the hearth, and the strongest young man brings in the log. He sprinkles wheat on the log in the fireplace and wishes everyone a Merry Christmas. The burning of the Yule log is to warm the Baby Jesus in the manger and symbolizes the light and warmth of faith that can never go out. Rural Yugoslavians also pour a little wine on each of the family's animals and wish it Merry Christmas and thank it for the hard work it performed all year. The Christmas Eve meal does not include meat or dairy products, but many families have twelve different dishes in honor of the twelve apostles.

✤ ROMANIA

Carolers carry a steava, a five-sided box on which there is a picture of the Virgin Mary or another religious figure. It is illuminated with a candle and carried on a pole.

✤ GREECE

On Christmas Eve morning, children go caroling from home to home to proclaim the birth of Christ. Greek families end a four-week fast with an elaborate Christmas Day dinner of pork or chicken and a special bread called *christopsomo* (bread of Christ), which is decorated with elaborate frosted ornaments representing some aspect of the family's occupation.

The Greeks celebrate New Year's Day with another special bread. This bread is marked with a cross and has a coin baked inside it. As the family breaks the bread, the first portion is given to St. Basil or to the Holy Virgin. (St. Basil, the patron saint of Greece, is believed to have arrived on a ship loaded with gifts on Christmas Day.) Pieces are set aside for the household animals, and what is left is shared among the family. The family member who finds the coin is destined for good fortune in the new year.

In many Balkan countries, priests bless a gold cross and throw it into the water. In some countries, boys dive for the cross because it is believed that the one who recovers it will have good luck.

✣ PHILIPPINE ISLANDS

Filipino households do not have Christmas trees, but the homes are decorated with colorful flowers, palms, and flags, and a candle is kept burning in a window all night. On Christmas Day, after attending mass, families join a parade, wearing wreaths and chains of bright flowers. A band accompanies the festive songs. Then people gather for family dinners with dancing and musical entertainment. Church bells ring to proclaim the end of Christmas Day.

ACTIVITIES FOR STUDENTS

Critical Thinking

1. Make a list of gifts (real or imaginary) you want to get for others for the holidays. Allow yourself a fixed sum to "spend" for the gifts. Check prices in stores, mail-order catalogs, and newspaper advertisements.

Information Gathering and Sharing

2. Look through an atlas to find place names that remind you of Christmas or winter, such as Santa Claus, Indiana; Snowball, Arkansas; Candle, Alaska; Christmas, Florida; Bethlehem, Pennsylvania; and Holly, Colorado. With your class, send letters and stamped, self-addressed envelopes to the postmasters of some of these towns, requesting that the envelopes be postmarked and sent back. Use the envelopes for a bulletin-board display or for trimming a classroom tree. (Be sure to put the zip code on your envelopes. Your post office has a zip code directory.)

3. Through discussion, share your family's special Christmas customs with the class. Interview people who have celebrated Christmas in other ways in foreign lands.

4. Make a study of the origin of some present-day Christmas customs for a special report to the class.

5. Investigate the gift-giving customs and legendary figures in different lands, such as King Balthazar in Spain (January 6) and La Befana in Italy (January 6).

6. Compile a list of traditional Christmas greetings from different lands.

7. With your class, make a large word-and-picture chart, comparing the ways Christmas is celebrated in different countries. Find information for the following categories: typical gifts, season, date, typical holiday food, customs, religious services, decorations, legendary figures, "Merry Christmas," or other season's greetings in the native language, and other fascinating facts.

Writing and Language Arts

8. Ask your teacher to write to a school official in a foreign land or a distant city to set up correspondence with a class or with individual students in order to learn about their Christmas practices.

9. With a small group, turn a Christmas story or poem into a playlet.

10. Write and tape a story, poem, or play to send to other classrooms or to the children's ward at a local hospital.

11. Write a short essay on the spirit of giving and goodwill.

12. Make a simple acrostic poem with appropri-

ate seasonal words beginning with each letter of the word Christmas. For example,

C—hurch

H—olly

R—eindeer

I—cicle

S—anta

T—ree

M—istletoe

A—ngel

S—tocking

Art and Visual Aids

13. Make an exhibit of Christmas plants and trees, such as spruce, holly, mistletoe, and poinsettia.
14. Decorate the class Christmas tree with large, colorful paper placards, each showing a contribution of another land to Christmas celebrations in America.
15. With your class, draw illustrations of representative Christmas scenes and national customs. Mount the pictures around a large wall map of the world, connecting each picture to its country with red or green string, yarn, or ribbon.
16. With your class, make a floor-to-ceiling frieze or mural, using a "Christmas in Other Lands" theme. Have a committee sketch the overall design. Divide the class into groups to paint or paste paper "tiles" in sections of the mural. This project could also be undertaken by several classes or the entire school.
17. Make personalized Christmas cards featuring your photograph or a scene from your neighborhood.

Music

18. Tape your favorite Christmas songs, or bring appropriate seasonal recordings to class.

Special Projects

19. As a class, construct, collect, and repair toys for needy families and community service centers.
20. As a class, have a simple grab-bag gift exchange of inexpensive presents that are typical of various foreign countries.
21. With your class, decorate a "giving tree" with nonperishable food items and warm hats, scarves, gloves, and mittens that can be donated to the local welfare department for needy people.

QUESTIONS FOR CLASS DISCUSSION

1. What is the origin of your favorite Christmas custom?
2. What is the most important message to remember about the meaning of Christmas?
3. Red and green are the colors associated with Christmas. Why is this so? What other holidays have certain colors identified with them? Can you name them?
4. How can you learn more about other people's religions or national backgrounds?
5. What do you know about the ways children in the Southern Hemisphere enjoy the Christmas season? How are their celebrations different?
6. What are some of the special ways children can help around the home during the holiday season?
7. Do you think the celebration of Christmas in the various regions of the world will become more or less different as time goes by? Explain.
8. What customs found in other countries are most appealing to you?
9. Why do people stress goodwill and peace on earth at Christmastime?

KEY VOCABULARY

bough	mistletoe
candle	nativity
card	Noël
carol	ornaments
ceremony	poinsettia
chimney	practice
Christmas	present (noun)
custom	reindeer
deck (verb)	Santa Claus
decorations	service
don	sleigh
eve	spirit
fir	star
garland	tinsel
goodwill	trim
greetings	universal
holly	wassail
icicle	Wise Men
ideal	wrappings
manger	wreath
Mass	Yule
merry	

RELATED CAREER EDUCATION TERMS

advertiser	package designer
baker	professional
craftsperson	shopping service
decorator	storekeeper
designer	wrapper
manager	

January

National Hobby Month

First Week:

1
* New Year's Day
* Abraham Lincoln issued Emancipation Proclamation, 1863
* Betsy Ross, flagmaker, born, 1752
Paul Revere, soldier and patriot, born, 1735
Tournament of Roses, Pasadena, CA, since 1886
First flag of George Washington's army completed, 1776

2
Winter Sports Day

3
Alaska admitted to the Union, 1959
Battle of Princeton, 1777
Lucretia Coffin Mott, women's rights advocate, born, 1793
March of Dimes established to raise funds for polio research, 1938

4
Louis Braille, inventor of braille alphabet system for the blind, born, 1809
Jacob Grimm, author of fairy tales, born, 1785
Sir Isaac Newton, discoverer of law of gravity, born, 1642

5
Great Northern Railway completed, 1893
Stephen Decatur, U.S. naval hero, born, 1779
Nellie Taylor Ross became first woman governor in U.S. (Wyoming), 1925
Bird Day—National Audubon Society founded, 1905

6
Carl Sandburg, poet and author, born, 1878
Pan American Airways achieved the first around-the-world commercial flight, 1942

7
Transatlantic telephone service began, 1927
President Millard Fillmore born, 1800
First national election in the U.S., 1789
First U.S. commercial bank opened, in Philadelphia, 1782
Eastern Orthodox Christmas

*A teaching unit is included on the following pages for each starred entry.

Second Week:

8
Andrew Jackson defeated British at Battle of New Orleans, 1815
World Literacy Day
President Washington delivered first State of the Union address, 1790

9
First balloon flight in the U.S., 1793
Carrie Chapman Catt, women's suffrage leader, born, 1859
President Richard Nixon born, 1913

10
Ethan Allen, leader of the "Green Mountain Boys," born, 1738
First Texas oil strike, 1901
League of Nations founded, 1920
First session of the United Nations, 1946

11
Alexander Hamilton, first secretary of the U.S. Treasury, born, 1757

12
John Hancock born, 1737
* First public museum founded, in Charleston, SC, 1773
Jack London, novelist, born, 1876

13
Horatio Alger, novelist, born, 1832
Stephen Foster Memorial Day

14
Albert Schweitzer, humanitarian, born, 1875

15
* Martin Luther King, Jr., leader of nonviolent civil rights movement in the U.S., born, 1929
Mathew B. Brady, first photographer to record Civil War battlefields, died, 1896

Third Week:

* World Religion Day (the 3rd Sunday in January)

16
Civil Service system established, 1883
National Do Nothing Day

17
* Benjamin Franklin, scientist and statesman, born, 1706

18
Daniel Webster, statesman, born, 1782
A. A. Milne, author of the *Winnie-the-Pooh* books, born, 1882

19
General Robert E. Lee born, 1807
James Watt, inventor of steam power, born, 1736

20
Presidential Inauguration Day (every 4th year), beginning in 1937
First basketball game, Springfield, MA, 1892

21
Nautilus, first atomic-powered ship, launched, 1954
Stonewall Jackson, Confederate general, born, 1824

22
* First postal route (Boston to New York) established, 1672

23
20th ("lame duck") Amendment ratified, 1933
Record ocean descent—U.S. Navy bathysphere, Trieste, went 24,000 feet to bottom of
   Mariana Trench in the Pacific Ocean, 1960

Fourth Week:

Chinese New Year (at 1st full moon after sun enters Aquarius—between January 21 and February 19)

24
Gold discovered in California, 1848
National School Nurse Day

25
Transcontinental telephone service established, 1915

26
General Douglas MacArthur born, 1880
Michigan admitted to the Union, 1837

27
Wolfgang Amadeus Mozart born, 1756
Lewis Carroll (Charles Dodgson), author of *Alice in Wonderland*, born, 1832
Samuel Gompers, first president of the American Federation of Labor, born, 1850
Vietnam Day—official signing of peace agreement ending the Vietnam War, 1973
Three Apollo I astronauts killed in fire during ground testing, 1967

28
Sir Francis Drake, English explorer, born, 1540
U.S. Coast Guard established, 1915
Seven astronauts killed in Challenger explosion, Kennedy Space Center, FL, 1986

29
Seeing Eye, Inc., first guide-dog foundation, organized, 1929
President William McKinley born, 1843
Common Sense Day—Thomas Paine, Revolutionary War patriot and writer, born, 1737

30
Baseball Hall of Fame established, 1936
President Franklin D. Roosevelt born, 1882

31
U.S. launched its first satellite, Explorer I, 1958

New Year's Day

THEMES AND THOUGHTS

Resolution, Progress, Reflection,
   Commitment

   Ring out the old, ring in the new,
   Ring, happy bells, across the
snow;
   The year is going, let it go;
   Ring out the false, ring in the
true.
                    —*Alfred Lord Tennyson*

   Should auld acquaintance be
forgot,
   And never brought to mind?
   Should auld acquaintance be
forgot,
   And days of auld lang syne?
                    —*Robert Burns*

   Time has no divisions to mark its
passage, there is never a thunderstorm or blare of trumpets to
announce the beginning of a new
month or year. Even when a new
century begins it is only we mortals
who ring bells and fire off pistols.
                    —*Thomas Mann*

FASCINATING FACTS

   The new year has not always begun on
January 1, and it doesn't begin on that date
everywhere today. It begins on that date only for
cultures, like ours, that use a 365-day solar
calendar. January 1 became the beginning of the
new year in 46 B.C., when Julius Caesar developed a calendar that would more accurately
reflect the seasons than previous calendars had.

   The Romans named the first month of the
year after Janus, the god of beginnings and the
guardian of doors and entrances. He was always
depicted with two faces, one on the front of his
head and one on the back. Thus he could look
backward and forward at the same time. At
midnight on December 31, the Romans imag-
ined Janus looking back at the old year and
forward to the new. The Romans began a
tradition of exchanging gifts on New Year's by
giving one another branches from sacred trees
for good fortune. Later, nuts or coins imprinted
with the god Janus became more common New
Year's gifts.

   In the Middle Ages, Christians changed
New Year's Day to December 25, the birth of
Jesus. Then they changed it to March 25, a
holiday called the Annunciation. In the sixteenth
century, Pope Gregory XIII revised the Julian
calendar, and the celebration of the new year
was returned to January 1.

   The Julian and Gregorian calendars are solar

calendars. Some cultures have lunar calendars, however. A year in a lunar calendar is less than 365 days because the months are based on the phases of the moon. The Chinese use a lunar calendar. Their new year begins at the time of the first full moon (over the Far East) after the sun enters Aquarius—sometime between January 19 and February 21. The Chinese celebrate the holiday by exchanging gifts, having parades, and exploding firecrackers. One of twelve animals, such as a tiger, a rooster, or a dog, is associated with each new year.

The Jewish New Year, Rosh Hashanah, is celebrated on the first two days of the Jewish calendar's first month, Tishri, which falls in September or October. The Jewish New Year is heralded by the rabbi blowing a shofar, or ram's horn, in the synagogue. The Islamic year starts anew every 354 days. Because there are no adjustments, like leap year, to make each calendar year correspond to the earth's cycle around the sun, the first month of the Islamic calendar, Muharram, is not in the same season every year.

Many Native Americans celebrate the new year toward the end of the summer. For the Creek Indians, for example, the ripening of the corn in July or August signals the end of the year. At this time, they replace their household goods and clothing and burn their old belongings and the grain and other food that has not been eaten during the previous year. Then each family's fire is extinguished, and a new one is started from a holy fire built by the chief priest. The Iroquois celebrate the new year for several days. Old disputes and grudges are settled by means of rituals that involve throwing water or ashes. The Iroquois also have a special New Year's ceremony to drive out evil spirits.

Although the date for New Year's Day is not the same in every culture, it is always a time for celebration and for customs to ensure good luck in the coming year. In France, families gather and exchange gifts and greeting cards. Children often present their parents with homemade gifts to wish them Bonne Année. In Italy, a piece of mistletoe is hung over the front door to bring good luck to the entire household. In Scotland, people bring delicious cakes and cookies to parties. It is believed that the first person to enter a house will receive good luck. "Auld Lang Syne," the traditional New Year's song, was written by a Scottish poet, Robert Burns, 200 years ago. In Japan, New Year's is celebrated for three days, starting on January 1. Everyone receives new clothes and little work is done. On New Year's Eve, Buddhist temples ring out the old year by letting passersby each ring a huge bell once until it has rung 108 times, one time for each kind of evil in the world. On New Year's Day, it is traditional to make a pilgrimage to a Shinto shrine or a Buddhist temple.

In the United States, the New Year's celebrations that are familiar to us today were originated in the 1750s by the Dutch in New Amsterdam. Today, we make New Year's resolutions. We decide to "turn over a new leaf" and improve ourselves in some way during the new year. Many people have big parties on New Year's Eve. Children are often permitted to stay up until midnight, when "Old Father Time" (with a long, white beard) is replaced by the "New Year's Child" (dressed only in diapers).

There are also special New Year's traditions in various parts of the country. In New York City, tens of thousands of enthusiastic celebrants crowd into Times Square to await the dropping of a large, lighted ball from the top of a skyscraper precisely at midnight on New Year's Eve. The occasion, shown on television, triggers celebrations all across the United States. On New Year's Day in Philadelphia, thousands of people dress in elaborate costumes and dance through the main streets in the daylong Mummers' Parade. In Pasadena, the Rose Bowl football game is preceded by the Tournament of Roses Parade—marching bands from all parts of the United States and hundreds of floats covered with fresh flowers. Several other bowl games are also played around the country to end of the college football season.

Another tradition is beginning to take root across the United States, too. In many communities, African-American families gather for a karamu, a special feast, on January 1, at the end of Kwanzaa. Kwanzaa is a seven-day celebration of African-American heritage that was originated by a university professor from California, Ron Karenga, in the 1960s. The celebration is based on a traditional African harvest ceremony, and the name comes from a Swahili phrase that means "first fruits." Each day of Kwanzaa is dedicated to one of seven principles of black culture. Each evening, family members light one of seven candles in a special candleholder called a kinara and discuss the principle for the day. The principles are Umoja (unity), Kujichagulia (self-determination), Ujima (collective work and responsibility), Ujamaa (cooperative economics), Nia (purpose), Kuumba (creativity), and Imani (faith). All seven principles are discussed at the karamu, the contributions of ancestors are remembered, the old year is assessed, and commitments are made for the new year. Some people exchange creative, homemade gifts at the karamu. The feast ends with music and dancing.

ACTIVITIES FOR STUDENTS

Critical Thinking

1. With your class, listen to recordings of bells and discuss the custom of bell ringing to welcome the New Year.
2. Make a list of "good citizen" resolutions for classroom and community improvement.
3. With your class, discuss the meaning of the seven principles of Kwanzaa: Umoja (unity), Kujichagulia (self-determination), Ujima (collective work and responsibility), Ujamaa (cooperative economics), Nia (purpose), Kuumba (creativity), and Imani (faith). Share examples that illustrate the application of these principles.

Art and Visual Aids

4. Make a community or class calendar for January through June. Highlight seasonal weather forecasts and local commemorative days.
5. Make a snapshot or picture calendar with an accompanying notepad.
6. With your class, make an illustrated timeline of days and events throughout the year, putting each event on a 5" x 8" index card. Mount the timeline cards on the walls around the room for ready reference. You can use the monthly calendars in this book as well as books in the library for your references.

7. With your classmates, choose one day in the upcoming month to illustrate on a sheet of 8 1/2" x 11" paper or a large poster board. Place all the drawings in a notebook or on a chart rack for timely viewing.
8. Divide your class into groups. Each group will be responsible for researching, designing, and illustrating a monthly mosaic, mural, or frieze depicting the events and anniversaries in one month.
9. Collect or draw pictures that represent a special day, a month, or a season. Mount your pictures on heavy paper. Write the name of the day, month, or season on the back of each picture. Show your cards to the rest of the class and let them guess what each picture represents.
10. Design and make individualized New Year's or Kwanzaa greeting cards.

Information Gathering and Sharing

11. Make a simple chart to indicate when and how other nations observe New Year's Day.
12. Read excerpts from the *Farmer's Almanac* and similar documents listing weather predictions for the coming year.
13. With your class, put together a "Did You Know Hour" of fascinating facts and customs about New Year's celebrations in other lands and historical oddities about the calendar.
14. Research the origins of the names of the days and months.

Writing and Language Arts

15. Start a daily diary or journal on New Year's Day. Try to record something every day so that at the end of the year you can look back on the activities and happenings in your life.
16. Write some humorous or serious predictions of things to come in the new year. Compile the class' predictions and make them available for reference.
17. As part of the Kwanzaa celebration, people talk about how their ancestors have contributed to who they and their family

members are today. Write a brief essay about how your ancestors influenced the kind of person you are and hope to become.

QUESTIONS FOR CLASS DISCUSSION

1. How does the climate of a region affect the manner in which a country celebrates New Year's Day? List some examples.
2. In this age of global travel and communication, why would it be advantageous to have a uniform time and calendar system throughout the world?
3. What would be some interesting and appropriate ways to celebrate New Year's Day?
4. Why did some early peoples rely on the celestial bodies (especially the moon) to make their calendars?
5. Why do grandparents or older people born in other countries sometimes have more than one birthday?
6. Compare the way you think New Year's Day was celebrated in 1800 to your prediction of the way people will observe it in the year 2000.
7. Is it a good idea to have everyone observe a special day like New Year's in the same fashion? Give your reasons.

KEY VOCABULARY

A.D.	leap year
anniversary	legal holiday
annual	lunar
auld lang syne	midnight
B.C.	millennium
celebration	New Year's Child
century	
Chinese	noisemakers
custom	Old Father Time
date	
decade	party
equinox	resolution
Gregorian calendar	ritual
Hindu	solstice
Jewish	Times Square
Julian calendar	

RELATED CAREER EDUCATION TERMS

historian	party-goods producer
musician	
newscaster	statistician
	writer

Emancipation Proclamation Issued

Freedom, Civil Rights, Humanitarianism, Fairness

On the first day of January in the year of our Lord, one thousand eight hundred and sixty-three, all persons held as slaves within any state, or designated part of a state, the people whereof shall then be in rebellion against the United States shall be then, thenceforward, and forever free.

—*Abraham Lincoln*

A house divided against itself cannot stand. I believe this government cannot endure permanently half slave and half free.

—*Abraham Lincoln*

In giving freedom to the slave, we assure freedom to the free—honorable alike in what we give and what we preserve.

—*Abraham Lincoln*

Free at last! Free at last! Thank God Almighty, we are free at last!

—*Spiritual*

Injustice anywhere is a threat to justice everywhere.

—*Martin Luther King, Jr.*

"We, the people." It is a very eloquent beginning. But when that document was completed on the seventeenth of September in 1787 I was not included in that "We, the people." I felt somehow for many years that George Washington and Alexander Hamilton just left me out by mistake. But through the process of amendment, interpretation and court decision I have finally been included in "We, the people."

—*Barbara Jordan*

FASCINATING FACTS

The first black people in America were twenty Africans brought to Jamestown, Virginia, on a Dutch pirate ship in 1619. They became indentured servants, like many of the white people living in the settlement at that time.

Slavery did not exist in the colonies until Maryland and Virginia enacted laws in the 1660s legalizing the practice of owning a person for life. Over the next 200 years, about 1 million Africans survived the trip across the Atlantic Ocean to be sold as slaves in the United States.

The first slave revolt took place in 1708 in Long Island, New York. A meeting of Quakers in Germantown (Pennsylvania) in 1688 was the first group to formally protest against slavery. The abolition movement continued to grow in the North and helped at least 100,000 slaves to escape. By the early nineteenth century, slavery had almost disappeared in the North, but it was essential to the South's plantation system.

Disagreements between the North and the South about slavery were a major cause of the South's secession from the United States and of the Civil War, which began in 1861. At that time, there were about 4 million black people who were slaves in the South.

On January 1, 1863, Abraham Lincoln publicly read the Emancipation Proclamation. It declared that all slaves in those territories still in rebellion (that is, in the states that were part of the Confederacy) would be free. This proclamation was issued to appease Northern antislavery opinion, even though it had no military significance for the Civil War. Because the Proclamation applied only to Confederate territory and could not be enforced, relatively few slaves were freed. By the end of 1863, however, some 50,000 black soldiers were fighting in the Union army.

The North won the Civil War in April of 1865. The complete abolition of slavery became law under the Thirteenth Amendment, which was ratified on December 18, 1865.

ACTIVITIES FOR STUDENTS

Critical Thinking

1. Complete the following sentence (in writing or orally) in 50 words or less: "I think slavery is wrong because…."
2. Learn and analyze the words to a number of spirituals.

Information Gathering and Sharing

3. Write a report about the life of Dred Scott, Frederick Douglass, Harriet Tubman, Sojourner Truth, Gabriel Prosser, Denmark Vesey, or Nat Turner.
4. Report on readings about life for slaves on Southern plantations.
5. Report on slavery in some other countries and how and when the slaves were freed.
6. Report on the African slave trade or on a slave auction.

Writing and Language Arts

7. Write a dialogue that might have taken place between a slave and his or her master after learning about the Emancipation Proclamation.

Art and Visual Aids

8. Design and draw a poster that might have been displayed in Southern cities and towns in 1863 announcing the order to release all slaves.
9. On a map of the United States, draw the routes of the Underground Railroad.

QUESTIONS FOR CLASS DISCUSSION

1. What is slavery? Are there any modern-day examples of slavery? Where?
2. In what ways is slavery wrong? How was it justified in the past?
3. What proclamations or laws do you think Abraham Lincoln would like to see passed if he were President of the United States today?
4. Why did some slaves choose to remain on their plantations even after they were given their freedom and could leave?
5. In what ways do the descendants of slaves still face deprivations and injustices? How have they experienced change and progress?
6. What was there about Abraham Lincoln's life and character that made him sympathetic to the idea of the Emancipation Proclamation?

KEY VOCABULARY

abolition	free
abolitionist	morality
antislavery	proclaim
auction	proclamation
bondage	rebellion
civil liberties	servitude
Confederacy	slave
Constitution	slave master
Declaration of Independence	slavery
emancipate	Union
equality	Thirteenth Amendment

RELATED CAREER EDUCATION TERMS

civil rights worker	historian
curator of archives	lawyer
	politician

Betsy Ross Born

THEMES AND THOUGHTS

Contribution, Dedication,
Creativity, Neatness

A thoughtful mind, when it sees
a nation's flag, sees not the flag
only, but the nation itself; and
whatever may be its symbols, its
insignia, reads chiefly in the flag of
the Government, the principles, the
truths, the history which belongs to
the nation that sets it forth.
—*Henry Ward Beecher*

Hats off!
Along the street there comes
A blare of bugles, a ruffle of
drums
A flash of color beneath the sky:
Hats off!
The flag is passing by.
—*H. H. Bennett*

Let our object be our country,
our whole country, and nothing but
our country.
—*Daniel Webster*

FASCINATING FACTS

Betsy Ross (1752–1836) was the daughter of a Quaker carpenter. Her husband, John Ross, was killed soon after their marriage in 1773. She took over his upholstery business and soon became an expert seamstress. She was an official flagmaker for the Pennsylvania Navy.

According to an account published in 1870 by a grandson, William J. Canby, Betsy Ross made the first official U.S. flag. Canby said his grandmother told him that in June of 1776, a committee headed by George Washington visited her with a rough design of a flag. One member of the committee was George Ross, a signer of the Declaration of Independence and an uncle of her husband, John Ross. According to Canby, Washington proposed a flag with six-pointed stars, but Mrs. Ross persuaded him to make them five-pointed instead. Historians have not been able to verify this incident, and there is no clear proof of who actually made the first U.S. flag.

On June 14, 1777, the Continental Congress adopted a flag with "13 stripes alternate red and white, and . . . 13 stars white in a blue field."

Today the legend of Betsy Ross persists, and her home in Philadelphia is a popular tourist attraction.

ACTIVITIES FOR STUDENTS

Art and Visual Aids

1. Design a flag that is appropriate for and symbolic of your school, community, or region. Take into consideration origin, motto, geography, and history of the area. Relate the colors and design of the flag to one or more of these factors. Explain your design.
2. Design a flag for the 13 colonies.
3. Make a roller movie or a videotaped reenactment of how the first flag was made. The narration may be recorded on a tape recorder.

Critical Thinking

4. Make a list of great women in U.S. history. Explain the reason for each of your choices.

Writing and Language Arts

5. Select your favorite story or poem about the U.S. flag. Write an original poem about our flag.
6. Write imaginary diary entries for a week in the life of Betsy Ross.
7. Write a dialogue between George Washington and Betsy Ross concerning the proposed design of the U.S. flag.

Information Gathering and Sharing

8. Research the meaning of the three colors of the U.S. flag.
9. Do some research into the number of U.S. flags that are manufactured each year.

QUESTIONS FOR CLASS DISCUSSION

1. Why was a woman asked to make one of our nation's first flags? In what other ways did women participate in the American Revolution?
2. There are many legends about the origin of the first flag. Why do you suppose the Betsy Ross story is the most familiar one?
3. Why do ordinary men and women, such as Betsy Ross, sometimes become famous in times of crisis, such as the Revolutionary War?
4. If you had been selected to design our country's first flag, what might you have felt and thought?
5. Why is it often difficult to verify facts about events that took place hundreds of years ago?

KEY VOCABULARY

colonial	measurement
colors	museum
design	Old Glory
dimensions	Quaker
honor	seamstress
legend	Stars and Stripes
material	

RELATED CAREER EDUCATION TERMS

artist	dyer
craftsperson	flagmaker
designer	manufacturer
dressmaker	tailor

First Public Museum Founded

THEMES AND THOUGHTS

Curiosity, Heritage, Remembrance

We live in time, and the past must always be the most momentous part of it.
—*Lionel Johnson*

For where your treasure is, there will your heart be also.
—*St. Matthew, 6:22*

A place for everything and everything in its place.
—*Isabella Mary Beeton*

To furnish the means of acquiring knowledge is . . . the greatest benefit that can be conferred . . . . It prolongs life itself and enlarges the sphere of existence.
—*John Quincy Adams*
(Report on the establishment of the Smithsonian Institution)

FASCINATING FACTS

The word *museum* comes from the Greek word *mouseion*, which meant "temple" or "sanctuary of the Muses," the Greek goddesses of the arts and sciences.

Alexander the Great, almost 2,400 years ago, is credited with being the first to have the idea of a museum. He would give his teacher, Aristotle, objects from the lands he conquered, such as plants, rocks, and animals. Aristotle collected these objects and kept them in one place.

Ptolemy I Soter, Alexander's successor as the ruler of Egypt, founded the first formal museum in about 307 B.C. in Alexandria, Egypt, and it was called a mouseion. Ptolemy's mouseion was primarily a research center. It had a temple, gardens, a zoo, a library, and even a place for scholars to live.

In the United States, the first museum was established in 1773 in Charleston, South Carolina. Here, materials and objects relating to the natural history of South Carolina were collected.

The first art museum in the United States was in an artist's home. In 1784, Charles Willson Peale displayed his paintings in his home in Philadelphia. Later, he moved his museum to Independence Hall, where items from the Lewis and Clark expedition were displayed. President Thomas Jefferson, who was a friend of Mr. Peale, also donated items to the collection.

There are three main types of museums: science, art, and history. Some museums are a combination of these types, and some specialize in a particular subject, such as automobiles, toys, or dolls. There are even children's museums, which are arranged from a child's point of view, with demonstrations and hands-on exhibits. The first children's museum in the United States, the Brooklyn's Children Museum, was founded in 1899 and still exists today. The largest children's museum in the world is the Children's Museum in Indianapolis, Indiana. You can walk through an 1890s firehouse and ride a 1900s merry-go-round right inside the museum.

There are also outdoor museums, such as Williamsburg, Virginia—a restored colonial town. The Galapagos Islands off the coast of Ecuador are called a "living museum." The many fossils found there tell us about extinct plants and animals.

The United States has a national museum. This is the Smithsonian Institution in Washington, D.C., established in 1846. Because the holdings of this complex of nearly a dozen art, science, and history museums are so enormous, the Smithsonian is sometimes called "the nation's attic."

Where do museums get their collections? There are many sources. Museums accumulate their collections through donations, loans, purchases, exchanges, bequests, and expeditions.

The value of a museum's collection, however, depends on information. A museum director's responsibilities go beyond simply acquiring objects. There must be a permanent means of identification—what the objects are, where they came from, and when they were created or found. The objects need to be displayed attractively and in a way that lets viewers appreciate and study them. The objects must also be preserved so that they can be kept for a long time.

Museums are important places in our communities. Today, museums not only display objects, but also offer educational and cultural services such as concerts, lectures, demonstrations, classes, and special publications. Museums are our link to other places, other times, and other people. Museums make us aware of the world around us.

ACTIVITIES FOR STUDENTS

Special Projects

1. With your class, take a field trip to a nearby museum. If possible, visit both a small, local museum and a large museum. Compare and discuss the differences and similarities of the two museums.
2. With your class, plan a museum for the school. Choose a board of directors to plan the museum and select a director, assistants, catalogers, researchers, exhibit designers, custodians, and lecturers. Select items that you think will appear in museums 100 years from now. The items can be displayed in a school showcase or a designated "museum" area in the library or media center. When items are added, a "lecturer" could provide information to other classes in the school.

Information Gathering and Sharing

3. Invite a museum director or staff person to come speak to your class about museums. Before the visit, formulate questions you would like to know about museums or the person's job responsibilities.
4. Compile a directory of museums in your county or city. Each entry should include a description of the type of museum and collection and other significant information. The directory can be duplicated for distribution to the students in the school.
5. For each of the related museum career occupations (listed on page 153), explain the main job responsibilities.
6. Divide your class into groups to write to various museums for copies of their brochures and special pamphlets.
7. Do research in encyclopedias about some of the world's most famous museums, such as the Smithsonian Institution, the British Museum, and the Hermitage.
8. Report orally about your experiences and impressions of a museum visit.

Critical Thinking

9. With your class, design a museum of the future—A Museum of the Year 2025. Indicate items that might be included in the museum collection and explain why each item has been selected. A floor plan and a building design could be made on a large piece of newsprint. You might want to

share your ideas with another class.
10. Write a list of rules for proper behavior and other suggestions for making the most of a museum visit.
11. Make a list of items that could be placed in a local time capsule to be opened in the year 2200.

QUESTIONS FOR CLASS DISCUSSION

1. Why do people collect things and display them in museums?
2. Why do you think the Smithsonian Institution is called "the nation's attic"?
3. Why do you think some museums are called "living museums"?
4. Why is it important to identify and provide some information about the objects in museum displays?
5. Why is it important for a museum to have a plan of organization?
6. Pretend that you are employed as a museum guide. What do you think your responsibilities would be?
7. How have museums changed over the years from their beginnings in Egypt and Europe?
8. Museums make us aware of the world around us. What would you put in a museum collection to tell about your area?
9. Most museums tell a story about certain aspects of natural history or human history. What kinds of special museums might be built to preserve aspects of today's society?
10. In what ways are places like Williamsburg, Independence Hall, the Presidential libraries, the California missions, Disneyland and Disney World, Epcot Center, the Alamo, and Sturbridge Village like museums? Can you name other such places that help us recapture the past?
11. The U.S. government has proclaimed certain buildings and locations as national historic sites. Why is this being done? Can you name some national or state historical sites near your home?
12. If the ten most important buildings in the United States' past could be moved to one central historical park, which buildings

would you select and where would you move them?
13. Museums often center around a theme. Name some themes or topics of special interest that would lend themselves to fascinating museum displays.
14. Give some examples of "outdoor" museums in the United States.
15. How can museums be made more interesting and exciting? What new types of museums would you recommend?
16. What is a "traveling museum"? Can you give some examples?

KEY VOCABULARY

acquisition	house (verb)
administrator	institution
art	interpret
artifact	lecture
authentic	natural history
catalog	nostalgia
collection	planetarium
concert	preserve
cultural	reconstruct
curator	research
diorama	restoration
display	science
document (verb)	security
	specimen
exhibit	

RELATED CAREER EDUCATION TERMS

accountant	director
archaeologist	exhibit designer
board of trustees	freelance designer
building superintendent	guard
	guide
cataloger	laboratory technician
conservator	
curator	lecturer
curatorial assistant	librarian

RELATED CAREER EDUCATION TERMS CONTINUED

photographer
researcher
restaurant worker
scientist
secretarial or
  clerical worker

security guard
taxidermist
teacher

Martin Luther King, Jr., Born

THEMES AND THOUGHTS

Hope, Perseverance, Justice, Vision, Fortitude, Peacefulness, Humanitarianism, Commitment

I have a dream that one day this nation will rise up, and live out the true meaning of its creed: We hold these truths to be self-evident; that all...are created equal.
—*Martin Luther King, Jr.*

Injustice anywhere is a threat to justice everywhere.
—*Martin Luther King, Jr.*

Thou shalt love thy neighbor as thyself.
—*Leviticus 19:18*

We shall overcome!
—*Spiritual*

Give to every other human being every right that you claim for yourself.
—*R. G. Ingersoll*

Nonviolence is the first article of my faith.
—*Mohandas K. Gandhi*

Rather than love, than money, than fame, give me truth.
—*Henry David Thoreau*

His headstone said
FREE AT LAST, FREE AT LAST
But death is a slave's freedom
We seek the freedom...
And the construction of a world
Where Martin Luther King could have lived
And preached nonviolence.
—*Nikki Giovanni*

FASCINATING FACTS

Martin Luther King, Jr., was a civil rights leader and clergyman. He received the 1964 Nobel Peace Prize for his leadership in attempting to bring about social, political, and economic equality for blacks through nonviolent means. King achieved a number of successes during the 1950s and 1960s for his crusade by combining peaceful mass action against racial discrimination and segregation with an appeal to his followers to bear no malice against those who opposed human and civil rights for all citizens. He used economic boycotts (Montgomery, Alabama, bus boycott), demonstrations against discrimination (Birmingham, Alabama), sit-ins (St. Augustine, Florida), voter rights marches (Selma to Montgomery, Alabama), and housing marches (Chicago, Illinois). On August 28, 1963, King captured the spirit of the civil rights movement with his "I Have a Dream" speech to 250,000 people assembled in Washington, D.C., at a rally for equality. This was the largest civil rights demonstration in history.

King derived his philosophy of nonviolence from the teachings of Christianity, Henry Thoreau's social writings, and the civil disobedience methods employed by the great

Indian leader, Mohandas K. Gandhi. King was arrested several times for leading protests against injustice and discrimination.

Martin Luther King, Jr., came from a family of Baptist ministers. He was born in Atlanta, Georgia, on January 15, 1929. He attended public schools in that city, Morehouse College, and Crozier Theological Seminary, and he received a Ph.D. from Boston University in 1955. He wrote several books about the quest and the need for equality for black people. He had millions of devoted followers among all races in all parts of the United States, though his approach was controversial within the black community.

Dr. King's life was constantly in danger. He experienced jeering, bombing, stabbing, stoning, and all types of derogatory and sometimes violent haranguing. He rejected the ideas of Black Power, separatism, and militancy for blacks. Paradoxically, violence cut short his mission when an assassin shot and killed him on April 4, 1968, in Memphis, Tennessee. In Atlanta, his tombstone reads "Free at last, free at last, thank God Almighty, I'm free at last!"

In November 1983, President Reagan signed a bill designating the third Monday in January, beginning in 1986, as an official federal holiday honoring Dr. Martin Luther King, Jr.

ACTIVITIES FOR STUDENTS

Information Gathering and Sharing

1. Make a five-column chart listing year, name, field of work, famous sayings, and miscellaneous facts for the recipients of the Nobel Peace Prize over the last 25 years.
2. Look in an encyclopedia for African-American firsts in various categories, such as sports, science, government, and arts and entertainment. Compile the information in a "Famous First Facts" booklet or a Hall of Fame exhibit. In this exhibit, label portraits of the selected history-making African-Americans with appropriate captions and display them in the classroom.
3. With your class, discuss the life and accomplishments of Martin Luther King, Jr. Work together to condense the class

contributions onto an experience chart. Use pictorial representations whenever possible.
4. With your class, research laws passed by Congress giving blacks many of the rights Martin Luther King, Jr., worked for. Make a book describing each law and the inequalities it was designed to erase. The book may be bound and later included in the school library.
5. Look for evidence in current newspaper and magazine articles that indicates the United States is striving to live up to its creed, "We hold these truths to be self-evident; that all…are created equal."

Writing and Language Arts

6. Compose a glossary of terms relating to the life of Martin Luther King, Jr., and the causes for which he fought.

Critical Thinking

7. Make a list of pictures and items that should be displayed at a Martin Luther King, Jr., Memorial Museum.

Dramatics and Role-Playing

8. With your class, simulate a "Meet the Press" program featuring Martin Luther King, Jr., being interviewed about timely issues by several newspaper reporters. The reporters should prepare their questions.

Art and Visual Aids

9. Compose slogans or design a placard that could have been used to announce one of the speeches given by Martin Luther King, Jr.
10. Select any letter in the name Martin Luther King, Jr. Write a word that begins with that letter and relates to Dr. King's life—for example, M for minister, T for truthful, H for honest, or K for kind. Then draw a picture illustrating that word.
11. Design, draw, and color a montage, mural, or painting commemorating the life of Martin Luther King, Jr.

QUESTIONS FOR CLASS DISCUSSION

1. Why do you suppose Martin Luther King, Jr., decided to embrace a philosophy of nonviolence in trying to achieve his goals?
2. What do you think historians in the year 2025 will say about Dr. King's contributions to society?
3. Why are certain people willing to risk jail, abuse, and even death in order to crusade for a cause, while others are content with letting things stay as they are?
4. Had Martin Luther King, Jr., been able to live out his life, what other programs do you think he would have embarked upon? Would they have been successful?
5. Do you think that Martin Luther King, Jr.'s, "dream" will one day come true? Why?
6. What is meant by the phrase "Injustice anywhere is a threat to justice everywhere"?
7. Why is it important to have a philosophy of life?
8. What was there about Martin Luther King, Jr.'s, life that had some bearing upon his ability to lead people? What influenced his ideas about how to bring about changes in the treatment of blacks in the United States?
9. Why do you think the Nobel Peace Prize Committee selected Dr. King to win this high award?
10. Why did the name Martin Luther prove to be an appropriate name for Dr. King?
11. Has King's work and accomplishments had any bearing on the women's rights movement? In what way?
12. What does the inscription on Dr. Martin Luther King, Jr.'s, tombstone imply?

KEY VOCABULARY

Bill of Rights	mission
Black Power	mourning
boycott	nonviolent
brotherhood	passive resistance
civil	peace
civil rights	political
clergyman	prize
creed	protest
crusade	racism
demonstrate	rally
derogatory	segregation
discrimination	separatism
dream	sit-in
equality	social
freedom	status quo
injustice	unconstitutional
malice	vision
march	voting
martyr	widow
militant	

RELATED CAREER EDUCATION TERMS

author	politician
cleric	public relations consultant
lawyer	
lecturer	social reformer
philosopher	theologian

World Religion Day

Understanding, Faith, Love,
Forgiveness, Tolerance,
Commitment

One religion is as true as
another.

—*Robert Burton*

How many are your deeds,
Though hidden from sight,
O Sole God beside whom there
is none!
You made the earth as you
wished, you alone.

—*The Great Hymn to the Aten
(Egypt, 1350 B.C.)*

Avoid what is evil; do what is
good; purify the mind—this is the
teaching of the Awakened One
[Buddha].

—*The Pali Canon (sacred
scriptures of the Theravada Buddhists)*

O our Mother the Earth, O our
Father the Sky,
Your children are we, and with
tired backs
We bring you gifts.

—*Song of the Sky Loom
(Tewa Indian)*

In the beginning God gave to
every people a cup of clay, and from
this cup they drank their life.

—*Northern Paiute proverb*

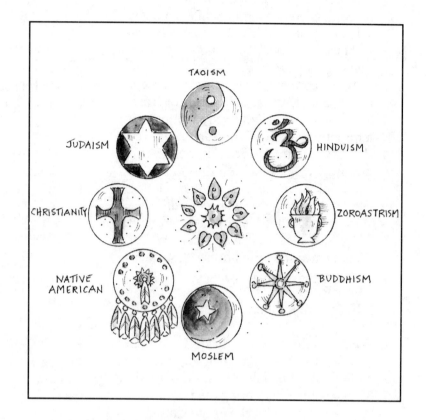

Most people of the world believe in a power or powers
greater than themselves, and they believe that following a
religion will lead to better conduct and a more fulfilling life.

The word *religion* probably stems from the Latin word
religare, which means "to bind tightly."

The ancient religions of the Egyptians, Babylonians,
Assyrians, Greeks, Romans, Celts, and Scandinavians are
reflected in some of the formal practices of many present-
day religions. These religions are credited with giving rise to
prayers and fundamental religious observances. Their
centuries-old religious shrines and sites are visited by
tourists the world over.

About one-third of the people of the world are believed to
be Christians. About half of the Christian population is
Catholic, and the rest are members of Eastern Orthodox and
Protestant denominations. Other major world religions
include Buddhism, Hinduism, Islam, and Judaism.

Primitive people believed in many spirits. They wor-
shipped animals, plants, rocks, rivers, and even the ele-

ments. Some early tribes paid homage to ghosts of the dead. Some isolated and remote groups still hold these beliefs.

Often in the past (and to a much lesser degree today), holy wars were fought over religious causes and ideals. In the thirteenth century, thousands of European children left their homes to embark upon a "children's crusade" to save the Holy Land from the "infidels" after previous adult crusades had failed.

ACTIVITIES FOR STUDENTS

Information Gathering and Sharing

1. Compare Christmas or Easter customs in many lands by making a "Here and There" booklet and summary chart.
2. Do a report about the ecumenical movement among the world's religions today.
3. With your class, visit a nearby house of worship.
4. Do a report about religious architecture throughout the world.
5. With your class, write to the headquarters of religious bodies (see listings in almanacs) for information.
6. Investigate and report on the story of the Four Chaplains during World War II and the Four Chaplains' Chapel in Philadelphia, Pennsylvania. (See February 3, page 167.)

Writing and Language Arts

7. Make a glossary of terms relating to important people, places, events, practices, and religious symbols found in the various living religions of the world.
8. Write a simple essay about a theme common to many religions, for example, kindness to others or the "golden rule."

Art and Visual Aids

9. With your class, design a pictorial chart entitled "Contributions of the World's Great Religions."
10. Cut out or draw pictures of some of the world's great churches, synagogues, mosques, temples, and other holy shrines. Make a picture display. Do the same for various religious symbols of the living religions.

Critical Thinking

11. Write a code for practicing proper ethical values.

QUESTIONS FOR CLASS DISCUSSION

1. What is the relationship of religion to the laws of the United States?
2. What are some general rules of good behavior, citizenship, and fair play that all people should practice no matter what their religious beliefs?
3. Can you think of some causes or "crusades" that young people could consider getting involved in today?
4. What kinds of beliefs, practices, and experiences are important and common to most religions?
5. It has been said that religion means different things to different ages. What does this statement mean?
6. In what ways does religion influence the literature, food habits, customs, and social and family life of a nation?
7. What are some ways in which religious beliefs are transferred from one area to another or are spread throughout the world?

KEY VOCABULARY

belief	cult
Bible	custom
brotherhood	doctrine
Buddhism	ecumenical
cathedral	ethical
Catholicism	evangelical
ceremony	faith
chapel	Hinduism
Christianity	holy
church	idol
clergy	Islam
convert	Judaism

KEY VOCABULARY CONTINUED

Koran	rite
legend	sacred
minister	seminary
missionary	service
monastery	shaman
monotheism	Shintoism
mosque	shrine
myth	symbol
observance	synagogue
prayer	Taoism
priest	temple
prophet	testament
proselyte	theology
pulpit	Torah
rabbi	worship
revelation	Zoroastrianism

RELATED CAREER EDUCATION TERMS

artist	nun
brother	organist
cantor	priest
choir director	rabbi
church architect	sexton
minister	theologian
monk	

Every Day's a Holiday

Benjamin Franklin Born

Intelligence, Inventiveness, Frankness, Creativeness, Patriotism

The body of Benjamin Franklin, printer,
   (Like the cover of an old book,
   its contents worn out,
   And stript of its lettering and
gilding)
   Lies here, food for worms!
   Yet the work itself shall not be
lost,
   For it will (as he believed) appear
once more
   In a new and more beautiful
edition,
   Corrected and amended
   By its Author!
                —*Epitaph for himself*

I succeed him; no one could
replace him
   But matchless Franklin! What a
few
   Can hope to rival such as you.
   Who seized from kings their
sceptred pride
   And turned the lightning's darts
aside.
                —*Philip Freneau*

A good name is rather to be
chosen than great riches.
                —*Proverbs 22:1*

As long as you live, keep learning
to live.
                —*Seneca*

FASCINATING FACTS

Few have done as much for their country and the world as Benjamin Franklin, friend of liberty, literature, business, science, philosophy, and humanity.

Born in 1706 in Boston, Massachusetts, Ben Franklin was the fifteenth of seventeen children. A man of many talents, Franklin was a self-educated man who had to quit school at the age of ten. He is credited with many firsts. As a printer, he was the first American to mold type from lead forms and set up the first press printing on copper plates. As an author, he wrote *Poor Richard's Almanac* and edited the *Pennsylvania Gazette.* As a scientist, he worked with electricity, colors, and heat relationships and developed a bookkeeping system for postal use. He gave us bifocals (invented at age 78), the condenser, lightning rods, and the Franklin stove. As a philanthropist, he is credited with beginning the first circulating library, the first volunteer militia, and the University of Pennsylvania. As a statesman, he served as Secretary of the Pennsylvania Assembly, played a leading role in colonial affairs and the writing of the Declaration of Independence, and served as the Ambassador to France.

Benjamin Franklin's last public service was to urge ratification of the Constitution. Just before he died, he asked Congress to abolish slavery. He lived long enough to see his friend of long-standing, George Washington, inaugurated as President of the new government to which he had contributed so much.

ACTIVITIES FOR STUDENTS

Critical Thinking

1. Explain and illustrate some of the sayings from *Poor Richard's Almanac*, such as "A stitch in time saves nine" and "One today is worth two tomorrows," as your contribution to a class booklet. Also, write your own sayings.
2. Make a then-and-now chart of Ben Franklin's contributions in various fields. Show how his inventions have been improved and are still used today.
3. Read and discuss *Poor Richard's Almanac*. Select your favorite story, joke, or proverb and explain it as you think Franklin intended it to be interpreted.
4. Rank any ten of Franklin's contributions in order of importance. Combine your list with those of the rest of the class for a composite list.
5. With your class, make a list of the ten most outstanding Americans of the past. Do the same for the ten most outstanding Americans of the present. Make a similar roster for world leaders.

Art and Visual Aids

6. With your class, prepare a tape and a roller movie about the life of Ben Franklin.
7. Draw a cartoon of Franklin that portrays an interesting aspect of his life.

Writing and Language Arts

8. Franklin wrote a series of satirical essays for his brother's paper, *The Courant*, and signed them "Mrs. Silence Dogood." These articles used humor to make Bostonians take a look at some of their attitudes and fads (such as hoopskirts). Write a humorous essay that would cause readers to see a current fad or attitude in a new way.
9. Construct a mystery sentence about a phase of Franklin's life. Compose one question about Franklin's life for each letter in the mystery sentence. The trick is that the first letter of each answer, when plotted vertically from left to right, should reveal the mystery sentence.
10. With your class, make a booklet about Ben Franklin, with stories, illustrations, and a glossary of terms and Franklin's sayings. Select an imaginative title.
11. Write a composition based on the theme "If Benjamin Franklin had never lived."
12. Write a eulogy of Benjamin Franklin's life that might have appeared in a Philadelphia newspaper in 1790.
13. With your class, write a brief biography of Franklin. Each class member may be responsible for one page about some aspect of or episode in this talented man's life.
14. With your class, write and "publish" a facsimile edition of the *Pennsylvania Gazette* or *Poor Richard's Almanac*.

Dramatics and Role-Playing

15. With your class, plan and present a program entitled "This Is Your Life, Ben Franklin."

Information Gathering and Sharing

16. Make a list of things and places named in honor of Benjamin Franklin.

QUESTIONS FOR CLASS DISCUSSION

1. Benjamin Franklin was an inventor, printer, philanthropist, statesman, author, and scientist. Do we have a "Benjamin Franklin" today?
2. What is the mark of a true genius? What habits and qualities did Franklin have to cause him to become such a great man?
3. Who today resembles Benjamin Franklin? Were there any other "Benjamin Franklins" in the past?
4. Some observers say that Franklin had

"nine lives." What do they mean by that?

5. Why is Franklin considered to be one of our greatest statesmen and ambassadors?

6. Would Benjamin Franklin have made a good President of the United States? Give your reasons.

7. If he were alive today, how could Franklin best serve our nation?

8. What do you think Franklin was like when he was a boy, a young man, a middle-aged man, and an elderly man?

9. What adjectives would you select to describe Benjamin Franklin?

10. Why is the Franklin Institute in Philadelphia such a perfect memorial tribute to Benjamin Franklin?

11. Why was Franklin so popular as America's representative abroad?

12. The following are some of Franklin's wise sayings. What does each one mean to you?

- The worst wheel of the cart makes the most noise.
- Plow deep while sluggards sleep and you shall have corn to sell and to keep.
- When you run in debt, you give another power over your liberty.
- We must all hang together, or most assuredly, we shall all hang separately.
- . . . in this world nothing is certain but death and taxes.
- A penny saved is a penny earned.
- Remember that time is money.
- Be in general virtuous, and you will be happy.
- Necessity never made a good bargain.

13. Hardworking Franklin ignored his own advice about going to bed early. Why do you think that was so?

14. It has been said that Benjamin Franklin lived a very full and meaningful life. List examples to prove this.

15. Which of Franklin's many contributions to the United States do you think were his greatest? Explain your answer.

16. Why do you think Benjamin Franklin changed his interests and careers so often?

17. At a time when most men died in their middle years, Benjamin Franklin lived to the ripe old age of 84. What might be the reasons that he lived so long?

KEY VOCABULARY

academy	lightning rod
almanac	minister
ambassador	octogenarian
anecdote	patriot
apprentice	philanthropist
author	philosopher
bifocal	principle
circulating library	printer
civic leader	prose
diplomat	research
editor	sage
electricity	scientist
epitaph	statesman
gazette	stove
genius	talent
insurance company	treaty
inventor	vegetarian
kite	

RELATED CAREER EDUCATION TERMS

accountant	opthamologist
ambassador	optometrist
author	philanthropist
bookkeeper	philosopher
business person	postal worker
diplomat	printer
electrician	publisher
inventor	scientist
librarian	statesman

First Postal Route Established

THEMES AND THOUGHTS

Service, Cooperation, Work, Efficiency, Organization

Neither snow, nor rain, nor heat, nor gloom of night stays these couriers from the swift completion of their appointed rounds.
—*Inscription on New York City Post Office, adapted from Herodotus*

For I'm going to run till she leaves the rail—or make it on time with the southbound mail.
—*Inscription on monument to John Luther (Casey) Jones*

Letters of thanks, letters from banks,
Letters of joy from girl and boy,
Receipted bills and invitations
To inspect new stock or to visit relations,
And applications for situations,
And timid lovers' declarations,
And gossip, gossip from all the nations.
—*W. H. Auden*

FASCINATING FACTS

Ancient civilizations had various means of communication, such as clay tablets, smoke signals, and drumbeats. They also used runners and horseback riders to deliver verbal or written messages over distances.

The Romans had a highly developed system of mail service using riders on horseback. Roadside stations were set up for the riders, which included places to eat and sleep as well as a stable for the horses. To mark these stations officially, a large post was set up by the roadside in front of each one.

It seems that early Spanish settlers in America had a mail service before 1600, but no attempt at regular delivery was made. Sometimes travelers would carry letters, which might or might not reach their destination.

The first real post office in America was established in Boston in 1639. One penny was collected for every letter handled. Other postal services began in Virginia in 1657 and in Connecticut in 1674. The first postal route was established in 1672 between Boston and New York City. Intercolonial postal service began in May of 1683. However, postal service in America officially began on February 17, 1692, when King William III appointed Thomas Neale to establish a postal system for all the colonies. Fast, young riders delivered mail once a week in summer and twice a month in winter.

On July 26, 1775, Benjamin Franklin became the first Postmaster General. His salary was $1,000 a year. In 1789, the Post Office Department was made a branch of the U.S. Treasury

Department. In 1829, the position of Postmaster General became a part of the cabinet of the President of the United States.

When Benjamin Franklin was Postmaster General, postal rates were high—6 cents for a 30-mile delivery and up to 25 cents to deliver a single page 450 miles. No envelopes were used, and the letters were folded to show the number of sheets. Congress issued the first postage stamps in 1847. Postage stamps were required for all letters starting in 1855.

Mail delivery in these years was very slow. It took over three weeks for a letter to go by stagecoach from Missouri to California. The Pony Express, with young riders like "Buffalo Bill" Cody, shortened the delivery time to eight days in 1860.

Over the years, mail delivery has become faster and more efficient. In 1864, the Post Office Department began using the railroads to transport mail. Earle Ovington made the first airmail flight in 1911, and planes were carrying mail regularly by 1918. The Postal Service began using automated equipment to process mail in the 1960s. Postal codes called zoning improvement plan (zip) codes were introduced in 1963.

Today the United States Postal Service employs over 700,000 postal workers and has more than 29,000 post offices and about 9,000 smaller postal centers. It is estimated that well over 100 billion pieces of mail are handled yearly. The process is mostly automated. Each year, however, millions of letters have to be routed to experts to be deciphered, because of poor handwriting, carelessness, or improper mailing addresses. More than 18 million letters are sent to the Dead-Mail Office each year.

A letter carrier is not allowed to carry more than 35 pounds in a mail bag while delivering mail on a route.

Certain mail is sent free by government workers corresponding about government business.

ACTIVITIES FOR STUDENTS

Dramatics and Role-Playing

1. With your class, dramatize various postal activities, with a class narrator or commentator elaborating on the scenes.

Information Gathering and Sharing

2. Pretend you are an "inquiring reporter" and develop an interesting question to pose to your letter carrier. Write down the response and report it to the class.
3. On a large outline map of the United States, show the zip codes assigned to several major cities throughout the country.
4. With your class, visit the local post office for a briefing and a tour. Each student can investigate one aspect of the functioning of a post office—volume, equipment, job responsibilities, the handling of unusual types of mail, a map of the post office, neighborhood route maps, or post office services, for example.
5. Do some research into how correspondence was handled in ancient times.
6. Research the history of airmail service in the United States. Make a timeline of major events.
7. Find out about each of the following U.S. mail services: express mail, post office boxes, zip codes, return receipts, mailing containers, and metered postage accounts.

Art and Visual Aids

8. Contribute to a bulletin-board display the different kinds of stamps, postmarks, letters, postcards, and classes and types of mail.
9. Make a picture diary or flow chart illustrating the steps involved in the sending of a letter from the time it is dropped into a mailbox until it is delivered to its destination.
10. Divide your class into groups to construct large oaktag posters of correct personal and business letter and envelope forms.
11. With your class, draw a mural depicting the early means of communicating by mail.
12. With your class, make a roller movie of a postal theme. Each student can paste an 8 1/2" x 11" picture and caption on the scroll backing. Narrate the movie on tape. Invite another class to attend the showing. Each

visiting student can bring one canceled stamp as an admission ticket.

13. Design an original commemorative stamp. Your class can send its designs to the U.S. Postal Service or your Congressional Representative to see if any might be adopted.

Writing and Language Arts

14. With your class, exchange letters with a class in another community, state, or country.
15. Write a report or a fictional story about the life of a Pony Express rider.
16. Write or tell a creative story about a letter's trip from sender to receiver, as if you were the letter. Use the first person singular ("I") for your story. It can be humorous (but not silly).
17. With your class, construct a glossary of postal terms.
18. Practice correct letter-writing form by writing a fictitious letter.
19. Use the letters in the term "postal worker" to make an acrostic puzzle relating to the postal system.

QUESTIONS FOR CLASS DISCUSSION

1. What means would you suggest for improving the postal service in the United States?
2. If telephone rates became very inexpensive, how might this affect the volume of mail being sent throughout the nation? Why?
3. Can you think of some ways you can ensure that a letter is delivered to the right place? What kinds of things cause problems for letter carriers?
4. What do you think mail delivery might be like in the year 2025?
5. What special qualifications should a person possess to be a good letter carrier?
6. What are the major differences in being a letter carrier in the city, in the suburbs, and in a rural area?
7. Some people think all letters mailed should only be of one class at a standard rate of postage. What is your opinion about this proposal?

8. What items are prohibited from being sent via the U.S. postal system?
9. How might computers in homes and offices in the twenty-first century change our means of sending mail?
10. Some citizens advocate the printing of a 1-cent stamp to be used solely for writing to their representative in Congress. What do you think of the idea?

KEY VOCABULARY

address
airmail
automation
cancellation
  machine
certified mail
civil service
classes of mail
courier
Dead-Mail Office
envelope
express mail
insurance
letter box
letter carrier
mail meter
mail pouch
money order

parcel post
Pony Express
post
postage
postal inspector
postmaster
  general
railway post
  office
registered letter
rural free
  delivery
separation clerk
sorting machine
special delivery
zip code
zone

RELATED CAREER EDUCATION TERMS

driver
engraver
envelope
  manufacturer
letter carrier
mail loader
mail tractor-trailer
  driver
philatelist
pilot
postal clerk
postal inspector

postcard
  manufacturer
postcard
  photographer
postmaster
postmistress
printer
sorter
stamp designer
stationery
  manufacturer

Every Day's a Holiday

February

Black History Month
American Music Month
Humpback Whale Awareness Month
National Dental Health Month
National Heart Month

First Week:

American History Week

1

National Freedom Day
Langston Hughes, poet, born, 1902
Julia Ward Howe's "Battle Hymn of the Republic" published, 1862
Robinson Crusoe Day—Alexander Selkirk, Scottish sailor and model for Daniel
 Defoe's *Robinson Crusoe*, rescued from Juan Fernández Islands, 1709

2

*Groundhog Day

3

Four Chaplains Memorial Day—four chaplains of different faiths lost at sea
 when the U.S.S. *Dorchester* was sunk in the Pacific, 1943
Horace Greeley, journalist, born, 1811

4

Charles A. Lindbergh, aviator, born, 1902
Rosa Parks, "mother of the modern civil rights movement," born, 1913

5

Roger Williams, founder of Rhode Island, arrived in America, 1631

6

Puerto Rico became U.S. territory with the ratification of Treaty of Paris, 1899
George Herman ("Babe") Ruth, home-run king of the New York Yankees, born, 1895

7

*Frederick Douglass born, 1817
Charles Dickens, English novelist, born, 1812
Sinclair Lewis, novelist, born, 1885

---

*A teaching unit is included on the following pages for each starred entry.

Second Week:

*National Crime Prevention Week

8

Boy Scouts of America founded, 1910
First opera performed in American colonies, 1735

9

U.S. Weather Service established, 1870
President William Henry Harrison born, 1773

10

The first singing telegram was sent, 1933

11

*Thomas A. Edison born, 1847
National Inventor's Day

12

*Abraham Lincoln born, 1809
National Association for the Advancement of Colored People (NAACP) founded, 1909
Thaddeus Kosciusko, Polish patriot and aide to Washington, born, 1746

13

Boston Latin Grammar School, oldest public school still in existence in U.S., began, 1635

14

*Valentine's Day
League of Women Voters founded by Carrie Chapman Catt, 1920

15

Cyrus McCormick, inventor, born, 1809
Galileo Galilei, Italian astronomer and mathematician, born, 1564
Susan B. Anthony, crusader for women's rights, born, 1820

Every Day's a Holiday

Third Week:

Presidents' Day (the 3rd Monday in February)
Mardi Gras (the Tuesday before Ash Wednesday)
Seminole Tribal Fair and Rodeo (4 days in mid-February)

16 Henry Adams, historian, born, 1838

17 PTA Founders Day—National Congress of Parents and Teachers founded, 1897
War of 1812 ended, 1815

18 San Francisco's Golden Gate International Exposition opened, 1939

19 Nicholas Copernicus, Polish astronomer, born, 1473

20 Lt. Col. John Glenn, Jr., became first American to orbit the earth, 1962
U.S. purchased the Virgin Islands from Denmark, 1917

21 Washington Monument dedicated, 1885

22 *George Washington born, 1732
Frank W. Woolworth opened his first 5-cent store, 1879

23 Marines raised the U.S. flag on Mt. Suribachi (Iwo Jima), 1945

Fourth Week:

National Future Farmers of America Week
International Friendship Week

24
Pope Gregory XIII established modern calendar, 1582
Mexican Flag Day
First rocket to reach outer space blasted off in New Mexico, 1949

25
Income tax law adopted, 1913
Francisco Coronado embarked upon exploration of Mexico and southwestern U.S., 1540
First Timberland Protection Act passed by Congress, 1779

26
William ("Buffalo Bill") Cody born, 1846
First around-the-world nonstop airplane flight took off from Fort Worth, Texas, 1949

27
Henry Wadsworth Longfellow, poet, born, 1807
Voting by women declared legal by Supreme Court, 1922

28
Republican Party organized, 1854
First televised baseball game, 1940

29
Leap year (every 4th year)

Groundhog Day

THEMES AND THOUGHTS

Conservation, Curiosity,
Affection, Patience

Everybody talks about the
weather, but nobody does anything
about it.
—*Charles Dudley Warner*

There is really no such thing as
bad weather, only different kinds of
good weather.
—*Lord Avebury*

Some are weather-wise, some are
otherwise.
—*Benjamin Franklin*

There is nothing more universally commended than a fine day;
the reason is, that people can
commend it without envy.
—*William Shenstone*

FASCINATING FACTS

The groundhog, known also as the wood-
chuck or the marmot, grows to be over two feet
long and weighs 8 to 12 pounds. The superstition that the groundhog can predict weather
was brought to this country by the British and
the Germans. They believed that if the groundhog saw its shadow, it would be frightened and
go back into its hole to hibernate for six more
weeks; it was believed that this meant more
winter weather. An early spring was anticipated
if the groundhog did not see its shadow.

This day, which is 40 days after Christmas,
is also called Candlemas Day, a Christian
festival of candle blessing. Punxsutawney and
Quarryville in Pennsylvania have a Groundhog
Banquet and shadow-forecasting festivities on
Groundhog Day.

ACTIVITIES FOR STUDENTS

Information Gathering and Sharing

1. Make a list of weather superstitions. With
   your class, illustrate the superstitions for a
   bulletin-board display. Discuss why these
   sayings are fiction and not fact. Here are
   some to start you off.

   If the rooster crows at night,
   He's trying to say rain's in sight.

   The hooting of an owl
   Says the weather will be foul.

   Wind before rain,
   Fair weather again.

   When you see a beaver carrying sticks in
       its mouth,
   It will be a hard winter—You'd better go
       south.

   Thunder at night,
   Traveler's delight.

Thunder in the morning,
All day storming.

When the chairs squeak,
It's about rain they speak.

When sheep gather in a huddle,
Tomorrow we'll have a puddle.

Expect the weather to be fair
When crows fly in pairs.

A circle around the moon,
'Twill rain soon.

When ladybugs swarm,
Expect a day that's warm.

Rainbow in the morning,
Shepherds take warning.

When chickens scratch together,
There's sure to be foul weather.

Flies bite more before a storm.

Frogs croak more and ducks quack louder
before rain.

2. With a small group, prepare a newscast to give to the class, reporting on the groundhog's activities on February 2. The newscast can be videotaped or broadcast over the school intercom system.

3. Invite a local meteorologist to come speak to the class on weather forecasting, records, and instruments.

4. Research and report on the history and methods of weather forecasting. The class can give its reports as a special television news report, with students playing the roles of the news anchor, reporters, announcers, and actors in commercials.

5. Construct a state or local weather map showing precipitation, temperature, and wind direction and speed. Consult newspapers and TV and radio weather reports for data.

6. Make a weather booklet that explains how rain, snow, clouds, rainbows, and thunder are formed. Use diagrams and pictures. Include a glossary of terms.

7. Keep a daily weather chart for a month. Compare the actual weather with the weather that was predicted. Make eight columns on a sheet of paper listing the following information:

Column 1— the date and time you make your record (try to make your record at the same time each day)

Column 2— the temperature outdoors

Column 3— the atmospheric pressure

Column 4— the humidity

Column 5— the direction and speed of the wind

Column 6— the cloud cover in the sky

Column 7— the weather conditions, such as rain, snow, clear, sleet, fog, or freezing rain

Column 8— the weather forecast cut out from the local newspaper.

Art and Visual Aids

8. Make a display about the characteristics and habits of the groundhog. To make a groundhog, cut out two groundhog patterns from brown construction paper, brown craft paper, or brown cloth. Then staple or sew the cloth together, leaving an opening large enough to stuff with cotton batting. With your class, list the groundhog's characteristics on chart paper. Put the chart paper on a bulletin board surrounded by the groundhogs made by the class.

9. With your class, construct a woodland scene or a mural, using colored construction paper. Research, draw, and cut out one animal that hibernates—a turtle or a beaver in the bottom of a pond or stream, a bear in a cave, or a skunk in the ground or a hollow log, for example. Report on your findings as you add your animal to the mural.

Creative Thinking

10. Rename the groundhog before it appears on February 2.

Writing and Language Arts

11. With a small group, write a comical story about a groundhog's reaction on Groundhog Day. Construct stick puppets out of

popsicle sticks and construction paper to use for dramatizing the story.

12. Finish this story about Max, the groundhog: "Max, the Groundhog, stirred from his sleep. He stretched and gave a big yawn. It was February 2 already. Wow! How time flies!"

Special Project

13. With your class, build a weather station by constructing simple weather instruments. Consult the school or public library for resource books. You will need a thermometer to record the temperature, a barometer to determine the air pressure, a weather vane or windsock to find the direction of the wind, an anemometer to find wind speed, a hygrometer to find relative humidity, and a rain gauge to measure rainfall. You can get weather maps from your local newspaper or weather bureau.

QUESTIONS FOR CLASS DISCUSSION

1. Why is the February groundhog often called "nature's alarm clock"?
2. Why do we give the groundhog so much attention on February 2, even though we realize that its appearance is only superstition?
3. What animals protect themselves against seasonal weather threats?
4. To what animal family does the groundhog belong?
5. Why do you think the people of Punxsutawney and Quarryville become so excited about Groundhog Day?

KEY VOCABULARY

anemometer	precipitation
barometer	predict
climate	rain gauge
degree	thermometer
forecasting	windsock
groundhog	weather
hibernate	weather station
hygrometer	weather vane
marmot	woodchuck
meteorology	

RELATED CAREER EDUCATION TERMS

environmentalist	veterinarian
meteorologist	wildlife ranger
reporter	zoologist
scientist	

Frederick Douglass Born

Liberty, Courage, Compassion,
Devotion, Helpfulness,
Perseverance

Every tone [of the songs of the slaves] was a testimony against slavery, and a prayer to God for deliverance from chains.
—*Frederick Douglass*

The history of the world is none other than the progress of the consciousness of Freedom.
—*Georg Wilhelm Frederick Hegel*

In giving freedom to the slave we assure freedom to the free— honorable alike in what we give and what we preserve.
—*Abraham Lincoln*

The Constitution does not provide for first and second class citizenship.
—*Wendell Willkie*

Freedom is an indivisible word. If we want to enjoy it, and fight for it, we must be prepared to extend it to everyone, whether they are rich or poor, whether they agree with us or not, no matter what their race or the color of their skin.
—*Wendell Willkie*

I swear to the Lord
I still can't see
Why Democracy means
Everybody but me.
—*Langston Hughes*

FASCINATING FACTS

Frederick Douglass was born into slavery in Talbot County, Maryland, in 1817. (Some history books say he was born on February 7, others say on February 14, but there is no official record.) His mother, a slave, named him Frederick Augustus Washington Bailey. His father was an unknown white man. He was taken from his mother while he was still an infant and sent to live with his grandparents, who were also slaves. His mother saw him only on the nights when she could find the strength to walk the twelve miles between the plantations after a long day of work. She died when Frederick was eleven.

When Frederick was eight, he was sent to Baltimore to be a house servant for one of his master's relatives. His new master's wife defied state law and helped him learn to read and write. At the age of 16, his master died, and he was returned to the plantation as a field hand. His slave master treated him cruelly. When Douglass tried to escape, he was sent to a "slave breaker" who specialized in beating slaves in

174

order to teach them to be obedient. But Douglass refused to be "broken." He was sent back to Baltimore and hired out as a caulker, working to make ships watertight.

When he was 21, Douglass finally was successful in his attempt to escape. Disguised as a sailor, he boarded a ship bound for New Bedford, Massachusetts. To elude the slave hunters, he changed his name to Frederick Douglass. He applied for a job as a ship caulker, but white men refused to work alongside him. He ended up working as a manual laborer for three years.

He became interested in the abolitionist movement. In 1841, Douglass was invited to address an anti-slavery convention about what life was like for slaves. He was so eloquent that he soon was asked to work for the Massachusetts Anti-Slavery Society. He challenged slavery and Jim Crow practices wherever he went. (The term *Jim Crow* came from a popular minstrel song about discrimination and segregation.) Douglass protested segregated seating on trains by deliberately sitting in the whites-only cars and had to be physically dragged off. He walked out of a church service that had separate services for "colored" people (the term for blacks in those days) and for whites. He spoke out against segregated schools in the North.

Douglass was tall, handsome, and articulate. Some people had trouble believing that this dignified man could have been a slave. So in 1845, Douglass published his autobiography, *Narrative of the Life of Frederick Douglass*, one of the most thoroughly authenticated books about slavery ever written from the slave's point of view. (In later years, he revised and expanded the book into two volumes, *My Bondage and My Freedom* and *Life and Times of Frederick Douglass*.) Because he revealed his real name in the book, he feared that some slave catcher might try to capture him in order to claim the bounty offered for returning fugitive slaves to the South. So he went on a two-year speaking tour of the British Isles. In 1847, Douglass returned with enough funds to purchase his freedom and to start his own newspaper, the *North Star*.

Because he believed that political action and resistance were necessary to end slavery, as well as racism directed at free blacks, Douglass sometimes found himself at odds with William Lloyd Garrison, another leading abolitionist, who edited the widely read anti-slavery newspaper, the *Liberator*. Garrison believed that the best way of ending slavery was to expose its evils and nonviolently resist them and thereby appeal to people's sense of what was right and just. Douglass believed that it was necessary to more actively oppose slavery, and he recognized that slaves might have to physically as well as morally resist their masters. But he did not advocate violence, and he advised against abolitionist John Brown's armed attempt in 1859 to help slaves escape.

Douglass' home in Rochester, New York, became a station on the Underground Railroad, the secret system that sheltered runaway slaves en route to Canada or safe areas in free states. He also was an early champion of equal rights for women. During the Civil War, he helped recruit blacks for the Union Army and his sons were among those who enlisted. He discussed the dilemma of slavery with President Abraham Lincoln several times. During the Reconstruction period at the end of the war and until his death, he held several important civil service posts. In 1877, President Rutherford B. Hayes nominated Douglass to be U.S. marshal for the District of Columbia, and he was confirmed after much debate in the Senate. He thus became the first black to receive a major government appointment. In 1889, Douglass received a presidential appointment as the U.S. minister and consul general to Haiti. Douglass died in 1895, after over half a century of distinguished leadership for human rights.

In 1926, black historian Carter G. Woodson organized a celebration during the second week of February "to include the birthday of [Abraham] Lincoln and the generally accepted birthday of [Frederick] Douglass." In the 1960s, this celebration was expanded into Black History Month.

ACTIVITIES FOR STUDENTS

Writing and Language Arts

1. Make a list of New Year's resolutions that Frederick Douglass might have made in

the year 1838, just before he turned 21 and escaped from slavery.

2. Write a dialogue that might have occurred between Frederick Douglass and Abraham Lincoln.
3. Use the first person singular ("I") to write a brief account of Douglass' autobiography, *The Narrative of the Life of Frederick Douglass.*

Critical Thinking

4. As a concerned citizen who opposes slavery, write a letter to William Lloyd Garrison, the editor of the *Liberator*, stating your position about what needs to be done to abolish slavery. Or write a letter expressing your views about why slavery is wrong.
5. Pretend that you are a politician in a southern or a northern town at the time of the great slavery debate just before the Civil War. Write a speech denouncing the institution of slavery.
6. Research, analyze, and interpret the meaning of the spirituals sung on the plantations of the South. Also, provide copies of the spirituals' words for your classmates to share and discuss.

Information Gathering and Sharing

7. Write a research report about one of the following topics:

   - indentured servants
   - slave catchers and kidnappers
   - the Dred Scott decision
   - Jim Crow
   - plantation life before the Civil War
   - the Missouri Compromise
   - the role of the Quakers in the Underground Railroad

8. Construct an illustrated, chronological chart or timeline for the years 1817–1895, depicting the events of that period and of Frederick Douglass' life.
9. Research the contributions of one or more of the following black Americans:

Alvin Ailey	Langston Hughes
Richard Allen	Rev. Jesse Jackson
Marion Anderson	Mahalia Jackson
Louis Armstrong	Percy L. Julian
Crispus Attucks	Martin Luther King, Jr.
James Baldwin	Theodore K. Lawless
Benjamin Banneker	Joe Louis
James Beckworth	Thurgood Marshall
Mary McLeod Bethune	Jan Ernest Matzeliger
James Bland	Garrett Morgan
Edward William Brooke	Jesse Owens
Ralph Bunche	Sidney Poitier
George Washington Carver	Salem Poor
Paul Cuffe	Leontyne Price
Countee Cullen	Norber Rillieux
Benjamin O. Davis, Jr.	Paul Robeson
Frederick Douglass	Jackie Robinson
Charles Drew	Peter Salem
E.B. Dubois	Robert Smalls
Paul Lawrence Dunbar	Sojourner Truth
John Hope Franklin	Harriet Tubman
Althea Gibson	Alice Walker
Alex Haley	Booker T. Washington
Prince Hall	Phillis Wheatley
W.C. Handy	Daniel Hale Williams
Matthew A. Hanson	Granville T. Woods
Lena Horne	Andrew J. Young

Art and Visual Aids

10. Draw a picture of plantation life, slaves escaping along the Underground Railroad, a meeting between Abraham Lincoln and Frederick Douglass, a lecture by Douglass, or some other scene from his life. Write an informational caption under each picture.
11. With your class or by yourself, make a replica front page of the *Liberator* or the

North Star. Design the newspaper's logo and masthead.

For additional activities about black history, see "Benjamin Banneker" (pages 88–91), "Emancipation Proclamation Issued" (pages 146–148), "Martin Luther King, Jr." (pages 155–157), "Crispus Attucks" (pages 210–212), "Harriet Tubman" (pages 216–218), and "Booker T. Washington" (pages 247–249).

QUESTIONS FOR CLASS DISCUSSION

1. Some slaves, like Frederick Douglass, fought back against slavery. Other slaves did not. What reasons might account for the different responses?
2. Why did many slave owners discourage or not allow their slaves to learn how to read and write?
3. Why did plantation owners often separate young children from their parents and send them off to other plantations to be raised by friends or relatives?
4. Why were some slaves singled out and treated especially harshly and even sent to "slave breakers" for beatings and severe punishments?
5. Caulking of boats was an important trade in the 1800s. Why is it now obsolete? Can you name other skills of that century that are no longer in use?
6. Slavery was economically not as popular in the northern states as it was in the South. List some reasons why this was so.
7. William Lloyd Garrison advocated moral persuasion to try to end slavery. Frederick Douglass believed in taking dramatic political and public action to change the system. How has history judged the effectiveness of both methods? What are your views about the success of each approach?
8. Douglass spoke eloquently and wrote movingly about the evils of slavery. Which of the two means of communication served his cause better in arousing the people's concern?
9. Why did southern plantation owners go to the trouble of hiring kidnappers and slave catchers to track down runaway slaves and bring them back?
10. Why did Douglass think it was important to recruit blacks to serve in the Union Army?
11. Which twentieth-century civil rights leaders are most like Frederick Douglass?

KEY VOCABULARY

abolitionist	narrative
anti-slavery	*North Star*
author	orator
autobiography	outlaw
caulker	philosophy
Civil War	plantation
conductor	protest
consul general	publisher
discrimination	Quaker
escape	rebel
freedom	Reconstruction
free state	recruit
fugitive	runaway slave
intolerable	segregation
Jim Crow	slave breaker
journalist	slave catcher
kidnapper	slave master
laborer	society
liberator	station
marshal	Underground
masthead	Railroad

RELATED CAREER EDUCATION TERMS

diplomat	marshal
editor	merchant seaman
foreign service officer	publisher
journalist	sailor
laborer	shipyard worker
	soldier

National Crime Prevention Week

THEMES AND THOUGHTS

Citizenship, Safety, Alertness,
Prudence, Discipline

For you'll ne'er mend your
fortunes, nor help just cause,
By breaking of windows, or
breaking of laws.
—*Hannah More*

An ounce of prevention is worth
a pound of cure.
—*Benjamin Franklin*

Honesty's the best policy.
—*Miguel de Cervantes*

Let the punishment fit the crime.
—*Cicero*

An eye for an eye, a tooth for a
tooth.
—*Exodus 21:24*

Guns don't kill—people do!
—*Popular slogan*

FASCINATING FACTS

"Crime does not pay" is an old saying that has often been repeated. It is a form of crime prevention. It tells us that crime does no one any good.

What is crime? In general, crimes are acts that society legally forbids. They are acts that are against the law. Crime prevention, then, includes measures taken to stop crime before it happens.

What is considered a crime has changed as times have changed. For example, horse theft was a capital (major) offense on the American frontier, and in colonial Massachusetts, witchcraft was a punishable crime.

In ancient times, most crimes were punished by execution or exile. In the Middle Ages, criminals were tortured. However, laws began to

be developed to deal with offenders according to the crime committed. Today, there are three main types of crimes with punishments to fit the deed: treason, felony, and misdemeanor. Treason and felony are serious crimes and are punishable by at least one or more years in prison. Sometimes these crimes are punishable by death. A misdemeanor is punished by a fine or by less than one year in prison.

Crime prevention is a part of criminology, which is the study of crime and what to do about it. Everyone agrees that crime prevention is needed, but no one really knows how to go about stopping crimes before they are committed. Most people believe that at least part of the solution is to do away with poverty, poor housing, poor educational programs, and unemployment. Also, there should be places for families in trouble to go to for help.

Local police departments advise people to take precautions in their homes. Some police departments offer a security check of homes and advise the owners about better security measures. Some towns have programs that teach people how to protect themselves and their homes against burglary. Drivers should always remove the keys from their cars and lock their cars in order to cut down on auto theft. Better lighting on city streets and in parks can reduce purse snatching. It is everyone's responsibility to guard against crime and to report any suspicious happenings. We all want to live in safe surroundings.

SAFETY TIPS ABOUT STRANGERS

A stranger is someone
- you don't know.
- you've never seen.
- your parents don't know.

Don't talk to or take rides from strangers.

Don't follow a stranger who wants to tell you "something" or give you "something."

ACTIVITIES FOR STUDENTS

Art and Visual Aids

1. Make a poster using a slogan about the prevention of vandalism, shoplifting, stealing, child abuse, or another form of crime in your school or community.
2. Create a mascot and a slogan for crime prevention—for example, McGruff, the national crime prevention mascot and the national slogan "Take the bite out of crime."

Information Gathering and Sharing

3. Go on a field trip with your class to the local police station for a briefing by a crime prevention officer.
4. With your class, compile a list of safety rules for children to follow while traveling to and from school.

5. Invite a police officer to come speak to your class to discuss children's roles and responsibilities in preventing various types of crime. Before the visit, have a class discussion to formulate "What shall I do if . . ." questions for the officer to respond to.
6. Invite representatives of agencies—such as the Division of Youth and Family Services, the state, county, or local mental health association, and the probation department—to come speak to your class and provide informative literature.
7. Refer to an up-to-date almanac for data about various kinds of crime. Construct a bar, line, or pie graph on graph paper to compare crime trends, locations, types, and so on.
8. Ask your teacher to contact local newspapers and distributors and arrange to have a copy of at least two or three different newspapers (including both national and local papers) delivered to the classroom for each student. As an integrated assignment (language arts, math, social studies), do the following:
   a. Identify crimes reported in the newspapers.
   b. Classify the crimes as to different types.
   c. Enumerate the various crimes within each classification.
   d. Prepare a bar or line graph that illustrates the frequency of each type of crime.
   e. Interpret the graph to the class in a 5-minute presentation. The graphs may be displayed on the bulletin board for comparisons of coverage in the different newspapers.

Dramatics and Role-Playing

9. With your class, put on a paper-bag puppet show to demonstrate safety rules for children, with emphasis on self-conduct. Your class can divide into groups to write the script, make the puppets, and design the scenery. Convert a large carton into a puppet stage. The puppet show could be performed for the primary classes in the school. A discussion should follow.

Writing and Language Arts

10. Use each of the following sentences as the topic sentence for a paragraph:
    - Crime does not pay.
    - Shoplifting raises the cost of goods for all.
    - Graffiti leads to other kinds of vandalism.
    - Cheating in school leads to greater troubles.
    - Petty thievery is the start of serious crime.
    - Apathy or indifference (not becoming involved) promotes increased crime.

Critical Thinking

11. With your class, develop a "Crime Alert Guide," listing ways children can detect potential criminal acts. You could also make an "Eyewitness Observation Guide," listing things to notice when a crime is being committed, such as license tag numbers, the appearance of the people involved, and the events.
12. Use an inked stamp pad to make fingerprints. Identify each student's prints by name. Compare the fingerprints. Employ a magnifying glass for close inspection.

Discuss how prints can be used as a detection technique.

13. Discuss with your class the qualities of a good school citizen, such as bringing found items to the lost and found and stopping possible acts of vandalism or violence. Make a list of these qualities and write them on a large scroll to be posted in a prominent place in the school.
14. Make a true-false test about safety rules. Let your classmates take your test. Discuss the answers. Here are some sample true-false questions:
    - It is a good idea to play by yourself in an empty building or lot.
    - "No Trespassing" means do not go near this area.
    - Playing with a group of friends in the street is all right because you are in a group and not alone.
    - Jaywalking is fine if you look both ways before you cross.
    - Report all crimes observed to the authorities.
15. Your teacher will set up a chart in which you match self-protection actions with problem situations. Discuss your answers and then add problems and solutions to the chart.

PROBLEMS

_____ 1. Someone is following you in a car.

_____ 2. A stranger telephones when you are home alone.

_____ 3. A stranger says that he or she has been sent to take you home from school.

_____ 4. You are playing in an empty building.

_____ 5. You need to call for help, but there is no telephone book.

SOLUTIONS

a. Call your parents to be sure.

b. Ask the caller to phone later because your parents are busy right now.

c. Dial "0" or 911.

d. You may be in possible danger.

e. Note the license plate number and type of car and call the police.

Every Day's a Holiday

16. Research and make a poster to promote "Night Out," a national crime prevention project in which community residents throughout the nation turn on their lights in solidarity against crime.

17. Your teacher will distribute the following profile to each student. With your class, discuss what authority figures are and how they affect our lives. Take time to read each statement on the profile, thinking in terms of the four categories, and then complete the profile. Try this profile early in the year and again near the end of the year. Compare the two and see if your attitudes have changed.

PROFILE OF PERSONAL REACTION TO AUTHORITY

Directions: Write the name of the authority in Column I. Check II or III as you see fit. In Column IV, describe how you show your resentment.

I resent:	I. Who is the authority figure?	II. I agree with and obey decision without a fuss.	III. I don't like decision, but I obey.	IV. I resent decision and show it by:
not being allowed to see a certain movie or TV program.				
having to finish all my homework before playing outside.				
being stopped by a police officer for jaywalking.				
having to get a haircut.				
having a babysitter even though I am old enough to stay alone.				

Special Projects

18. With your class, organize a schoolwide crime prevention fair. Collect literature to be distributed and design booths to highlight ways of preventing crime. The local police can be contacted for assistance. The fair can be held during open house. Invite parents and friends to attend.

QUESTIONS FOR CLASS DISCUSSION

1. What are some of the causes of crime in our society?
2. What are some of the best ways to prevent a crime from taking place?
3. How do computers help the police in their fight against crime?
4. Why are more juveniles involved in crime than ever before?
5. The list of acts considered to be crimes is constantly changing. Why is this so?
6. Can you name crimes of the past that are no longer considered crimes (witchcraft, heresy, for example)?
7. What are some crimes today that were not crimes in the early days of our nation?
8. Why is evidence needed to convict a person of a crime?
9. Citizens throughout the country have long debated whether the death penalty (capital punishment) is a reasonable punishment. What is your opinion?
10. Why do some people fail to report crimes to the police?
11. Crime is not only costly to the victim, but also to all of society. Explain why this is so.
12. Why is it important to dial 911, or the police, when a crime is suspected?
13. What does the expression "The punishment should fit the crime" mean? Explain the saying "An eye for an eye, a tooth for a tooth."

KEY VOCABULARY

abuse	indictment
arrest	kidnapping
arson	larceny
assault	law enforcement
blackmail	lie detector test
break-in	lineup
burglar alarm	manslaughter
conviction	misdemeanor
counterfeiting	mugging
criminal	murder
detective	organized crime
drugs	patrol
embezzlement	police officer
evidence	racketeer
Federal Bureau of Investigation (FBI)	robber
	sentence
felony	shoplifter
fingerprint	smuggling
forgery	vandalism
fraud	victim
Helping Hand Program	vigilante
	watchdog
homicide	white-collar crime

RELATED CAREER EDUCATION TERMS

attorney	guard
auxiliary police officer	judge
	police clerk
counselor	police dispatcher
crime laboratory technician	police officer
	probation officer
crossing guard	prosecutor
detective	Secret Service agent
FBI agent	sheriff

Thomas A. Edison Born

Creativity, Innovativeness, Perseverance, Organization, Commitment

Genius is one percent inspiration and ninety-nine percent perspiration.
—*Thomas A. Edison*

Necessity is the mother of invention.
—*Anonymous saying*

Invention breeds invention.
—*Ralph Waldo Emerson*

Nothing is invented and perfected at the same time.
—*Anonymous Latin saying*

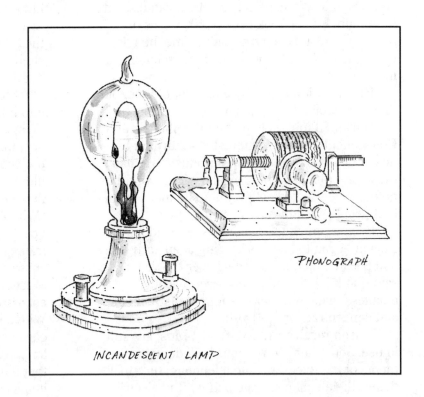

PHONOGRAPH

INCANDESCENT LAMP

FASCINATING FACTS

Thomas Alva Edison was born in Milan, Ohio. As a young boy, he was curious and outspoken. After only three months in school, the headmaster decided that he was a problem child. So his mother, a former teacher, decided to teach Alva, as she called him, at home. Edison's mother encouraged him to explore and enjoy learning. At the age of 9, he tested every experiment in a chemistry book his mother bought for him.

At 12 years of age, he got a job selling newspapers and snacks on the train that went from Port Huron, Michigan, to Detroit. Edison was still interested in chemistry and set up a laboratory in the baggage car on the train. In 1862, he bought an old printing press and installed it in the baggage car, too. He sold his newspaper, the *Grand Trunk Herald,* for 3 cents. It contained news he gathered on the Port Huron–Detroit run. His career on the train ended when he accidentally started a fire during one of his experiments. This, however, did not stop his inventiveness.

While he was working on the train, Edison also became interested in telegraphy and taught himself this skill. He became a telegraph operator and, as a young man, drifted to many cities (including Toledo, Indianapolis, Memphis, Louisville, Boston, and New York). In his spare time, he continued learning and experimenting. He gained the reputation of being able to repair all sorts of machines. After repairing a stock ticker, he discovered several ways of improving it. A stock company bought the patents for his improvements for $40,000.

Edison used the money to set up a laboratory in Menlo Park, New Jersey, so that he could work full time on his inventions. He often worked on as many as 40 different projects at the same time with the help of a staff of 20 or more people. He also established a library of scientific publications. Edison became known as the "Wizard of Menlo Park." Today Menlo Park is a section of Edison, New Jersey.

Edison was persistent. He rarely gave up on an invention until it turned out the way he wanted it. When he was working on a project, he would sleep only a few hours a day until he completed it. While perfecting the incandescent light bulb, Edison took over 40,000 pages of notes on the subject. Over his lifetime, he filled more than 3,400 notebooks with his scientific investigations.

His inventions not only took a lot of time, but they also took a lot of money. For example, he spent over $3 million to perfect the phonograph. Consequently, he was interested in turning his inventions into profit-making products. He had the ability to make impractical devices work, but before he perfected an invention, he made sure that people would want to use it.

Because of childhood illness or accidents, Edison began to lose his hearing at an early age and became increasingly deaf over the years. He said that he didn't mind, however, because deafness made it easier to shut out distractions and concentrate on his work.

Edison received 1,093 patents. Most are still in use. Some of his inventions include improvements of the telegraph, the telephone, the stock ticker, the alkaline storage battery, the electric light, and the motion picture projector and camera. He experimented with talking motion pictures, but was unable to come up with a workable machine. His most original invention was the phonograph.

In 1887, he moved his workshop from Menlo Park to West Orange, New Jersey, where he built a much larger laboratory. The Edison Laboratory is now a national monument housing many of his original inventions. Many of Edison's inventions are also on display at his winter home and laboratory in Fort Meyers, Florida.

ACTIVITIES FOR STUDENTS

Art and Visual Aids

1. Alone or with a partner, design a "Famous Person and Inventions Riddle" for a class filmstrip. On each of the first five frames, show details about various inventions by the person. On the sixth frame, show the question "Who Am I?" Each "frame" should be drawn on an 8 1/2" x 11" sheet of paper. You can use a commercial filmstrip-making kit. Or you can make a roller movie. Cut a "screen" in a cardboard box. Then paste the 8 1/2" x 11" pictures on a long sheet of shelving paper in sequential order. Number all of the frames. Tape or glue each end of the paper to a dowel. Insert the dowels into holes in the top and bottom of the box. To show the movie, roll the scenes past the opening. Focus on the "screen" with a projector's light. Place the projector and film in a central spot. After viewing the film, students can deposit answers to the "Who Am I?" questions in a special answer box. The answers should be identified by frame number. After a few days, open the answer box and discuss the answers.

2. Museums are places where items of interest are collected, classified, and exhibited. With a small group, pretend you are curators or staff members of a museum and create a display of drawings or pictures that illustrate Edison's inventions. The items can be displayed on a table, in a showcase, or on a bulletin board. Classify and label each item and explain it with a caption. Place the inventions in the order in which they were invented.

Critical Thinking

3. Think about the devices people use to communicate. Alone or with a partner, construct a model of some kind of communication device, such as a telegraph or telephone, using the following materials: a piece of wood, a strip of tin, nails, tin cans, and string. Think of the important elements of your invention in order to arrange the materials into a model. Look up the method of communication in the library in order to get a clear idea of how the device actually works.

4. Thomas A. Edison was called the "Wizard of Menlo Park." Think about what you have learned about Edison. With your class, come up with a list of other nicknames he could have had. When you

suggest a nickname, explain the reason for it.

5. Pretend that Edison has just asked you to lay out a newspaper advertisement designed to sell one of his inventions. Alone or with a partner, decide on the invention and then lay out the ad. Try to find a nineteenth- or early twentieth-century ad—from an early Sears and Roebuck catalog or from the *New York Times*, for example—to use as a model. Your goal is to persuade people to buy Edison's product because of your advertisement.

6. The use of science equipment and instruments requires safe practices. With your class, compile a list of safety slogans. Discuss why each slogan is important. For example:

   - Keep your eyes on the job.
   - Better to be safe than sorry.
   - An ounce of prevention is worth a pound of cure.
   - Stop, look, and listen.
   - Wear goggles at all times.
   - Don't disturb the operator while working.

Information Gathering and Sharing

7. Edison achieved great things despite his deafness by a strong will and a purposeful life. Research and discuss some other handicapped individuals who also rose above their difficulties—Helen Keller, Stevie Wonder, Beethoven, Ray Charles, Franklin D. Roosevelt, Theodore Roosevelt, George C. Wallace, Tom Dempsey, Kate Adams, Lord Byron, Harold Russell, Gilbert Ramirez, Sarah Bernhardt, Winston Churchill, Ben Hogan, Glenn Cunningham, Elizabeth Barrett Browning, Francisco Goya, Robert J. Dole, Daniel K. Inouye, Jim Dickson, Itzhak Perlman, and Mel Tillis, for example.

8. Use a number of references to make a list of famous American inventors. Select one or two inventors who are especially important and prepare a short oral report about their background and inventions. You could use a "This Is Your Life" or a "You Are There" format for your report. Enhance your presentation with illustrations and charts.

9. Alone or with a partner, make a chart to illustrate some of Edison's inventions that we use in an improved or changed form—the phonograph, the movie camera, the motion picture projector, and the light bulb, for example. Include a description of how the inventions have been improved or changed.

Dramatics and Role-Playing

10. Write a scenario about Edison and two assistants experimenting with a musical recording on the phonograph in Edison's laboratory. Rehearse the scenario and perform it for another class.

11. Transform your classroom into a sales demonstration center. Choose a partner and decide which of Edison's inventions (or one of your own) you're going to sell. Then decide which of you will be the salesperson and which will be the difficult customer—the kind of shopper who gives the salesperson many obstacles to overcome. The salesperson must know the product thoroughly and learn as much as possible about the invention chosen. A good sales pitch depends on knowledge and planning!

Writing and Language Arts

12. Edison created many inventions. Which one do you consider his most important one? Do some research about the invention and write a brief report, using these guidelines:

    a. name of invention
    b. description of invention
    c. purpose of invention, and
    d. reasons why you selected it as the most important invention.

For additional activities about people with handicaps, see "National Employ the Handicapped Week" (pages 46–48) and "Helen Keller" (pages 303–305).

QUESTIONS FOR CLASS DISCUSSION

1. Do you think Edison would approve of our highly technical world? State your reasons.
2. What are some common steps an inventor needs to take in order to start and complete an invention? What is the "scientific method"?
3. It is said that necessity is the mother of invention. What are some inventions needed in the world today?
4. Thomas A. Edison had little formal education. Do you think his lack of schooling would prevent him from becoming an important inventor today? Why or why not?
5. Edison's laboratory in West Orange, New Jersey, is a national historical site. It remains exactly as he left it after completing 44 years of work there. How do you picture the laboratory in your mind's eye?
6. In what ways have Edison's inventions made your life more comfortable?
7. Why is Edison called the "Wizard of Menlo Park"? Can you think of any other appropriate titles for him?
8. What qualities does a person need to become an inventor?
9. What are the major differences between a scientist and an inventor?

KEY VOCABULARY

chemical
deaf
device
dictating machine
dynamo
genius
incandescent lamp
instrument
inventor
laboratory
manufacture
motion picture projector

necessity
patent
phonograph
power station
publisher
stock ticker
storage battery
telegraph
telephone transmitter
tutor
wizard

RELATED CAREER EDUCATION TERMS

chemist
electrician
inventor
laboratory technician
manufacturer

photographer
projectionist
scientist
teacher
telegrapher
vendor

Abraham Lincoln Born

THEMES AND THOUGHTS

Honesty, Compassion, Leadership, Understanding, Integrity

A great man, tender of heart, strong of nerve, boundless patience and broadest sympathy, with no motive apart from his country.
—*Frederick Douglass (about Abraham Lincoln)*

It is true that you may fool all the people some of the time; you can even fool some of the people all the time; but you can't fool all the people all the time.
—*Abraham Lincoln*

The ballot is stronger than the bullet.
—*Abraham Lincoln*

A house divided against itself cannot stand.
—*Abraham Lincoln*

It is not best to swap horses while crossing the river.
—*Abraham Lincoln*

As I would not be a slave, so I would not be a master.
—*Abraham Lincoln*

He went down
As when a lordly cedar, green with boughs,
Goes down with a great shout upon the hills,
And leaves a lonesome place against the sky.
—*Edwin Markham*

FASCINATING FACTS

Three states can claim Abraham Lincoln as a favorite son. Born in a log cabin near Hodgenville, Kentucky, on February 12, 1809, young Lincoln moved with his family to Indiana when he was 7 years old, and then to Illinois when he was a young man of 21. His childhood was spent on the American frontier.

As he grew, two characteristics set Abe aside from other boys his age. One was his size and strength, and the other was his eagerness for knowledge. Growing to a height of 6 feet 4 inches, Lincoln rivaled his peers in rough frontier sports. At the age of 22, he was able to throw the strongest man of the neighborhood in a wrestling match.

Lincoln's uneducated parents encouraged his eagerness for knowledge. They saw to it that he and his sister attended schools organized by wandering teachers, regardless of the cost. Unfortunately, such schools never continued for very long.

Lincoln was mostly self-educated. He read over and over the few books he could find. These included Aesop's fables, *Robinson Crusoe*, a biography of George Washington, a history of the United States, the laws of Indiana, and the Bible.

As a young man, Abe realized that his success in life would depend upon his education. With each new job, Lincoln searched for and borrowed books that would help him learn about his work. Between the ages of 22 and 27, he was a storekeeper, a postmaster, and a surveyor. In 1836, he became a lawyer in Springfield, Illinois.

Lincoln was elected to the Illinois state legislature in 1834, where he served four two-year terms and became known for his frankness, honesty, and ability to tell droll stories. He then served one term in the U.S. House of Representatives—from 1847 to 1849. Lincoln opposed the extension of slavery and debated Stephen A. Douglas over the injustice of slavery in an unsuccessful bid for the U.S. Senate in 1858. After much hard work, he was elected President of the United States in 1861, just a few months before the Civil War began. He was the wartime leader of the country.

Believing that slavery was wrong, he put forth the Emancipation Proclamation, which freed all slaves, in 1863. Later that year, he gave the immortal Gettysburg Address during the dedication of the national cemetery at the site of a great, but costly, Union victory.

Lincoln was the first President to be assassinated. He was shot by actor John Wilkes Booth in Washington, D.C., on April 14, 1865, while watching a play at Ford's Theater. Lincoln is considered one of America's greatest and most loved leaders.

ACTIVITIES FOR STUDENTS

Art and Visual Aids

1. Make a diorama of Lincoln's early home life. Give the diorama authentic details by researching Lincoln's life and the period in which he lived. Make the diorama in a shoebox using colored construction paper. Add three-dimensional details, such as a log cabin made of twigs or craft sticks and trees made of sponge pieces painted with green tempera paint and a twig. People, animals, and farm equipment can be modeled from clay.

2. With your class, make a mural depicting Lincoln's life. The mural can be drawn on a long roll of white or tan craft paper or newsprint. The class can be divided into committees to draw each special event. Assemble pictures and reference books as well.

3. The log cabin is often associated with the spirit and independence of the pioneers. Build a miniature log cabin. You can use corrugated paper or craft sticks for "logs" and make the roof out of cardboard or oaktag.

4. Construct a 6-foot-4-inch cutout of Abe Lincoln for classroom or school display using oaktag or cardboard. This is an opportunity to apply measurement skills. The figure could be placed on a bulletin board with this story starter: "In my eyes, Abe Lincoln stands tall because. . . ." Write a brief paragraph to complete the story. Display the paragraphs around the figure of Lincoln.

Information Gathering and Sharing

5. Do some research to answer the following questions:

   - Why were log cabins used?
   - How were they constructed?
   - In what parts of the country were log cabins most commonly found?

   Design a chart to compare your home or school with Lincoln's home or school, using information you learned in answering the above questions. Here's an example:

LINCOLN'S LOG CABIN	MY HOME
No running water—water brought in from well.	Running water is available.
Light provided by candles and fire in fireplace.	Light provided by electricity.
Heat provided by fireplace.	Heat provided quickly by central heating.

6. With your class, compile a timeline of important changes that occurred during Lincoln's lifetime (1809–1865). Present the timeline on a long strip of 12-inch-wide paper and hang at eye level on a classroom wall or in the school corridor. Or each student can draw a captioned illustration (on 8 1/2" x 11" paper) about a particular aspect of Lincoln's life. Arrange the pictures in chronological order and hang across the room on a string or wire, using spring clips.

The events on the timeline could include some or all of the following:

- 1806 — Noah Webster publishes his first dictionary

- 1806 — completion of Lewis and Clark expedition

- 1816 — camera invented by Nicephore Niepce

- 1821 — first U.S. women's college founded by Emma Willard

- 1822 — automatic loom for textile manufacturing invented by R. Roberts

- 1824 — first public opinion poll taken in U.S. during presidential election campaign

- 1825 — steam locomotive invented by John Stevens

- 1828 — combine harvester patented by John Lane

- 1831 — horse-drawn reaping machine designed by Cyrus McCormick

- 1831 — lawn mower designed by Ferrabee Budding

- 1833 — Oberlin College became first coeducational college

- 1836 — railroad sleeping car invented by George Pullman

- 1837 — telegraph invented by Samuel F. B. Morse

- 1840 — first electric clock built by Alexander Blain

- 1841 — Thomas Cook organizes first vacation tour (for 500 people)

- 1841 — first wagon train to California

- 1842 — first use of anesthetic

- 1844 — safety match invented

- 1846 — sewing machine invented by Elias Howe

- 1847 — alarm clock invented by Antoine Redier

- 1848 — gold discovered in California

- 1849 — safety pin invented

- 1850 — first mail-order catalog

- 1859 — first commercially productive oil well in U.S.

- 1860 — Pony Express service started

- 1861 — Civil War began

- 1861 — U.S. income tax was established

- 1863 — slaves freed by Emancipation Proclamation

- 1863 — first underground railway built in London

- 1865 — Civil War ended

- 1865 — slavery abolished by 13th Amendment

7. Research information about Presidents who have been assassinated while serving in office. You may also research attempts made on the lives of other presidents, including Franklin D. Roosevelt, Harry Truman, Gerald Ford, and Ronald Reagan.

8. Refer to maps and atlases to locate places in the United States that commemorate Lincoln by name. Locate buildings, memorials, streets, and other places in your state or region.

Role-Playing and Public Speaking

9. Study the famous and colorful Lincoln-Douglas debates. List specific details and points made during the debate. Reenact some of the highlights. You might want to wear a costume, such as a bow tie and a stovepipe hat, to add to your characterization.

Critical Thinking

10. Collect and discuss quotations by and anecdotes about Abraham Lincoln.
11. Learn songs popular during Lincoln's time, such as "John Brown's Body," "Yankee Doodle," and "The Battle Hymn of the Republic." Discuss the historical and underlying meanings of the lyrics.

Writing and Language Arts

12. Write an acrostic poem using the letters in the word *Lincoln*. For example:

    L—eader

    I—nspiring to all

    N—oble and truthful

    C—alm and fair in all he said

    O—pen-minded in his thoughts

    L—oved by the people

    N—ever unkind in his deeds

13. Write a short paragraph depicting, but not naming, one of Lincoln's famous moments in history. You can include dialogue in the paragraph. Read the paragraph to the class and have them identify the event, explain why it occurred, and name where it took place.
14. Write a newspaper headline and account of Lincoln's assassination. Your article should answer the questions "Who?" "What?" "When?" "Where?" "Why?" and "How?" Try to obtain copies of newspaper articles from April 14–15, 1865, from the public library. Compare the articles with your account. Are there differences in language, presentation, or detail?
15. Write a eulogy for Abraham Lincoln.

16. Write an essay interpreting several quotations by Abraham Lincoln that express his attitudes about life and the world.

Questions for Class Discussion

1. Why was Lincoln a great man? (Consider personal traits as well as events of the time.) How do we judge greatness?
2. Abe Lincoln was known for his sense of humor and his wisdom. Why were these characteristics especially important during his presidency?
3. What do you think are the four most important contributions that Abraham Lincoln made to U.S. history? Rank them in order of importance.
4. Explain the meanings of the quotations on page 187.
5. Why are Presidents often the targets of assassins?
6. Lincoln's second inaugural address included the memorable phrase "With malice toward none, with charity for all." This phrase expressed his hope for the nation after the Civil War. Had he lived after the war, how might our nation's history have been different?
7. Why was Lincoln's life rather sad and troubled?
8. It has been said that Lincoln was both ugly and beautiful. How could that be explained?
9. Abe Lincoln was fondly called "Honest Abe." What other nicknames could be devised to describe Abraham Lincoln's life or character?

KEY VOCABULARY

address
administration
assassinated
ax
backwoods
border state
carpenter
civil
client
common man
Confederate
Congress
debate
Emancipation
    Proclamation
honesty
humble

inauguration
lawyer
legislature
log cabin
nominate
politics
president
rail splitter
Reconstruction
slavery
sportsmanship
statesmanship
statue
stump
Union
widow
witty

RELATED CAREER EDUCATION TERMS

farmer
lawyer
legislator
President

store clerk
surveyor
teacher
writer

Valentine's Day

Be slow in choosing a friend, slower in changing.
—*Benjamin Franklin*

A friend is a present which you give yourself.
—*Robert Louis Stevenson*

Kind hearts are more than coronets.
—*Alfred Lord Tennyson*

A good heart helps in misfortune.
—*Plautus*

Home is where the heart is.
—*Pliny*

Absence makes the heart grow fonder.
—*Thomas Haynes Bayly*

A good heart is worth gold.
—*William Shakespeare*

That which cometh from the heart will go to the heart.
—*Jeremiah Burroughs*

FASCINATING FACTS

No one really knows the actual origin of Valentine's Day. Many historians, however, seem to trace it to an ancient Roman festival called Lupercalia. This was held on February 15 to honor Faunus, the god of animal life, hunting, herding, the patron of husbandry, and the guardian of the secret lore of nature. After Christianity spread, some think this pagan festival eventually became Valentine's Day.

Other experts connect Valentine's Day with two saints of the early Christian church. According to one story, St. Valentine was a priest who would marry young couples against the orders of the Roman Emperor Claudius II, who believed that single young men made better soldiers. This story goes back to about A.D. 200.

There also was another St. Valentine who was a good friend to children. Because he would not worship the gods decreed by the Roman emperor, he was put in prison. While he was imprisoned, the children that he had befriended missed him and brought him loving notes. Many of the notes expressed the thought that "absence makes the heart grow fonder." He was supposedly executed on February 14 in A.D. 270. Some people think this is why we exchange friendly and caring messages on this day.

Others believe that the word *valentine* came from a Norman word *galatine*, which means a "gallant" or a "lover."

Some people connect the celebrating of Valentine's Day with an old English belief that birds choose their mates on February 14. This, too, is possible, since spring was less than a month away. The calendar used before 1582 was slightly different from the one we use now. Spring arrived on March 11 on the old calendar.

Many old-fashioned Valentine's Day customs involved ways single women could learn who their future husbands might be. In England in the 1700s, women wrote men's names on scraps of paper, rolled each in a ball of clay, and dropped them into water. The first paper that surfaced supposedly had the name of the woman's true love. It was also believed that if a woman pinned five bay leaves to her pillow on Valentine's Eve, she would dream of her future husband.

The saying "wearing his heart on his sleeve" probably came from a valentine custom where a young man would draw a woman's name out of a lot and pin it on his sleeve to wear for the next few days.

The custom of sending valentine cards started in Europe in the 1700s. Commercial valentines were first made in the early 1800s. Kate Greenaway, a British artist, was one of the leading makers of valentines. Her valentines are known for her drawings of little children and the varied shades of blues and greens that she favored.

Esther A. Howland of Worcester, Massachusetts, was one of the first U.S. manufacturers of valentines. In 1847, she began making hand-made valentines in her home, using one of the first assembly lines. She built her business into sales of $100,000 a year. Her cards ranged in price from 3 cents to $30.

Howland is credited with many firsts in card making. She was the first to use colored wafers of paper under lacy paper valentines, printed verses on the inside of the cards rather than the outside, and is also credited with the "lift-up" valentine card. Her trademark was a small "H" stamped in red on either the upper or lower corner of her valentines.

Whatever the origin, Valentine's Day is celebrated in many parts of the world today and is a holiday for both young and old.

ACTIVITIES FOR STUDENTS

Writing and Language Arts

1. Some greeting cards quote well-known sayings, and others use original verses. Some are humorous, others are serious. Compose an original valentine poem for a greeting card.
2. Study the first line in the chart below to see how a word can be made from syllables. Add syllables from Column 2 to the syllable in Column 1 to create a word. Circle the proper syllables. Put the new word in Column 3 and the number of syllables in Column 4. Make up some multisyllable valentine puzzlers yourself. Ask a classmate to figure out your mixed syllables.

1	2	3	4
fa	an i vor ta ite	favorite	3
ad	mir bit a tor tion		
friend	er ship ment on et		
com	en pan ite i on		
ap	pre es ci a tion ive		
ex	ton ive ble change est		
af	fec is iou ton tion		

Art and Visual Aids

3. Every poem written to celebrate Valentine's Day deserves a proper setting. Design a card that will eventually include an original poem. Refer to illustrations of antique cards as well as various types of modern valentines. Use a variety of materials, such as wrapping paper, doilies, stickers, yarn, and ribbons.

4. In Wales, an interesting way of showing affection was to give one's sweetheart a wooden "love spoon." Find samples in reference books in the library. The shape of the spoon bowl represented a special message. Try making a spoon out of clay, soap, or if you are really ambitious, out of soft wood.

5. Construct a colorful valentine tree by decorating a tree branch that can be placed in a free-standing container. Or make a tree out of construction paper that can be posted on a bulletin board. Write a poem or sentence that conveys the thoughts of generosity, friendship, and concern for others. Hang these papers on the tree.

6. Make a heart-shaped bag or envelope for receiving your class valentines.

7. With your class, make a post office where valentines can be sent and delivered.

8. With your class, hold a valentine-card contest. Decide on the categories, such as most loving, most humorous, most clever, most artistic, and best surprise ending. Vote on the cards. Display all entries.

9. Cut out a large paper heart. Use it to design a happy valentine face, adding small hearts for ears, eyes, lips, and nose.

10. Make special valentines to take home to parents and other family members.

Information Gathering and Sharing

11. Attics, cellars, and libraries are great places to scrounge around for hints of the past. With a small group, try to locate samples or reproductions of antique valentines. Or look for samples in your attic or cellar at home and bring them to class to share. Make a chart that compares a present-day valentine with one from the 1600s, 1700s, 1800s, or early 1900s. Display the chart on a bulletin board.

12. Research how other countries and cultures celebrate their Valentine's Day.

Critical Thinking

13. Read the myth of Cupid and Psyche. Discuss in class how this myth can be connected to Valentine's Day. Draw Cupid.

14. Do some research into why the symbol of the heart is used to represent Valentine's Day. Can you think of any other symbols that would be fitting? Explain why they could be used.

Music

15. Listen to the 1987 Grammy award–winning song, "That's What Friends Are For." Learn the words to the song. Learn other appropriate songs of love and friendship, such as "My Funny Valentine."

QUESTIONS FOR CLASS DISCUSSION

1. In what ways can Valentine's Day make someone either happy or sad?
2. How should you select a friend?
3. In what ways can you make and keep friends? How are they lost?
4. What does "You are wearing your heart on your sleeve" mean?
5. "A friend in need is a friend indeed." What do you think this means? Give some examples.
6. Why is the heart an appropriate symbol for Valentine's Day?
7. What are some of the most popular gifts given to loved ones and friends on Valentine's Day? What feelings do these gifts usually express?
8. Why is it customary to send greeting cards to real or pretend sweethearts on Valentine's Day?
9. What is meant by the term "heartbreaker"?
10. What makes a person popular?

KEY VOCABULARY

admiration
affection
appreciation
beau
beloved
bouquet
candy
compassion
Cupid
devotion
exchange
feast day

flowers
fondness
friendship
gift
gods
greeting
greeting card
heart
love
sweetheart
token

RELATED CAREER TERMS

artist
cartoonist
chocolate
  manufacturer
craftsperson
florist

greeting card
  designer, writer
historian
poet
writer

George Washington Born

Truthfulness, Respect, Courage, Reliability, Patriotism, Idealism

I hope I shall possess firmness and virtue enough to maintain what I consider the most enviable of all titles, the character of honesty.
—*George Washington*

Obedience is yielded the more readily to one who commands gently.
—*Seneca*

Oh, Washington! thou hero, patriot sage,
Friend of all climes, and pride of every age!
—*Thomas Paine*

FASCINATING FACTS

George Washington was born on February 22, 1732, near Bridges Creek, Westmoreland County, Virginia, where he spent the first three or four years of his childhood. His home, known as the Wakefield Estate, was accidentally burned during the Revolutionary War.

After his father's death, 11-year-old George became the ward of his half brother, Lawrence. Washington's favorite subject in school was arithmetic. When he was 14, he wanted to become a sailor, but his mother would not allow it. Instead, he decided to explore the frontier, and at the age of 15, became an assistant to local surveyors. At the age of 20, George began managing Mount Vernon. He enjoyed farming. Later in his life he took great pride in being regarded as the "first farmer" of the land.

His interests included riding, fox hunting, duck hunting, fishing, dancing, and theatrical performances. He also played billiards and cards and ran his own horses in races. He excelled in all outdoor activities. As a member of Virginia society, Washington insisted on the best clothes, which he bought in London.

As a landowner, he owned slaves, as was the custom of the times, but was a model master. He took care in feeding and clothing his slaves, always had a doctor at hand, and refused to take part in selling any of his slaves. He was totally against such behavior.

George Washington was a respected military leader, having distinguished himself during the French and Indian War, and did much to help our young nation achieve its independence. Washington became the successful and beloved Commander-in-Chief of the Continental Army during the Revolutionary War (fought against the British, 1775–1781). He was also called upon to lead the Constitutional Convention in 1787, whose purpose was to create a proper constitution for the newly formed Union.

Because of the leading role he had played in

the Revolution and in defining the new government, George Washington was unanimously elected first President of the United States and served two terms. When Washington was first elected, the nation's capital was New York City. In 1790, the capital was moved to Philadelphia. Congress agreed to move the capital to a federal district on the Potomac River in 1800. Washington spent much time on the plans for this city that would later bear his name.

On December 12, 1799, he rode his horse for several hours in cold, snowy weather and returned home quite ill. He died two days later. The news of his death was received with sorrow both in the United States and in Europe. Washington was one of the United States' greatest heroes. That is why he is called the Father of His Country.

ACTIVITIES FOR STUDENTS

Critical Thinking

1. Restate, in your own words, at least four of the following quotations which are found in Washington's writings and correspondence and reflect his philosophy. For example, "Speak no evil of the absent, for it is unjust" could be rewritten as "Do not talk behind other people's backs."

   - Think before you speak.
   - Let your conversation be without malice or envy.
   - Detract not from others, but neither be excessive in commending.
   - Be not hasty to believe flying reports to the disparagement of anyone.
   - Undertake not what you cannot perform, but be careful to keep your promise.
   - Labor to keep alive in your breast that little spark of celestial fire, called Conscience.

2. Pretend you are in the militia and write a secret-code letter to George Washington. Exchange messages with a classmate. (Your message can be humorous, if you like.) You can substitute numbers or symbols for letters or use letters to represent other letters.

Information Gathering and Sharing

3. Draw a picture chart of Washington's life or historical events that took place during his term of office. Events that happened while Washington was President include the following examples:

   - Kentucky, Vermont, and Tennessee became states
   - Bill of Rights was ratified
   - cotton gin was invented
   - Cabinet was established
   - first cotton mill was opened
   - Supreme Court met for the first time
   - U.S. Mint was established
   - first census was taken—about 4 million people
   - first bank of the U.S. was established

4. Do a report on Revolutionary War battles and how wars were fought in the late 1700s.

Art and Visual Aids

5. Construct a then-and-now chart, comparing the present-day United States with the 13 colonies. Include the first flag and our present-day flag on the chart.

6. Make a flip story of pictures and captions depicting George Washington's life. Make two holes in the top of the sheets of oaktag or construction paper so that the pages can be fastened with large rings. The booklet could also be stapled or attached by a paper fastener. The story can be put on a chart holder for display.

7. Draw pictures of various Continental Army uniforms and weapons.

8. Draw a large pictorial map that highlights important places in Washington's life. Your map should include (but not necessarily be limited to) the states of Virginia, Pennsylvania, New Jersey, and New York. It should show such places as Mount Vernon, Valley Forge, Morristown, Trenton, the Delaware River, Yorktown, and New York City.

Dancing

9. Learn how to do the dances of Washington's time, such as the minuet and the Virginia reel. The physical education or music teacher might be a resource.

Writing and Language Arts

10. Keep a diary for a week, pretending to be George Washington, one of his soldiers, Martha Washington, or the wife, sweetheart, or child of one of his soldiers.

11. Write a report about Mount Vernon, pretending to be a tour guide showing the home to a group of visitors. Use library references. You can also write for brochures from the Chamber of Commerce, 26 East First Street, Mount Vernon, VA 10550.

12. A word that is formed by rearranging some of the letters in another word is called an anagram. Make as many anagrams as you can from the letters W-A-S-H-I-N-G-T-O-N, such as sing, not, shot, and saw. Then use as many of these words as you can to write appropriate sentences, a poem, or a story about Washington's life and deeds.

QUESTIONS FOR CLASS DISCUSSION

1. Which of Washington's contributions to the United States were the most important? Tell why.
2. Why did so many colonists select George Washington for their leader?
3. How did Washington's contributions during the Revolutionary War help the colonists win their freedom? Explain your answer.
4. Think of at least five ways we commemorate George Washington today.
5. What are some questions about the life of George Washington that you would like to have answered?
6. Washington has often been called the "Father of His Country." Why? Do you think this is an appropriate name for him? Explain your answer. What other appropriate nicknames or expressions could describe George Washington?
7. Washington, in his farewell address, warned the nation against becoming involved in "foreign entanglements." Do you think his advice holds true today? Why or why not?
8. Could the Revolution have been successful without Washington's leadership? Explain your answer.
9. At the outbreak of the war, Washington could have continued to live comfortably on his Virginia farm. Why did he become a patriot and choose to go to war against the British?
10. A number of myths and legends have grown up around Washington (such as the cherry tree story and the coin toss across the Potomac River). What are some other stories that have been handed down about Washington? Why do such stories develop about a nation's heroes?

KEY VOCABULARY

campaign	integrity
cape	king
character	leader
colonial	militia
colony	oath
commander-in-chief	patriot
	plantation
counterattack	resident
farewell address	revolution
general	surveyor
headquarters	

RELATED CAREER EDUCATION TERMS

architect	sailor
farmer	soldier
politician	surveyor

March

First Week:

Newspaper in Education Week
Drug and Alcohol Awareness Week
Save Your Vision Week
Foreign Language Week
Return the Borrowed Books Week (March 1–7)

1

First U.S. national park, Yellowstone, established in Idaho, Wyoming, and Montana, 1872
U.S. Census authorized by Congress, 1790

2

Sam Houston, frontiersman, born, 1793
*National Teacher's Day
Theodor Seuss Geisel ("Dr. Seuss") born, 1904

3

Alexander Graham Bell, inventor of the telephone, born, 1847
President Hoover signed bill making "Star-Spangled Banner" the national anthem, 1931
Adhesive postage stamp first approved by Congress, 1847

4

Casimir Pulaski, Polish military hero of American Revolution, born, 1747
Constitution Day—U.S. Constitution went into effect, 1789
Garrett Morgan, inventor of the "gas inhalator" and traffic signal, born, 1877

5

Gerard Mercator, Flemish mapmaker, born, 1512
Boston Massacre, first bloodshed of the American Revolution, 1770
*Crispus Attucks Day

6

The Alamo was captured, 1836
Michelangelo Buonarroti, Italian artist, born, 1475
U.S. Bureau of Census established, 1902

7

Luther Burbank, botanist and horticulturist, born, 1849

*A teaching unit is included on the following pages for each starred entry.

Second Week:

Girl Scout Week (the week including March 12)

8
International Women's Day
Oliver Wendell Holmes, Jr., jurist, born, 1841

9
Monitor and *Merrimac* battle, 1862
*Amerigo Vespucci born, 1451

10
First word spoken over the telephone, 1876
Start of the Salvation Army in the U.S., 1880
*Harriet Tubman Day

11
First snowfall in the famous blizzard of 1888
John Chapman ("Johnny Appleseed"), frontier hero and horticulturist, died, 1845

12
Girl Scouts of America founded, 1912
U.S. Post Office Department established, 1789

13
First earmuffs patented, 1877

14
Albert Einstein, mathematician and physicist, born, 1879
Eli Whitney patented the cotton gin, 1794

15
President Andrew Jackson born, 1767

Third Week:

*National Wildlife Week (the week including March 19)
National Poison Prevention Week
Camp Fire Girls Birthday Week (the week including March 17)

16

U.S. Military Academy established, 1802
President James Madison born, 1751

17

*St. Patrick's Day
Camp Fire Girls founded, 1910

18

*Statehood granted to Hawaii, 1959
President Grover Cleveland born, 1837

19

Cliff swallows make their annual return to San Juan Capistrano, California

20

Uncle Tom's Cabin, by Harriet Beecher Stowe, published, 1852

21

Spring begins (traditional date)

22

U.S. granted independence to the Philippines, 1934

23

"Give me liberty or give me death" speech by Patrick Henry, 1775
John Wesley Powell, geologist, ecologist, and explorer, born, 1834

Fourth Week:

*Art Week (the last full week of March)

---

24 Robert Koch announced the discovery of the tuberculosis germ, 1882
Agriculture Day

---

25 Lord Baltimore's colonists landed in Maryland, 1634

---

26 Robert Frost, poet, born, 1874

---

27 Wilhelm Roentgen, discoverer of the X-ray, born, 1845
First coast-to-coast color TV broadcast, 1955

---

28 Gunpowder first used in Europe, 1380
Nuclear accident at Three Mile Island power plant near Harrisburg, Pennsylvania, 1979

---

29 President John Tyler born, 1790
Hyman Lipman patented the first pencil with an eraser, 1858
Vietnam Veterans Day

---

30 National Shut-in Day—for visiting the sick and disabled
U.S. acquired Alaska from Russia, 1867

---

31 Commodore Matthew C. Perry arranges "Open Door" treaty with Japan, 1854

Every Day's a Holiday

National Women's History Month

THEMES AND THOUGHTS

Commitment, Inspiration, Capability, Equality, Perseverance

For my part I distrust all generalizations about women, favorable and unfavorable, masculine and feminine, ancient and modern.
—*Bertrand Russell*

Social science affirms that a woman's place in society marks the level of civilization.
—*Elizabeth Cady Stanton*

One is not born a woman, one becomes one.
—*Simone de Beauvoir*

In the new code of laws which I suppose it will be necessary for you to make I desire you would remember the ladies, and be more generous and favorable to them than your ancestors. Do not put such unlimited power into the hands of the husbands. Remember all men would be tyrants if they could. If particular care and attention is not paid to the ladies we are determined to foment a rebellion, and will not hold ourselves bound by any laws in which we have no voice, or representation.
—*Abigail Adams (in a letter to John Adams, March 31, 1776)*

Success comes to those who believe in the beauty of their dreams.
—*Eleanor Roosevelt*

SUSAN B. ANTHONY

FASCINATING FACTS

Almost every society throughout history has defined what is and is not appropriate for women to do. Women in ancient Egypt, unlike women elsewhere in the world at that time, could work outside the home and own property. In ancient India, women could also own property and take part in public debate, but about 200 B.C., laws were passed taking away many of their rights. In Europe in the Middle Ages, a nobleman could end his marriage if his wife did not give birth to a son.

Until the 1800s, women in most European countries generally worked only in their homes and were not permitted to enter professions. Few women were able to have a formal education. But conditions for women began to change as a result of the Industrial Revolution. The new factories in Europe and North America needed more workers than the male work force could provide. More and more women began to work outside the home. They began to demand more rights, such as the right to spend the wages that they earned.

Women's rights movements began to develop in Europe and the United States in the early 1800s. On July 19–20, 1848, women (and some men) from throughout the United

States held a Women's Rights Convention in Seneca Falls, New York. The convention issued a Declaration of Independence for Women, pointing out that all "men and women are created equal" and that women as well as men are entitled to "Life, Liberty, and the Pursuit of Happiness." The Declaration proclaimed that women would never be free until they won the right to vote, to own property in their own names, to get a thorough education, to work at any job or profession they chose, and to be treated as the equals of men both outside and inside the home.

Women's right to vote was a battle that was fought for many years. The Nineteenth Amendment (known as the "Anthony Amendment" in honor of suffrage leader Susan B. Anthony) was introduced in Congress in 1878. But it was defeated in every session until 1919. The necessary number of states ratified the amendment by 1920, and it finally became law. The struggle took 42 years. The active role that women played in World War I helped persuade Congress to give them the right to vote.

One of the most successful women's rights demonstrations took place in New York City on March 8, 1908. The demonstration was called by women who worked in the needle trades—they were demanding a union and the right to vote. The news of this demonstration reached women in Europe, and a conference of European women in Copenhagen, Denmark, agreed that every year, March 8 should be International Women's Day, dedicated to women's struggle for equal rights.

One of the results of the women's movement fifty years later, in the 1960s and 1970s, was the growth of women's studies programs at colleges and universities around the country. People were beginning to realize that the role that women played in shaping U.S. and world history had often been overlooked, just as the rights of women had often been ignored. National Women's History Month was established as a time to learn more about our foremothers.

ACTIVITIES FOR STUDENTS

Information Gathering and Sharing

1. As a class, write a letter to your congressional representative and senators, requesting a copy of the congressional resolution establishing National Women's History Month.
2. Make a list of some special-issue campaigns of concern to women's organizations. Explain their goals.
3. Write to the women's center at a nearby college or university for information about its Women's History Month programs. You might also ask if the center could supply a speaker for a school presentation.
4. List some biographical information about each of our nation's first ladies.
5. Examine the *Guinness Book of World Records* in order to make a list of world records held by women, including those held in competitions with men.
6. Write a report about a leader who struggled for equality, such as Susan B. Anthony, Sojourner Truth, Lucy Stone, Lucretia Mott, Elizabeth Cady Stanton, Harriet Tubman, or Alice Paul.
7. Write a report about astronauts Sally Ride and Judith Resnik.
8. Write a report about an outstanding woman, such as:

Jane Addams	March Fong Eu	Molly Pitcher
Clara Barton	Helen Keller	Pocahantas
Mary McLeod Bethune	Dorothea Lange	Eleanor Roosevelt
Elizabeth Blackwell	Queen Liliuokalani	Betsy Ross
Lucy Burns	Nancy Lopez	Sacajawea
Rachel Carson	Clare Boothe Luce	Deborah Sampson
Shirley Chisholm	Sonia Manzano	Harriet Beecher Stowe
Carmen Delgado	VotawVilma Martinez	Maria Tallchief
Dorothea Dix	Christa McAuliffe	Sarah Winnemucca
Amelia Earhart	Rosa Parks	Chien-Shiung Wu

9. Compile a list of contemporary women who have been leaders in various fields, including government, science, business, the arts, and education. For contemporary women, you may need to refer to the Readers' Guide to Periodical Literature.

Writing and Language Arts

10. With your class, organize a school essay contest. The essays could be about special women in your lives or significant women of the past or present.
11. Write a poem about some aspect of women's rights, such as voting or equal job opportunities.
12. Select a woman of any calling from any place in the world—a woman in a village in India, a member of a railroad-building crew in Siberia, or a public-health nurse in Ghana, for example. In a composition, a narrative account, or an illustrated time-line, trace her daily activities from the time she gets up to the time she goes to bed.
13. Write an essay about the amendment that has been proposed to the U.S. Constitution: "Equality of rights under the law shall not be denied or abridged by the United States or by any state on account of sex."

Art and Visual Aids

14. Create a poster for National Women's History Month. Display your class' posters at school or in a local bank or store.
15. Make a picture chart of the accomplishments of outstanding women in world history. Use these headings: name, country, contributions, benefits to civilization.
16. Make a poster depicting women throughout the world or women who have advanced women's rights.

Critical Thinking

17. Select the ten most outstanding women of the century. Explain your reasons for each choice in a brief paragraph.

Special Projects

18. With your class, plan a school assembly about women's contributions to society, past and present. Or present the assembly to another class in your school.
19. Ask your school librarian to put up a special display for National Women's History Month. Ask your local librarian to do the same.
20. Contact local media (TV, radio, newspapers) to make sure that they know about National Women's History Month. Ask if they will interview local women who have made contributions to the community.

QUESTIONS FOR CLASS DISCUSSION

1. Who was Susan B. Anthony?
2. How did women contribute to the good of our country during the world wars?
3. Name some women who have served the nation in a political role. What were their leadership roles?
4. What do you think of the Equal Rights Amendment (ERA)?
5. Would the ERA benefit men as well as women? How?
6. Should a woman be paid the same salary as a man to do the same job? Explain your answer.
7. Should women be permitted to serve as combatants in war zones as members of our armed forces? Explain.
8. Why have we never had a woman President? Do you think a woman will become President in your lifetime? Explain.

KEY VOCABULARY	
achievement	feminist
activist	labor force
affirmative action	motherhood
awareness	opportunity
contribution	role
discrimination	sexist
equal rights	suffrage
ERA	women's liberation

RELATED CAREER EDUCATION TERMS	
advocate	journalist
author	lawyer
historian	politician

National Teacher's Day

THEMES AND THOUGHTS

Dedication, Enlightenment, Commitment, Creativity, Understanding

Those having torches will pass them on to others.
—*Plato*

There is only one good, knowledge, and one evil, ignorance.
—*Socrates*

Learning without thought is labor lost; thought without learning is dangerous.
—*Confucius*

Learning is not attained by chance, it must be sought for with ardor and attended to with diligence.
—*Abigail Adams*

Leadership and learning are indispensable to each other.
—*John F. Kennedy*

I am convinced that it is of primordial importance to learn more every year than the year before. After all, what is education but a process by which a person begins to learn how to learn?
—*Peter Ustinov*

Only the educated are free.
—*Epictetus*

Education has for its object the formation of character.
—*Herbert Spencer*

The love of money and the love of learning rarely meet.
—*George Herbert*

People learn while they teach.
—*Seneca*

Learning is not child's play; we cannot learn without pain.
—*Aristotle*

It is the supreme art of the teacher to awaken joy in creative expression and knowledge.
—*Albert Einstein*

If you love instruction, you will be well instructed.
—*Isocrates*

FASCINATING FACTS

The word *teach* is of Teutonic derivation, meaning "to show or instruct."

In ancient Greece, a trusted slave was assigned the education of the boys of the family. Slaves were responsible for the instruction, as well as making sure that lessons were studied. They also corrected the children's speech and taught them manners.

The first school in America was established by the Dutch West India Company on Manhattan Island in 1633. The first schoolhouse west of the Allegheny Mountains was established by Moravian missionaries in Schoenbrunn, Ohio, in 1773. The first law requiring communities to provide public education was passed in Massachusetts on November 11, 1647. It dictated that a schoolteacher be hired for every 50 families and that every town of 100 families was to establish a secondary school. The wages were to be paid by the town or the families. The first schoolbook was the New England Primer of 1689–90, printed by R. Pierce. The first normal school for the preparation of teachers, the Concord Academy in Concord, Vermont, was started by the Reverend Samuel Read Hall in 1823.

During colonial times, the three most common qualifications for teachers were that they be religious, loyal to the government, and morally acceptable to the community employing them. A New England grammar school teacher was paid approximately $50 to $100 a year, plus board. Salaries were often paid in produce or livestock, as well as cash.

Discipline was severe. A classroom not only had a dunce cap and stool, but the teacher always had a bundle of switches on hand to impose order. The teacher's responsibilities were to lecture, hear lessons, keep order, and make quill pens. Today, teaching is sometimes described as a social-service profession because teachers assist others—and gain personal satisfaction from doing so.

Teaching is the world's biggest profession. In the 1980s, there were about 30 million teachers throughout the world. Although teaching was once considered a woman's profession, there are now nearly equal numbers of male and female teachers in the world. In the United States, there were approximately 2.25 million classroom teachers in the 1980s.

ACTIVITIES FOR STUDENTS

Information Gathering and Sharing

1. Invite the president of the local teachers' association to speak to your class about teaching as a career.
2. Invite other teachers to visit your class and have a panel discussion about teaching.
3. Obtain literature, posters, and visual aids about the teaching profession from the local or state teachers' association.
4. Go to the local library or central school office for information about the history of education in your school district.
5. Investigate famous teachers, such as Horace Mann, Anne Sullivan, Plato, Johann Pestalozzi, Booker T. Washington, Christa McAuliffe, and John Dewey. Report on your findings.
6. Interview teachers in your school about why they became teachers. Discuss the results of your interviews in class.
7. Investigate and report on Presidents of the United States who were once teachers.
8. Interview your parents, grandparents, and older friends and neighbors to determine what schools, subjects, and teachers were like in the past.
9. Make a then-and-now chart that compares teaching and education in ancient Greece, colonial times, and today. The categories in your chart can include preparation, class size, school buildings, public support of schools, teaching aids, books, curricula, goals, philosophy, and dress.
10. Do a report on Christa McAuliffe, the first teacher selected to be a member of a space shuttle crew.
11. Compile a list of famous Americans who were once teachers.

Writing and Language Arts

12. Write an essay to finish the thought "If I were the teacher. . . . "
13. Write about one of these topics:
    - My Favorite Teacher
    - Why I Think Teachers Are Important
    - Why I Would Like to Be a Teacher
    - What It Takes to Be a Good Teacher
14. Write an original skit, "A Day in the Life of a Teacher: Past, Present, and Future."
15. Use the words *teaching* or *education* to form anagrams. Then compose sentences about education using your anagrams.

Art and Visual Aids

16. With your class, create a giant mural depicting an educational theme or scene. Each student can sketch one portion of the picture before it is colored.

Special Projects

17. Organize an after-school future teachers club. If interested, volunteer to help kindergarten and primary teachers during free time.
18. Prepare to teach something to the rest of the class.

QUESTIONS FOR CLASS DISCUSSION

1. In what ways are teachers examples to their students?
2. What qualities and qualifications are necessary to be an effective teacher?
3. In what ways can a teacher affect learning?
4. Why are teachers important to society?
5. In what ways has teaching changed in the last 25 years? How will teaching change over the next 25 years?
6. Why is there a teacher shortage throughout the world?
7. What is a teacher's most important purpose?
8. How can teachers help students find answers for themselves?
9. What daily preparations do teachers have to make for teaching?
10. What are some of the common problems that teachers often face?
11. What types of activities and teaching procedures would you use as a teacher?
12. Some people think that teaching is the most important profession of all. What is your opinion?
13. What does the phrase "Education for all the children of all the people" mean?
14. What does the expression "Teachers open doors of learning" mean?
15. What does the expression "Experience is the best teacher" mean?

KEY VOCABULARY

administrator	primer
aptitude	principal
Board of Education	principle
career	private school
certificate	procedure
creative	profession
curriculum	psychology
education	public school
elementary school	pupil
examination	rod
grammar school	secondary school
guidance counselor	special education
headmaster	student
hornbook	subject matter
instruct	syllabus
instructor	teacher
lecture	technique
lesson	vocational education
pedagogy	
philosophy of education	

RELATED CAREER EDUCATION TERMS

attendance worker	school nurse
guidance counselor	school psychologist
librarian	school secretary
media specialist	social worker
principal	teacher
professor	teacher aide
school bus driver	tutor

Crispus Attucks Day

THEMES AND THOUGHTS

Courage, Freedom, Sacrifice, Equality

And honor to Crispus Attucks, who was leader and voice that day:
   The first to defy, and the first to die, with Maverick, Carr and Gray.
   Call it riot or revolution, or mob or crowd as you may,
   Such deaths have been seed of nations, such lives shall be honored for ay [always].
                        —*John Boyle O'Reilly*

FASCINATING FACTS

Crispus Attucks (1723–1770) was a black slave who ran away from his master in Framingham, Massachusetts. Despite the advertisement in the *Boston Gazette* offering 10 pounds for his return, he succeeded in his escape, spending many years at sea working as a part of a ship's crew. About 20 years after his escape, this ex-slave was to become one of the first men killed in the American Revolution.

As the colonial spirit of resistance and independence began to run high against the British in Boston, British soldiers wearing bright scarlet uniforms were stationed there to maintain order. Tension grew between patriots and British soldiers. An excited crowd gathered in the streets on the night of March 5, 1770, after a fire alarm was sounded. The soldiers arrived at the same time and were greeted by catcalls and jeers of "redcoats" and "lobster-

backs." One British sentry, who may have struck a young boy, became the target of the crowd's wrath, and they pelted him with snowballs and stones.

A squad of soldiers came to his rescue. In the resulting fracas, a soldier who had been hit with a club fired his musket. Leading the crowd confronting the British was Crispus Attucks. He was the first of several citizens to fall from the gunfire. He died instantly. Four others were also killed, and six were injured. The incident, called the "Boston Massacre," forced the British troops to leave Boston and to withdraw to a fort in the harbor. This incident also rallied greater support among the colonials against the British.

Crispus Attucks' death is significant in that it demonstrated his strong loyalty to a country in which he was not actually free. Today, there is a Crispus Attucks Monument in Boston Commons to honor the five men who were killed in the Boston Massacre.

ACTIVITIES FOR STUDENTS

Dramatics and Role-Playing

1. With some classmates, dramatize the events of the Boston Massacre.
2. With your class, compose a written narration of the events leading up to the massacre. Organize the class into groups, each having a specific responsibility for some aspect of the narrative. You could present the narrative in the form of a radio or television special. Make sure each group's segment logically connects to the segments before and after.

Information Gathering and Sharing

3. Write a brief biography of Crispus Attucks.
4. Research the role of blacks in the Revolution. People you might include in your report are Peter Salem, Salem Poor, Lemuel Haynes, Pompey, and James Armistead.

Writing and Language Arts

5. Write an editorial about the Boston Massacre as if you were writing for the *Boston Herald* on March 6, 1770.
6. Write two headlines about the Boston Massacre, one as if you were writing for a colonial newspaper and then one for a British newspaper.
7. Construct an acrostic from the letters in the name Crispus Attucks to help recall some of the events, items, and issues of the Revolutionary era. For example:

    C—olonies

    R—edcoats

    I—ndependence

    S—ailor

    P—atriot

    U—nited

    S—tates

Art and Visual Aids

8. Design and draw a commemorative stamp in honor of Crispus Attucks. With your class, select the most appropriate designs to send to the Post Office Department in Washington, D.C., with an accompanying letter explaining why you think Crispus Attucks should be so honored.

For additional activities about black history, see "Benjamin Banneker" (pages 88–91), "Emancipation Proclamation Issued" (pages 146–148), "Martin Luther King, Jr." (pages 155–157), "Frederick Douglass" (pages 174–177), "Harriet Tubman" (pages 216–218), and "Booker T. Washington" (pages 247–249).

QUESTIONS FOR CLASS DISCUSSION

1. Why would an ex-slave be in the forefront of a revolutionary movement? Was Crispus Attucks' presence in the taunting mob a coincidence?
2. Why was the owning of slaves less profitable prior to the year 1793?
3. Why were the shots fired at the Boston Massacre "heard" throughout the 13 colonies?
4. Why did many leaders of the American Revolution support freedom for the slaves?
5. Do you think Crispus Attucks and other African-Americans experienced much or little discrimination during the Revolutionary period? Explain your answer.
6. Name other courageous historical figures who could be compared to Crispus Attucks. Discuss the comparisons.

KEY VOCABULARY

African-American	protest
courage	redcoat
crew	representation
demonstration	resistance
massacre	revolution
master	sacrifice
militia	slave
mob	struggle
musket	taunt
patriot	taxation
petition	troops

RELATED CAREER EDUCATION TERMS

military officer	sailor
reporter	soldier

Amerigo Vespucci Born

Resourcefulness, Curiosity, Exploration, Discovery

The winds and waves are always on the side of the ablest navigators.
—*Edward Gibbon*

They are ill discoverers that think there is no land, when they can see nothing but the sea.
—*Francis Bacon*

Those new regions [America] which we found and explored with the fleet . . . we may rightly call a New World . . . a continent more densely peopled and abounding in animals than our Europe or Asia or Africa; and, in addition, a climate milder than any other region known to us.
—*Amerigo Vespucci*

If European discovery had been delayed for a century or two, it is possible that the Aztec in Mexico or the Iroquois in North America would have established strong native states capable of adopting European war tactics and maintaining their independence to this day, as Japan kept her independence from China.
—*Samuel Eliot Morison*

FASCINATING FACTS

Question: If Columbus discovered the New World, then why isn't it known as the Columbias rather than the Americas? Answer: Because Amerigo Vespucci discovered that the lands of the New World belonged to a new continent. He made it clear that these lands were not part of Asia, as Columbus had thought.

The contributions that this Italian navigator and merchant made to our knowledge about the world are just as important as those made by Columbus, yet he has not been given the same place in history. Vespucci was not only the first to use the term *continent* in reference to the New World, but he also revealed that an antipodes existed and was habitable. The discovery that a land existed on the opposite side of the earth challenged centuries-old beliefs about the world.

Vespucci participated in at least two voyages to the southern part of the New World. He traveled down the coast of South America in 1501–1502 as far south as the Rio de la Plata, which he discovered. He developed an original method of celestial navigation that enabled him to locate the longitude of points in the New World. He compared the hour at which the moon was seen in a particular position in relation to a given planet and the hour at which the moon and the planet were seen in the same positions in Spain.

The name America was not given to the New World until 1507, when Martin Waldseemüller, a German cartographer, created and used the name for a map of the new land. He felt that America was a good name because Vespucci had proved the existence of a new continent.

Vespucci was well respected by the court of Spain and served as astronomer to the king of Spain until his death in 1512.

ACTIVITIES FOR STUDENTS

Information Gathering and Sharing

1. Look up the meaning of the word *antipodes*. With a small group, use a globe to identify the antipodes of five locations named by your teacher. Create a three-dimensional illustration, such as a Styrofoam ball with color-coded pin flags, of your findings. Then make a comparative chart for each antipodal pair, showing the similarities and differences in their way of life. The class' completed charts may be arranged in a bulletin-board display.
2. Select 20 places in the United States and research the origin of their toponymy (place names).

Critical Thinking

3. Answer the following questions with the help of a globe:
   - Where would Leif Ericson, Christopher Columbus, and Amerigo Vespucci have landed had they been able to sail west in a straight line?
   - Determine where these explorers would have landed on the West Coast of the Americas had they been able to sail east around the world in a straight line. How might landing in these different places have changed the course of history?

Stargazing

4. On a clear night, find the Big Dipper. Draw a sky map showing the position of the Big Dipper. Imagine how the Big Dipper would change if you were farther to the east, west, north, or south. Make a sky map for each different perspective.
5. Study a star chart (from a newspaper, almanac, or science book) for a particular time of the year and locate various celestial bodies during the early evening. Report your observations about their relative positions.

Writing and Language Arts

6. Use the letters in the word *America* as the first letters of appropriate words relating to Amerigo Vespucci's life and contributions to science and history. Here's an example:

   A—stronomer

   M—ariner

   E—xplorer

   R—io de la Plata

   I—talian

   C—ontinent

   A—ntipodes

Map Reading

7. Locate and write down the coordinates of latitude and longitude for 20 countries, cities, or places in the world. Write the answers on a separate sheet of paper. Exchange lists with another member of your class and locate the places on each other's lists.

QUESTIONS FOR CLASS DISCUSSION

1. What is a continent? How many continents are there in the world and what are they?
2. Why do you suppose Amerigo Vespucci called the New World a continent?
3. What knowledge is needed in order to use celestial navigation?

4. Does an explorer today experience the same difficulties and obstacles that Vespucci and Columbus did? Explain.
5. Our new frontier is space. How can we determine if a place in space is habitable?
6. How do you think Vespucci might have felt about having the New World named for him? If he were to visit the Americas today, what might some of his impressions be?

RELATED CAREER EDUCATION TERMS

adventurer	mariner
astronomer	merchant
cartographer	navigator
explorer	

KEY VOCABULARY

antipodes	cosmographer
astronomer	expedition
cartographer	habitable
celestial	longitude
century	navigator
circumference	star chart
continent	telescope

Harriet Tubman Day

THEMES AND THOUGHTS

Courage, Compassion, Commitment, Empathy, Helpfulness

I believe this government cannot endure permanently half slave and half free.

—*Abraham Lincoln*

If slavery is not wrong, nothing is wrong.

—*Abraham Lincoln*

I had reasoned this out in my mind; there was one or two things I had a right to, liberty or death; if I could not have one, I would have the other...I should fight for my liberty as long as my strength lasted, and when the time comes for me to go, the Lord would let them take me.

—*Harriet Tubman*

FASCINATING FACTS

Harriet Tubman (1821?–1913) was born a slave in Bucktown, Maryland. She became the courageous rescuer of hundreds of black slaves from bondage. She also served as a nonpaid scout, cook, nurse, soldier, and spy for the Union Army during the Civil War. It is said that she received a medal for her exploits from Queen Victoria of England.

Harriet Tubman's given name was Araminta Ross. As a young girl, she was required to go into the fields to pick the crops. In 1844, she married John Tubman, a freed slave.

Harriet Tubman managed to escape to the North in 1849, and from that time on she devoted herself to leading other slaves to freedom via the Underground Railroad, which featured "lines" and secret relay "stations" en route to the North and Canada. She forcefully urged on fugitives who were frightened by the hardships and dangers of their flight and were tempted to give up and return to slavery. Many Quakers and the abolitionist, John Brown, aided her with the rescue operations.

Harriet Tubman is credited with winning freedom for 300 to 400 slaves, including her own parents. She made 19 journeys to the deep South in her quest for "passengers" or "freight." In 1850, Congress passed a law making it a crime to help runaway slaves. Because she helped so many slaves, the reward for Harriet Tubman's capture once totaled $40,000.

Harriet Tubman, sometimes called the "Conductor," "Moses," or "Joan of Arc," could neither read nor write, but she spoke eloquently at numerous anti-slavery and women's rights rallies in the North. Upon her death, the citizens of Auburn, New York, the town where she lived after the Civil War, erected a monument to her memory. She was buried in Ohio with military honors for her contributions and devotion to the cause of freedom.

ACTIVITIES FOR STUDENTS

Writing and Language Arts

1. Write a play about a slave's escape from slavery or one of Harriet Tubman's journeys back to the South. You can do this project alone, or write one scene as part of a group effort. When the play is finished, present it to the class and videotape it.
2. Create some daily entries in an imaginary diary of a runaway slave.
3. Write a speech that might have been delivered by a rebellious slave leader trying to induce other slaves to rise up against their masters and strike out for freedom. The speech should discuss the advantages of being free.
4. A proverb tells a truth in a short sentence. Write some proverbs about freedom, as opposed to slavery—"He who enslaves has no conscience," for example. The proverbs could be compiled into a class book. You might want to "age" the paper by tearing the edges, wrinkling the paper, and soaking it in a solution of tea. After the paper is dry, you can iron it with a warm iron.

Art and Visual Aids

5. Design what you think the medal from Queen Victoria honoring Harriet Tubman may have looked like. You can use drawing paper or modeling clay. The medal should include an appropriate tribute or slogan.
6. Do some research about Harriet Beecher Stowe, Sojourner Truth, Nat Turner, David Walker, David B. Ruggles, John Brown, Denmark Vesey, Gabriel Prosser, Frederick Douglass, or another abolitionist. Report to the class about who the person was and how he or she helped in the freedom movement. These reports can be given orally as a special "television" program. Or written reports can be compiled in a "Who's Who" booklet.

Critical Thinking

7. Make a lifestyle contrast chart of a slave (man, woman, or child) and a member of a plantation owner's family. Here is an example contrasting two children.

PLANTATION SLAVE'S CHILD	PLANTATION OWNER'S CHILD
Does not attend school	Attends school
Works during the day	Practices the piano or goes riding
Cannot leave the plantation	Can visit friends on other plantations or go to the city or abroad
Has few clothes	Wears nice clothes
Gets only the food the master provides	Has food prepared and served by servants

Role-Playing and Public Speaking

8. With your class, role-play a mock trial of an abolitionist in a Southern courthouse in 1857. Students can play the roles of the judge, lawyers, and jury members.
9. Have a debate between one group of students representing plantation owners who find slavery a necessity for their way of life and another group representing citizens who are opposed to slavery. The moderator will keep a tally of the number of points each group discusses to support its viewpoint. Or you could divide the class into two groups to write opposing editorials about slavery as they might have been written before the Civil War. One group could write for an imaginary Northern newspaper, the *Boston Beacon*, and the other group for an imaginary Southern newspaper, the *Savannah Sun*.

For additional activities about black history, see "Benjamin Banneker" (pages 88–91), "Emancipation Proclamation Issued" (pages 146–148), "Martin Luther King, Jr." (pages 155–157), "Frederick Douglass" (pages 174–

177), "Crispus Attucks" (pages 210–212), and "Booker T. Washington" (pages 247–249).

QUESTIONS FOR CLASS DISCUSSION

1. Why was Harriet Tubman sometimes referred to as the Black Moses, the Conductor, the Heroine in Ebony, the Abolitionist, and the American Joan of Arc?
2. Why do you think Harriet Tubman chose to keep returning to the South (19 times) in order to help other slaves escape?
3. During the Civil War, Harriet Tubman served as an unpaid scout and spy for the Union Army. Why do you think she did this?
4. What problems do you think slaves faced while escaping to the North? What problems did they face upon their arrival as free men and women?
5. Why was such a high price put on Harriet Tubman's head for her capture? Who would want her work destroyed? Who would have been willing to turn her in?
6. Harriet Tubman was described as "strong as a man, brave as a lion, cunning as a fox." How do you explain these comparisons? Can you think of other adjectives that might also be appropriate?
7. Harriet Tubman's method of secretly helping slaves escape was called the Underground Railroad or the Freedom Train. Why do you think these are appropriate names?
8. Where in the world is freedom still somewhat restricted? Identify some of these restrictions. Why do these restrictions exist?
9. If Harriet Tubman were alive today, how do you think she would be using her courage, talents, and leadership?
10. Who was Dred Scott? Why was the verdict in his case so significant for U.S. history?

KEY VOCABULARY

abolitionist	lynch
activist	Mason-Dixon Line
bondage	master
conductor	Quaker
courageous	rebellion
escape	refuge
exodus	relay
freight	rescue
fugitive	slavery
humanitarian	spy
illiterate	station
Jim Crow	underground

RELATED CAREER EDUCATION TERMS

armed forces personnel	nurse
cook	politician
farmer	scout
lawyer	sociologist
lecturer	soldier

National Wildlife Week

THEMES AND THOUGHTS

Conservation, Compassion, Respect,
Caring, Empathy

I think I could turn and live with
animals, they are so placid and self-
contained.
— *Walt Whitman*

In all things of nature there is
something of the marvelous.
— *Aristotle*

We need the tonic of wildness....
We can never have enough of
nature.
— *Henry David Thoreau*

The cricket's gone, we only hear
machines;
In erg and atom they exact their
pay.
And life is largely lived on silver
screens.
— *David McCord*

FASCINATING FACTS

When all the animals or plants of a particular species die, that species becomes extinct. Throughout the history of the earth, many species have gradually become extinct. Over many centuries, a species adapts itself to changes in the environment. Sometimes, it changes so much that it becomes a new species, and the older, less well-adapted version dies out.

In recent history, however, many species of animals and plants have become extinct as the result of human activity, not as the result of natural processes. Because there are no new species to replace the ones that have become extinct, the variety of life on our planet is decreasing. Since the late 1600s, over 300 species and subspecies of plants and animals have become extinct. The passenger pigeon and the California grizzly bear are among these numbers.

Some species of plants and animals became extinct because human beings used them for food, clothing, or shelter (and sometimes sport) without realizing that too few of the species were left to reproduce and create a new generation. Other species became extinct when their habitats were destroyed or polluted because of the spread of cities, industries, or agriculture. Because of the destruction of their habitats and changes in the environment, 25 forms of birds in the Hawaiian Islands have become extinct. Humans continue to use plants and animals and change the environment out of necessity, but steps must be taken to assure that no more species are destroyed in the process.

National and international agencies have begun to keep records of endangered species (those in danger of extinction) and threatened species (those that may become endangered). Today, over 830 animal species and over 200 plant species are on the endangered and threatened list. Some endangered animal species are:

blue whale	Asian elephant
humpback whale	brown or grizzly bear
corn snake	giant panda
American crocodile	gorilla
bald eagle	orangutan
condor	sea otter
peregrine falcon	black rhinoceros
brown pelican	gray wolf
leopard	mountain zebra
tiger	shortnose sturgeon
cheetah	

The St. Helena redwood, the Ozark chestnut, and several varieties of California manzanita are among the plant species facing extinction.

Private organizations and government bureaus help educate the public about preserving the wildlife population. The National Wildlife Federation, for example, was founded in 1936 to encourage the intelligent management, appreciation, and use of wildlife. This group publishes educational materials, such as *Ranger Rick's Nature Magazine*, and promotes conservation projects. The Department of the Interior in Washington, D.C., oversees wildlife management in the United States. Throughout the world, national parks and nature reserves have been established to help save plants and animals.

Wildlife conservation is important for several reasons. First, every plant and animal species is unique—this variety contributes to the beauty of nature. Second, the economies of many nations and groups of people depend on products made from wild plants and animals. Third, by studying plants and animals, scientists have learned much that has improved the quality of human life. Fourth, every species of plant and animal plays a role in the survival of its ecosystem—the extinction of just one species can have unknown consequences for the other life forms that are directly or indirectly dependent on it.

ACTIVITIES FOR STUDENTS

Public Speaking

1. In many areas of the world, there are people who make their living by hunting animals for food, clothing, and other human needs or uses. With some classmates, formally debate the merits of such an occupation. Divide into groups to represent the two positions in the argument.

Art and Visual Aids

2. Make a large poster for a class display that advocates the need for conserving our nation's wildlife. Write a caption or short poem about the illustration on your poster.
3. Design a postage stamp depicting the need for national wildlife conservation. You might send a copy to the Postal Service or to your congressional representative.

Information Gathering and Sharing

4. Write to one of the following organizations or government agencies for informational materials about its work:

National Wildlife Federation
1400 16th St., NW
Washington, D.C. 20036

Izaak Walton League of America
1401 Wilson Blvd., Level B
Arlington, Virginia 22209

Environmental Protection Agency
401 M St., SW
Washington, D.C . 20460

Fish and Wildlife Service
Department of the Interior
C and 19th Sts., NW
Washington, D.C. 20240

National Audubon Society
950 Third Ave.
New York, New York 10022

Greenpeace
1436 U St., NW
Washington D.C. 20009

Department of the Interior
C and 19th Sts., NW
Washington, D.C. 20240

National Oceanic and Atmospheric
 Administration
6010 Executive Blvd.
Rockville, Maryland 20852

5. Investigate and report on ways various organizations and governmental agencies are employing and promoting conservation measures throughout the nation and your state.

6. Investigate and report on why certain animals and wildlife have become associated with certain ideas (the dove with peace), states and countries (the bald eagle with the United States), flags, recreation, customs, holidays, and other forms of human endeavors.

7. With a small group, make a three-part chart for at least ten different fishes, birds, amphibians, mammals, reptiles, or insects. Column A should identify animals that are now extinct (dinosaurs), Column B should list various endangered species, and Column C should list kinds of animals that seem to be safe from extinction. For each animal chosen, write a brief explanation about why you placed it in Column A, B, or C.

8. Compile a list of products made from animal materials that are used for food, clothing, and shelter.

9. Investigate and report on how a specific environmental problem—such as acid rain, the greenhouse effect, or water pollution—is an international (not just a national or local) concern.

Special Projects

10. Create a class nature magazine. Each student can be responsible for writing or illustrating an article about some form of wildlife. Editorials, feature articles, and advertisements highlighting special problems should be included.

11. Have the class or school "adopt" an endangered species. Draw up resolutions; sponsor fund-raising programs; write letters to the editor of local newspapers, members of Congress, state legislators, and government agencies; and sponsor other school activities and learning experiences dealing with the theme of "Save Our _____."

QUESTIONS FOR CLASS DISCUSSION

1. How do some animals camouflage themselves?
2. What is the difference between a plant and an animal?
3. Prove the expression "Animals are everywhere."
4. What are the main classes of animals?
5. What makes a bird different from other animals?
6. What is the difference between a mammal and a fish?
7. What are the names of some reptiles? How are they different from fish and birds?
8. What are the names of some sea animals?
9. What are the names of some animals that lived long ago, but no longer inhabit the earth?
10. What are some ways animals can be protected through wise management?
11. How can people enjoy viewing or living with animals without endangering them?
12. What are the positive and negative aspects of zoos insofar as wildlife is concerned?
13. It has been claimed that wildlife conservation is not only a national issue, but an international problem as well. Explain why this is the case.
14. What kinds of groups and businesses might oppose wildlife conservation? Explain their motives. What could be done to change their attitudes or positions?

amphibian
animal
animal kingdom
biology
bird
colony
conservation
contaminate
creature
deforestation
diminish
ecology
endangered
extinction
fauna
federal lands
fish
flock
flora
game
game farm
habitat
herd
hibernation
human destruction
hunting
inheritance
insect

Interior Department
mammal
migration
naturalist
overkill
pesticide
plant
preservation
preserve
prevent
poison
pollute
pollution
protect
protective law
ranger
rare
reptile
school
species
tame
trapping
urban development
vanishing
weapon
wild
wildlife
zoology

animal artist,
  photographer
animal scientist
biologist
botanist
conservationist
environmentalist

game warden
ranger
taxidermist
veterinarian
zookeeper
zoologist

St. Patrick's Day

THEMES AND THOUGHTS

Pride, Loyalty, Tradition,
Heritage, Spirit

Oh! St. Patrick was a gentleman
Who came of decent people;
He built a church in Dublin town,
And on it put a steeple.
—*Henry Bennett*

Ireland is a country in which the probable never happens and the impossible always does.
—*John P. Mahaffey*

FASCINATING FACTS

Though it is a holiday associated with the country of Ireland, St. Patrick's Day is welcomed by people from every background, not just the Irish.

St. Patrick, the patron saint of Ireland, was not Irish, but thought to have been born in Britain. No one knows for sure, but it is believed that March 17 was the date of St. Patrick's death rather than his birth. There are many legends about St. Patrick. The most popular one is that he drove all the snakes out of Ireland and into the sea.

How did St. Patrick come to be associated with Ireland? Legend has it that, as a young man of 16, St. Patrick was captured by pirates from his father's farm in Britain and kept as a slave for six years, working as a shepherd in Ulster, Ireland. After escaping back to Britain, St. Patrick devoted his life to God. He was a deeply religious man and dreamed of returning to

Ireland to bring Christianity to the Irish. He did—as a monk—and is said to have established over 300 churches and baptized over 120,000 people. The historical records from that era are incomplete, but the surviving writings of St. Patrick show that he was a devout man and tireless missionary. (The largest Catholic church in the United States, St. Patrick's Cathedral in New York City, was named for him.)

St. Patrick's Day has been observed in the United States and Canada since colonial days. It started as a religious holiday, when people went to church, and later it became festive as well. It is a day when the Irish show their unity by the "wearing of the green." Some people think that green became the color of St. Patrick's Day because it occurs at the beginning of spring, when all turns green. Green is also a color connected with hope and nature.

Today, major cities in at least 30 of the 50

states have St. Patrick's Day parades and celebrations. The biggest parade takes place each year in New York City. More than 200,000 marchers and spectators are on hand for the parade, which is said to have started in 1761. The center stripe down Fifth Avenue is painted green. In Chicago, which boasts the nation's largest population of Irish descent (with 1.1 million people), the Chicago River is dyed green on St. Patrick's Day. All around the country, merchants sell special green hats, buttons, flowers, shamrocks, and other wares to make it a "great day for the Irish." People often celebrate this day by having corned beef and cabbage, Irish stew, Irish soda bread, or mulligan stew—popular foods in Ireland.

The shamrock is one of the most popular symbols associated with St. Patrick's Day. According to legend, St. Patrick used the shamrock in Ireland (Eire) to explain the Trinity, a basic principle of the Catholic faith. The word *shamrock* comes from the Gaelic word *seamrog,* which means "trefoil" or "little clover." The shamrock is the national flower of Ireland. It appears on the coat of arms of Great Britain along with the thistle and the rose, the national flowers of England and Scotland. There is a town named Shamrock in Florida, where people send letters to be postmarked.

ACTIVITIES FOR STUDENTS

Special Projects

1. Learn Irish songs and the Irish jig.
2. With your classmates, analyze the lyrics of the Irish song "McNamara's Band." Then have a parade, using band instruments, as described in the song.

Art and Visual Aids

3. Make shamrock people. Cut shamrocks (any size) out of paper and add faces, arms, and articles of clothing.
4. Make leprechauns out of green paper, pipe cleaners, and cloth.
5. Design an original coat of arms or flag for Ireland.

6. Design and draw a travel poster depicting some of the sights in Ireland.

Information Gathering and Sharing

7. Report on the way St. Patrick's Day is celebrated in different countries.
8. With your classmates, discuss the legends about the "wee folk."
9. With your class, compile a list of outstanding Americans of Irish extraction, such as the Kennedy family. Make a bulletin-board "hall of fame" display about them.
10. Make a list of some of Ireland's most famous poets and playwrights and their works.

Writing and Language Arts

11. Compile and explain a list of common Irish expressions, such as "The top of the morning to you."
12. The limerick probably got its name from an Irish refrain that contained the name of County Limerick, which is in southwest Ireland. The limerick is a five-line nonsense poem, with the rhyme scheme aabba—the first, second, and fifth lines (a) have three stresses; the third and fourth lines (b) each have two. Select your favorite limerick for recitation. Then compose a limerick of your own.
13. Compose an acrostic using Irish names or Irish terms.

QUESTIONS FOR CLASS DISCUSSION

1. How is St. Patrick's Day celebrated in your home community?
2. Why do you think Irish-Americans show so much pride on St. Patrick's Day?
3. In what ways do the modern-day celebrations of St. Patrick's Day differ from the original significance of St. Patrick?
4. Why do so many people who are not Irish-Americans choose to wear green on St. Patrick's Day?
5. How do you explain that sometimes a holiday or custom started in one country

takes on a different meaning, purpose, and form of celebration in another?

6. What does the expression "When Irish eyes are smiling, all the world seems bright and gay" mean? What does "Luck of the Irish" imply? What does "Everyone is Irish on St. Patrick's Day" mean?

7. Name some of the performers and musicians often found in a marching band.

8. What are the major differences between Northern and Southern Ireland?

9. What does this Irish blessing mean?

> May the road rise to meet you
> May the wind be always at your back.
> May the sun shine warm upon your face,
> The rains fall soft upon your fields and
> Until we meet again,
> May God hold you in the palm of his hand.

KEY VOCABULARY

bagpiper	island
bishop	isle
Blarney Stone	jig
brogue	Killarney
cabbage	laddie
Celtic	lass
clan	leprechaun
coat of arms	limerick
colleen	missionary
corned beef	parade
county	patron saint
devout	pride
Eire	reel
emerald	saint
Erin Go Bragh	shamrock
ethnic	shillelagh
festive	spirit
Gaelic	stew
grand marshal	thistle
harp	unity
herder	vision
immigrant	wit

RELATED CAREER EDUCATION TERMS

caterer	public relations consultant
musician	uniform maker
public events coordinator	

Statehood Granted to Hawaii

THEMES AND THOUGHTS

Beauty, Tranquility,
Resourcefulness, Friendliness,
Courtesy

Hawaii is the loveliest fleet of
islands that lies anchored in any
ocean.

—*Mark Twain*

The life of the land is perpetu-
ated in righteousness.
(Ua mau ke ea o ka aina i ka
pono.)

—*Hawaii's state motto*

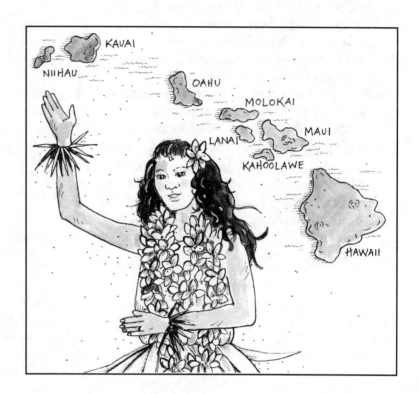

FASCINATING FACTS

Eight green gems, lying almost in the center of the Pacific Ocean as a crossroads, send forth the scent of thousands of flowers into the air. These are the main Hawaiian islands, known for their natural beauty and mild, semitropical climate.

The first inhabitants were Polynesians who sailed from the Marquesas Islands probably as early as A.D. 400. Many others followed from Tahiti during the ninth or tenth century. Hawaii consists of a 1,523-mile-long chain of 132 islands, including the eight main islands. When Captain James Cook of the British Navy arrived at the islands in 1778, the natives at first believed that he was a reincarnated Hawaiian god. Cook named the islands the Sandwich Islands after the Earl of Sandwich, the head of the British navy.

Hawaii, proclaimed the fiftieth state on August 21, 1959, is the only state that is not situated on the mainland of North America. It is our most western and southern state. Hawaii's friendly people have given it the nickname "The Aloha State." Aloha means "greetings" in Hawaiian. The capital, Honolulu, is on the island of Oahu.

Hawaii provides 70 percent of the world's supply of pineapple. Other important products include sugar, tuna, cement, and clothing. Coffee, rice, sisal, and cotton are also grown there. An oil refinery produces many petroleum products. Tourism and defense are also important income producers. Pearl Harbor is the headquarters of the Pacific fleet.

Hawaii is the only state that was once an independent monarchy. The last monarch,

Queen Liliuokalani, was deposed in 1893. The Iolani Palace is now a museum.

Only traces now remain of the cherished native culture. Some of these are the flower leis, colorful symbols of the Hawaiian welcome; the hula dance; and the luau, or feast.

Hawaii is a land of volcanoes. Haleakala, on the island of Maui, is the largest dormant volcano in the world. Its crater is seven miles long and two miles wide. Diamond Head Crater became a registered natural landmark in 1970. Two volcanoes on the island of Hawaii are still active—Mauna Loa and Kilauea.

ACTIVITIES FOR STUDENTS

Art and Visual Aids

1. Make a picture book about Hawaii. Draw the pictures or clip them out of old magazines or travel brochures.
2. Make a Hawaiian lei with paper flowers. Make flowers from colored tissue paper or crepe paper and thread them on a string. You can thread pieces of plastic straws between the flowers so that they do not bunch up.
3. Use native Hawaiian materials, such as beach pebbles, coconut shells, seeds, coral, driftwood, and shells for a craft project.
4. The long, slender leaves of the hala, or pandanus, tree are used to weave many articles, such as mats, hats, and coasters. Weave a lauhala mat from strips of construction paper in place of the leaves. Use a basic weaving pattern—odd-numbered rows go in an under-over-under-over pattern, and even-numbered rows go in an over-under-over-under pattern.
5. Make a sand sculpture in a large wooden or strong cardboard box about six or ten inches deep. Shells, pebbles, marbles, and paint may be added for decoration.
6. Sculpt a Hawaiian object or scene from wood, soap, clay, or firebrick. Or mold it from papier-mâché.
7. Make a batik design with a Hawaiian theme on paper or cloth.
8. Tapa is made from the bark of the paper mulberry. A patterned cloth, tapa, is made by pounding the bark flat and thin. Tapa cloth is used for clothing and floor coverings. Research Polynesian tapa cloth designs (refer especially to books about Polynesian or South Pacific art). After learning about tapa designs, create your own adaptation of tapa design on paper or cloth.
9. Make a model of a volcano from papier-mâché using a tin can for the base. Put sand inside. Take the model outside and, with adult supervision, make it "erupt" by placing 1 1/2 tablespoons of ammonium dichromate on top of the sand and lighting it. You can also use an old lamp shade, covered and painted, or chicken wire covered with molding material, or even a flowerpot.
10. June 11 is Kamehameha Day in Hawaii. (This day was established by the last king of Hawaii, Kamehameha V, to honor his grandfather.) All kinds of festivities occur on this day, including luaus and parades in which floats depict the history of the islands. Celebrate Kamehameha Day with your class. Divide into five committees. Each committee will make a model of a float to represent one of the five biggest islands (Hawaii, Maui, Molokai, Oahu, and Kauai). The base of the float can be a shoebox or a carton. Trees, people, land forms, and other items on the float can be made from construction-paper cutouts.

Information Gathering and Sharing

11. Collect information about travel to Hawaii from periodicals and local travel agencies. With a small group, make a quiz for the class about traveling to Hawaii.
12. Prepare a travelogue about Hawaii. With a small group, you might also prepare a pocket guide and duplicate it for the rest of the class.
13. Research and illustrate the unusual system of directions used in Hawaii (mauka, makai, ewa, and waikiki).

14. Write a report of the events that took place at Pearl Harbor on December 7, 1941.
15. Make a monthly graph of the climate (rainfall and temperature) of Honolulu. Refer to geography books and almanacs that include climate information.

Writing and Language Arts

16. Create a journal about an imaginary trip to Hawaii.

Dramatics and Role-Playing

17. Ki'i plays are similar to vaudeville, with lots of jokes, sarcasm, and songs. Write a ki'i play or adapt a legend of Hawaii for a puppet show. To find out more about ki'i plays, look in library reference books under the headings of "legends of Hawaii" or "arts of Hawaii."

Special Projects

18. With your class, plan a Hawaiian luau. Parents could be invited. You could teach your audience some Hawaiian words and tell some Hawaiian legends. Some class members could also perform Hawaiian songs and dances.
19. With your class, exchange recorded tapes, local or school newspapers, postcards, or letters with a class in Hawaii.

Crossword Puzzle

20. Work the crossword puzzle on page 229. Refer to an encyclopedia or a book about Hawaii, if necessary.

QUESTIONS FOR CLASS DISCUSSION

1. What are some of the main reasons that Hawaii is an important tourist attraction?
2. Why is the geographic location of Hawaii both an asset and a hindrance to the people who live there?
3. Why do you think there are so many stories, songs, and legends about Hawaii's past?
4. Can you think of some reasons why Hawaii could be called "The sweetest place on earth"?
5. What are the principal products and industries of Hawaii?
6. Why are so many ethnic and cultural groups represented in the population of Hawaii?
7. Why would you like or dislike living in Hawaii?

KEY VOCABULARY

aloha	mountain
bat	muumuu
batik	native
beach	natural landmark
canyon	naval base
catamaran	outrigger canoe
coconut	palace
coral	palm tree
crater	pineapple
descendant	Polynesian
exotic	rainbow
hula	ranch
husk	resort
immigrant	royal
island	statehood
lava	surfboard
leeward	taboo
lei	territory
luau	tidal wave
mainlander	tropics
monarch	volcano

Every Day's a Holiday

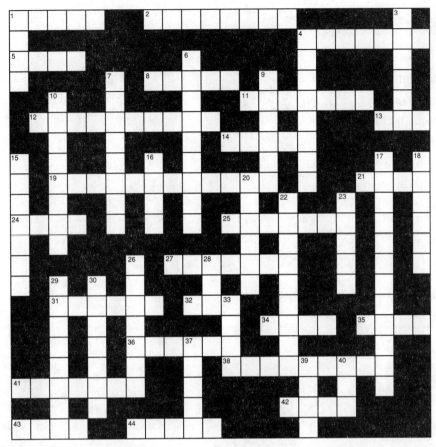

Across

1. Hawaii became the fiftieth _____ in 1959.
2. State flower of Hawaii.
4. Fifth largest island.
5. State bird of Hawaii.
8. First island visited by Captain Cook; location of the Grand Canyon of the Waimea.
11. Ocean in which Hawaii is located.
12. Hawaii was first settled by _____ people.
13. Mauna _____: Highest point in the state of Hawaii.
14. _____ Harbor: Attacked by Japanese on December 7, 1941.
19. Queen _____: Last Hawaiian ruler, whose rule ended in 1893.
21. Because Hawaii is of volcanic origin, _____ covers the ground.
24. "Orchid Capital of the World."
25. One of Hawaii's two remaining active volcanoes.
27. Source of lava; source of Hawaiian Islands.
31. A loose dress worn by women in Hawaii.
32. Only animal definitely known to be indigenous to Hawaii.
34. Location of Honolulu.
35. A Hawaiian feast.
36. The name of the royal palace in Hawaii.
38. In 1921, James Dole started full-scale _____ growing.
41. The fruit of a type of palm tree, which is filled with milk.
42. Island second in size and third in population.
43. Most of Hawaii's coffee comes from the _____ Coast.
44. _____ waves cause much damage to islands.

Down

1. Some beaches in Hawaii are covered with black _____.
3. The Parker Ranch in Hawaii is the second largest _____ ranch in the U.S.
4. Hawaii was made a U.S. Territory in 1898 when _____ was President.
6. _____ occupies almost three-quarters of Hawaii's cropland.
7. _____ Islands: Original name of Hawaiian Islands.
9. Largest island.
10. Capital of Hawaii.
15. Flowers widely grown in Hawaii.
16. Captain James _____ discovered the Hawaiian Islands in 1778.
17. U.S. mainland ships _____ goods to Hawaii.
18. _____ forests are found on the islands; mats are made from this plant.
20. Island completely devoted to cattle raising.
22. Smallest of the eight main islands.
23. Island whose name also means a veranda or open-sided living room.
26. _____ trade constitutes an important part of Hawaii's economy.
28. Mauna _____: An active volcano.
29. Hawaii was made an _____ Territory in 1900.
30. A favorite sport in Hawaii.
33. Many people's dream vacation is a _____ to Hawaii.
37. Hawaiian word meaning "welcome" or "good-bye."
39. Channel between Lanai and Maui.
40. Taro-root paste.

RELATED CAREER EDUCATION TERMS

anthropologist
botanist
builder
chef
clothes designer
cultivator
customs agent
entertainer
entrepreneur
explorer
farmer

harvester
hotel manager
industrialist
manufacturer
navigator
navy base worker
plantation owner
surfboard
  manufacturer
tour guide
travel agent

ANSWER KEY

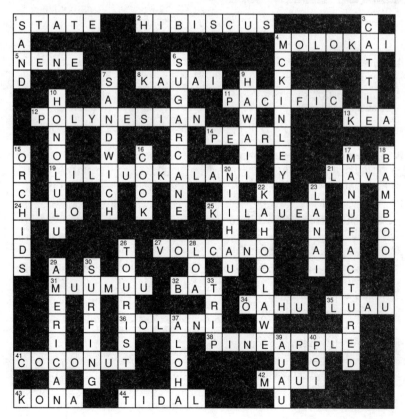

Art Week

THEMES AND THOUGHTS

Self-Expression, Beauty,
Legacy, Creativity

As the sun colors flowers, so does art color life.
—*Sir John Lubbock*

All nature is but art, unknown to thee; All change, direction, which thou canst not see.
—*Alexander Pope*

Art is art because it is not nature.
—*Johann Wolfgang von Goethe*

Art is long and Time is fleeting.
—*Henry Wadsworth Longfellow*

Artists, like the Greek Gods, are only revealed to one another.
—*Oscar Wilde*

To me Art's subject is the human clay,
And landscape but a background to a torso;
All Cézanne's apples I would give away
For one small Goya or a Daumier.
—*W. H. Auden*

It's clever, but is it Art?
—*Rudyard Kipling*

Conception, . . . fundamental brainwork, is what makes the difference in all art.
—*Dante Gabriel Rossetti*

Life without industry is guilt, and industry without art is brutality.
—*John Ruskin*

Every artist was first an amateur.
—*Ralph Waldo Emerson*

FASCINATING FACTS

Art is a common experience to all peoples everywhere throughout history. Scientific evidence shows that all human tribes, no matter how isolated, independently developed ornamentation and graphic representation. Art is found in every place where human beings ever have been. Achievements of past civilizations are judged by the art that lives on. Art thus becomes a source of inspiration and enjoyment to those who encounter it.

Pictures of animals are the oldest known paintings. Some of the best examples are found in caves in Lascaux, France, and Altamira, Spain. These paintings were made 10,000 to 15,000 years ago. Historians believe that prehistoric people made these paintings as part of magical or religious ceremonies. Throughout history, art has been used to represent important events and ideas, as well as to beautify objects of daily life—prehistoric people carved patterns in the handles of their hunting knives. Art is universal and an important part of our lives.

Every work of art has a different effect on each beholder, creating an infinite number of different interpretations and impressions. The artist sees things from a different perspective, and each artist sees differently from all other artists. This unique vision gives individuality and a special kind of life to each visual image.

The eye is the precious instrument through which visual impressions reach us, but it is the mind that sees. The Chinese believe that the outer eye merely sees and that the "inner eye" must be used for understanding and enjoyment.

The National Gallery of Art, a branch of the Smithsonian Institution, was created by Congress in 1937 to assemble and maintain a national collection of paintings, sculpture, and the graphic arts representing the best in the artistic heritage of America and Europe. Its building and a collection of American portraits were donated by financier and industrialist Andrew W. Mellon.

ACTIVITIES FOR STUDENTS

Information Gathering and Sharing

1. With a small group, collect colored reproductions of works of art or student art for a monthly display. Each month a different group can create a display around a theme, such as art about animals, art by Spanish artists, or art by early American artists. The display, entitled "Art Gallery," can be hung on a bulletin board or a plastic clothesline or card holder strung across the room.
2. With your class, visit a local art gallery or art museum.
3. Invite a local artist or an art teacher to give a demonstration to your class.
4. With your classmates, take turns selecting a picture of the week to be displayed in the classroom. The picture can be by a professional artist or a student. Give a brief oral report about the work of art and the artist. An opaque projector may be used for class viewing if you have only a small reproduction of the picture.
5. Experiment with combining paint colors.

Start with a small amount of each of the primary colors in a small jar or cup (such as a paper cup or a spray-can lid). Combine various pairs of the primary colors in other cups or on a sheet of paper. After experimenting, the class can summarize its findings. For example, blue + yellow = green.

6. With your class, go on a treasure hunt for beauty in nature—natural art. Keep a written and illustrated record of what you find, such as a cobweb or a tree.
7. With your class, discuss reproductions of art from a museum or a series of art appreciation slides. In your discussion, remember that interpretations and opinions may vary because people see things differently and also see different things.

Art and Visual Aids

8. Before a holiday, such as Halloween, Christmas, or Easter, prepare an art project with a small group to demonstrate to the class. You can be the "artists of the day."
9. Make a modern painting, using three colors of tempera paint, newsprint, and large brushes. Bright colors, such as orange, yellow, and red, will make interesting and bold designs.
10. With your class, compile a list of words that suggest motion, such as run, jump, and wiggle. Use colored chalk, paint, or crayons on large newsprint to illustrate the words. Display the finished product on a bulletin board under the title "We Were Moved" or "Move, Move, Move." An attractive border could be made by writing the words on 2-inch-wide strips of construction paper.
11. After your teacher reads a poem to the class, use crayons, pastels, or watercolors to paint an appropriate picture.
12. Make a self-portrait with crayons on a large sheet of construction paper. Add colored yarn for hair and scraps of cloth for clothing. Cut out your self-portrait and tape it to your chair for an open-house night.
13. Make a self-portrait on large white construction paper with a charcoal pencil. As you draw, look at your face in a mirror.

14. Use spools, pipe cleaners, buttons, yarn, tempera paint, and other odds and ends to create fanciful animals and people. The class' creations may be displayed on a table with a title, such as "The Land of Odd" or "A Strange Gathering."

15. Make an animal puppet from a brown lunch bag that has a flap folded over the bottom seam. Use paper or fabric scraps and crayons to add the features. With your class, plan a puppet show using your creations. You might name the program "At the Zoo" or "Animal Crackers."

16. Make a hand puppet from two gelatin boxes. Cover the boxes with colored construction paper, or paint them with tempera paint (to which a little liquid detergent has been added to make the paint adhere to the waxy surface). Add ears and facial features with colored construction paper. Tape the two boxes together. Insert a piece of red paper between the boxes for a tongue.

17. A small cone made of sturdy paper, such as oaktag or poster paper, may be used to make a variety of characters and animals by just adding or changing features. For example, you can make a turkey by adding a fanlike tail (baking cup), feet (pipe cleaners), and a head (almond) to the basic cone.

18. Make a simple scrapbook of examples of artistic expression that you like. You can cut pictures and ads out of magazines, take photographs, or draw pictures. Display the class' scrapbooks for a parent open house.

QUESTIONS FOR CLASS DISCUSSION

1. What makes a work of art great?
2. What kinds of things can be learned from a work of art? For example, what can be learned about a period of time, a country, and the artist's personality?
3. What temperament or personality is often associated with artists? Can you give examples of artists who fit this stereotype and examples of artists who do not?
4. What are some ways an artist can convey a message or impression to the viewer?
5. What do each of the following art terms mean?

architecture	crafts
engraving	tapestry
etching	enameling
lithography	carving
painting	still life
perspective	gallery
sculpture	photographic

6. What does the expression "A study of the arts is a study of mankind" mean?
7. Where can you see works of art (or reproductions) besides art museums and galleries? Are there works of art in public places in your community? In your home?
8. Is the message of a work of art more important than the technique or quality?
9. What subjects, colors, and medium would you use to create a calm picture? An exciting picture?
10. Why is the work of an artist sometimes judged against the background of the time in which he or she lived?
11. Can you think of some ordinary manufactured objects that can be considered handsome or artistic?
12. Some paintings and drawings are not intended to be faithful likenesses of reality and come primarily from the artist's imagination. What are some reasons that an artist might not want to make a completely true-to-life picture?
13. Why do exceptional art works tend to increase in value over time? Who really determines the value or worth of a piece of art?
14. Why is the production or collecting of art a worthwhile leisure hobby?
15. What are some of the world's most outstanding works of art? Who are some of the world's greatest artists? Who are some highly regarded U.S. artists?
16. What are some ways that art can be beneficial to individuals and to the community?
17. What are some basic rules to remember when drawing or painting a picture?
18. What is art therapy?

19. What is meant by the expression "Beauty is in the eye of the beholder"?

KEY VOCABULARY

abstract	medium
appreciation	modern art
art	mood
artist	mural
creative	museum
curator	palette
design	palette knife
dimension	perception
easel	perspective
exhibit	portrait
expression	primary color
frame	represent
freehand	representation
fresco	scale
gallery	secondary colors
graphic	shading
illusion	shadow
imagination	silhouette
impression	sketch
landscape	studio
master	style
mat	surface
matting	trace
media	two-dimensional

RELATED CAREER EDUCATION TERMS

artist	illustrator
art teacher	jewelry designer
cartoonist	painter
commercial artist	potter
display artist	sculptor
engraver	set designer
fashion designer	textile designer
graphic artist	

Every Day's a Holiday

April

First Week:

National Cherry Blossom Festival in Washington, DC (April 1–8)
National Laugh Week (April 1–10)
Be Kind to Animals Week (the first full week of April)
Daylight Savings Time (the 1st Sunday in April)

1

*April Fool's Day

2

*U.S. Mint established, 1792
*Hans Christian Andersen born, 1805
International Children's Book Day

3

Pony Express began, 1860
Washington Irving, humorist and writer, born, 1783

4

Dorothea Dix, welfare reformer, born, 1802
Congress decreed that the flag should have 13 stripes and a star for each state, 1818

5

*Booker T. Washington born, 1856
Joseph Lister, founder of modern antiseptic surgery, born, 1827

6

Admiral Robert E. Peary, Matthew Henson, and four Eskimos reached the North Pole, 1909
Launching of first commercial communication satellite, Early Bird, 1965

7

World Health Day
Mountain Folk Festival Day

*A teaching unit is included on the following pages for each starred entry.

Second Week:

National Garden Week

8

Ponce de Leon, Spanish explorer, landed in Florida, 1513

9

End of Civil War—Lee surrendered to Grant, 1865

10

U.S. patent system established, 1790
Humane Day—American Society for the Prevention of Cruelty to Animals chartered, 1866

11

Civil Rights Act signed by President Lyndon Johnson, 1968

12

Civil War began at Fort Sumter, 1861
Henry Clay, the Great Compromiser, born, 1777
Soviet cosmonaut Yuri Gagarin became the first human to orbit the earth, 1961

13

*Thomas Jefferson born, 1743
Frank W. Woolworth, merchant, born, 1852

14

*Pan-American Day
S.S. *Titanic* sank, 1912
Assassination of Abraham Lincoln, 1865
Pocahontas married John Rolfe, 1614

15

Thomas Hart Benton, painter, born, 1889
Revolutionary War ended, 1783
Income Tax Day

Third Week:

National Coin Week

16
Wilbur Wright, aviation pioneer, born, 1867

17
Giovanni Verrazano discovered New York Harbor, 1542

18
Paul Revere's ride, 1775
San Francisco earthquake and fire, 1906

19
Patriots' Day—the Battle of Lexington, first major battle of the American Revolution, 1775

20
Supreme Court decides that busing should be the primary way to integrate schools

21
Spanish-American War began, 1898
John Muir, naturalist, born, 1838
Kindergarten Day—Friedrich Froebel, founder of the first kindergarten, born, 1782

22
Oklahoma opened to settlers, 1889
Earth Day

23
William Shakespeare born, 1564
President James Buchanan born, 1791
First public showing of a motion picture, in New York City, 1896

Fourth Week:

National Library Week
Professional Secretaries Week
National Youth Fitness Week
*Arbor Day (the last Friday in April)
National YMCA Week

24
Library of Congress founded, 1800
Secretaries' Day

25
Guglielmo Marconi, inventor of wireless telegraphy, born, 1874
United Nations formed, 1945

26
John J. Audubon, ornithologist, born, 1785
Confederate Memorial Day
Nuclear accident at Chernobyl, USSR, 1986

27
National Youth Workout Day
President Ulysses S. Grant born, 1822
Samuel Morse, inventor of the Morse Code, born, 1791

28
President James Monroe born, 1758
WalkAmerica

29
William Randolph Hearst, newspaper publisher, born, 1863

30
President George Washington inaugurated, 1789
First public broadcast of television, from the Empire State Building, 1939

Every Day's a Holiday

April Fool's Day

THEMES AND THOUGHTS

Humor, Consideration, Manners

True humor springs not more from the dead than from the heart.
—*Jean Paul Friedrich Richter*

Some think the world was made for fun and frolic, and so do I.
—*"Funiculi, Funicula"*

Laugh, and the world laughs with you;
Weep, and you weep alone.
—*Ella Wheeler Wilcox*

Humor is a serious thing. I like to think of it as one of our greatest and earliest national resources which must be preserved at all costs.
—*James Thurber*

If anything is spoken in jest, it is not fair to turn it to earnest.
—*Plautus*

Play with me and hurt me not,
Jest with me and shame me not.
—*Gabriel Harvey*

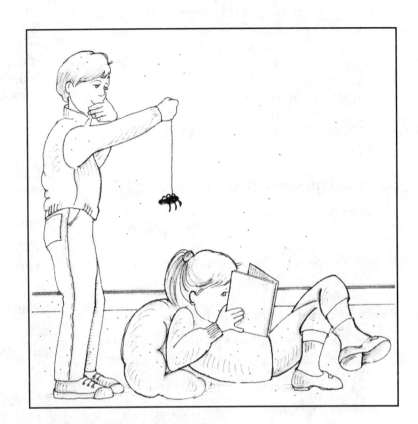

FASCINATING FACTS

The custom of playing practical jokes on friends was part of the celebrations in ancient Rome on March 25 (Hilaria) and in India on March 31 (Huli). The timing seems related to the vernal equinox and the coming of spring—a time when nature fools us with sudden changes between showers and sunshine.

April Fool's Day is thought to have originated in France. Before the use of the Gregorian calendar, New Year's celebrations ended on April 1. When New Year's Day was changed to January 1, the people who still celebrated it on April 1 were called April fools.

In France, the victim of a joke is called an "April fish" (poisson d'avril). In England, tricks can be played only in the morning. If a trick is played on you, you are a "noodie." In Scotland, you are called an "April gowk," which is another name for a cuckoo bird. In Portugal, April Fool's is celebrated on the Sunday and Monday before Lent. The traditional trick there is to throw flour at your friends. Humor and practical jokes are universal.

ACTIVITIES FOR STUDENTS

Critical Thinking

1. Read the classic parable about the boy who cried "wolf." Explain the parable in terms of a real-life situation.
2. With your class, discuss tricks you most enjoy playing. What tricks do you enjoy that are played on you?
3. With your class, discuss the difference between harmful and harmless practical jokes.

Information Gathering and Sharing

4. Interview your parents and older friends for their accounts of April Fool's tricks practiced years ago.
5. With your class, make a list of popular April Fool's Day tricks that are appropriate.

Writing and Language Arts

6. Write a story or draw a picture to illustrate one of these titles: "The Best Trick I Ever Played," "April Fool's Day," or "A Joke on Me."
7. Write a fictional story about April Fool's Day that has a theme or a message.
8. Compose a four-line poem about April Fool's Day.

Special Project

9. Design or construct a positive April Fool's Day trick.

QUESTIONS FOR CLASS DISCUSSION

1. In what ways can a joke be harmful?
2. What makes a good trick?
3. What type of person would say "Some think the world was made for fun and frolic, and so do I"?
4. Why is it a good idea to set one day aside each year for tricking and fooling?
5. Sportsmanship is a two-way street. One must learn how to take a joke as well as play one—that is, one must learn how to be a good loser as well as a gracious winner. Why is this quality important?
6. The word *trick* has different meanings. What's the difference between playing a trick on another person and a magician's trick?
7. What does the term "Watch him, he's tricky" mean?
8. What's the main difference between a trickster and a liar?

KEY VOCABULARY

deceit	humor
decoy	joke
dupe	mirth
fakery	mischief
fate	mischievous
feelings	outwit
fool	prank
fool's errand	ruse
frolic	sportsmanship
harmless	trick
hoax	

RELATED CAREER EDUCATION TERMS

comedian	magician
comedy writer	recreation director
humorist	

U. S. Mint Established

Value, Usefulness, Enterprise,
Trust, Integrity

A penny saved is a penny earned.
—*Proverb*

The love of money is the root of all evil.
—*Timothy 6:10*

Lack of money is the root of all evil.
—*George Bernard Shaw*

Put not your trust in money, but put your money in trust.
—*Oliver Wendell Holmes*

Money is a good servant but a bad master.
—*French proverb
(translated by Francis Bacon)*

Never spend your money before you have it.
—*Thomas Jefferson*

You're worth what you saved, not the million you made.
—*John Boyle O'Reilly*

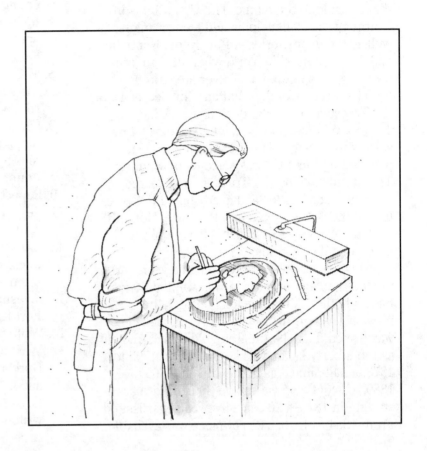

FASCINATING FACTS

A coin is a piece of metal stamped by the authority of a government as a guarantee of its value. The first known coins in the West were Lydian, around 700 B.C. In the East, the first coins were Chinese, before 700 B.C. Early coins, which were made by hand, show many variations. Standardized coins began to be made with a mill-and-screw machine in the seventeenth century.

The real value of any coin is determined by the stability, prosperity, and gold reserves of a country. A mint is a place where coins are manufactured. All U.S. coins are made at two government mints in Philadelphia, Pennsylvania, and Denver, Colorado. A third mint in San Francisco, California, discontinued making coins in 1955.

The first U.S. coins were minted in 1652 by John Hull for the colony of Massachusetts, which paid him one coin for every forty he minted. When the first federal mint was established in Philadelphia in 1792, George Washington provided silver for the coins from his own household silver. In 1873, the Bureau of the Mint was created by Congress. In 1984, its name was changed to the United States Mint. The

Mint produces U.S. coins and also makes engraving stamps (dies) and tools used in minting. It mints coins for some foreign governments as well as coin sets and commemorative medals that are sold to the public. The U.S. Mint is in charge of the Philadelphia and Denver mints, as well as the depositories at Fort Knox, Kentucky, and West Point, New York, where the government's stocks of gold and silver are stored.

The director of the Mint and the Secretary of the Treasury select the designs for U.S. coins. There are times, however, when Congress selects the design. The Washington 25-cent piece minted in 1932 was selected by Congress. The motto "In God We Trust" first appeared on a 2-cent piece in 1864 and is attributed to Secretary of the Treasury Salmon P. Chase. Not until 1955 did Congress establish a law requiring this motto on all U.S. coins.

More pennies—over 10 million a year—are minted than any other coin. The United States has had other denominations besides the present ones. From 1793 to 1857, the half-cent was issued. In 1849, the first gold dollar, known as the Liberty Head, was struck. From 1792 to 1873, a half-dime was minted. From 1865 to 1889, a 3-cent coin was made. For three years, starting in 1875, a 20-cent silver coin was issued. From 1864 to 1873, a 2-cent piece was available.

ACTIVITIES FOR STUDENTS

Art and Visual Aids

1. With your class, make a bulletin-board display of money from around the world.
2. Design a coin or bill. Submit outstanding designs from your class to the Bureau of Mints.

Critical Thinking

3. With your class, discuss the meaning of an allowance and a budget.
4. Make a personal budget based on your weekly allowance or earnings.
5. With your class, discuss and list the things money can buy and the things money cannot buy.

Information Gathering and Sharing

6. Make a chart or "money line" showing the history and development of money exchange systems.
7. Invite an accountant or local banker to speak to your class about money exchange and banking.
8. Make a collection of popular sayings about money, such as "The love of money is the root of all evil."
9. List songs that have some form of money denominations in the title, such as "Pennies from Heaven" or "Three Coins in the Fountain."
10. Report on the history of currency.
11. Report on how trade is carried out in remote parts of the world today.
12. Examine a dollar bill closely (even under a microscope) for interesting features. List them.
13. Investigate and report on the importance of Fort Knox, Kentucky, to our money system.
14. Write to the U.S. Mint (501 13th St., NW, Washington, D.C. 20220) or to the U.S. Bureau of Engraving and Printing (14th and C Sts., SW, Washington, D.C. 20228) for supplemental literature on money. Or write to the Mint in Philadelphia (Fifth and Arch Sts., Philadelphia, Pennsylvania 19106) or in Denver (320 W. Colfax, Denver, Colorado 80204).
15. With your class, make a flow chart illustrating the steps in the process of making and distributing new currency.
16. Write a report about the first state mint (in Asia Minor early in the seventh century), other early mints, and the art of coining in ancient Greece, Rome, Persia, India, China, and Japan.
17. With your class, take a week to find the oldest penny, nickel, dime, quarter, and half dollar that you can.
18. Investigate the symbols and persons pictured on various coins or bills. Chart the information. Explain the meaning of the symbols.
19. Compile a lexicon of popular names for various kinds of currency and coins (past and present)—such as buck, C-note, and fin.

Mathematics

20. With your class, set up an "international bank," using replica money for exchanging currencies. Refer to an almanac or the newspaper for current exchange rates and names for established units of currency, such as pound, yuan, lira, mark, franc, peso, and yen. A table of current exchange rates is also available at banks.
21. Compute interest rates for imaginary savings, based on local bank rates for a period of time.
22. With your class, set up a pretend grocery store. Take turns being clerks and customers. Use real or play money.
23. Draw a pie chart of the national, state, town, or school budget. Be prepared to discuss it.
24. Make a chart to indicate the exchange rate of the U.S. dollar in other countries. Use newspapers as your resource.

QUESTIONS FOR CLASS DISCUSSION

1. Every country has its own coins and bills. Why is this necessary? Why can't all nations have a universal money system?
2. How can we identify different U.S. coins?
3. Why are some old coins valuable?
4. Why does the Mint continue to make new coins each day?
5. Why is there a growing interest in collecting coins?
6. How is the dollar supported? Why is it used as a standard for trade throughout the world?
7. In the future, do you think we will still use coins and bills for business transactions? How might new technology change the way we buy and sell things?
8. What does the term "mint condition" mean?
9. What are the modern processes used for minting coins?
10. What are some ways of detecting counterfeit currency?

KEY VOCABULARY

alloy	gold
bank	half dollar
barter	issue
cent	loan
coin	mint
copper	money
counterfeit	motto
currency	nickel
debt	paper money
denomination	penny
design	precious
dime	quarter
dollar	savings
engrave	serial number
exchange	silver
face value	silver dollar
Federal Reserve note	tender
	treasure
forgery	treasury

RELATED CAREER EDUCATION TERMS

artist	engraver
banker	government official
bank teller	miner
cashier	silversmith
clerk	skilled machinist
designer	treasurer

Hans Christian Andersen Born

THEMES AND THOUGHTS

Persistence, Communication,
Innovativeness, Imagination

Life is the most wonderful fairy
tale of all.
—*Hans Christian Andersen*

First you suffer terrible things,
Then you get to be famous.
—*Hans Christian Andersen*

Nothing in the world can take
the place of persistence.
—*Calvin Coolidge*

FASCINATING FACTS

Though Hans Christian Andersen is best known as a writer of stories for young children, he is also respected as a scholar and ranks among the great writers of the world. His works have been translated into most major languages and are popular with millions of children and adults worldwide, particularly in the United States.

Andersen was born into a very poor family in Odense, Denmark. His father read endlessly to him and encouraged his interest in stories by building him a puppet theater. Andersen learned much folklore from his mother, who was very superstitious. He received little formal education during childhood and was very poor at spelling. He was, however, a dreamer and had a most creative ability to imagine story plots and to tell them in unusual ways. He was 11 when his father died. At the age of 14, he set out for Copenhagen to become famous.

While in Copenhagen, he suffered "terrible things." He lived in dark, dreary surroundings, wore hand-me-downs, and nearly starved while trying to make his living as an actor, singer, and ballet dancer. At 17, he received a grant and was sent to grammar school. Andersen was very tall and was self-conscious about his strange, stork-like looks. He was placed in a lower-level class and teased by his headmaster and teachers. With the help of an influential friend from the theater, he eventually gained admission to Copenhagen University, where he completed his education and was free to write. At first, he wrote plays, novels, and travel books. In 1835, he wrote his first fairy tales.

More copies of Hans Christian Andersen's 168 beloved tales have been sold than any other book in the world, except the Bible. Over 2,000 editions have been published in 80 languages. Among his most famous stories are "The Ugly Duckling," "The Brave Tin Soldier," "The Little Mermaid," and "The Red Shoes."

Statues of Hans Christian Andersen are located in Central Park in New York City and in

Copenhagen, Denmark. A statue of the Little Mermaid is in Copenhagen's harbor.

ACTIVITIES FOR STUDENTS

Dramatics and Role-Playing

1. With a group of classmates, dramatize one of Andersen's fairy tales using puppets, flannel-board, or pipe-cleaner figures.

Writing and Language Arts

2. Write an original fairy tale.

Information Gathering and Sharing

3. With your class, compile a "Who's Who Book of Fairy-Tale Land," listing characters generally found in fairy tales, such as a king and a princess. Or list specific Andersen characters, such as the ugly duckling. Pictures and short character descriptions could be included.
4. Read one of Hans Christian Andersen's famous tales, such as "The Ugly Duckling," "The Red Shoes," or "The Emperor's New Clothes," and make an illustrated report about your selection.

Art and Visual Aids

5. With your whole class or a committee, make a roller movie of one of Andersen's tales. The narration may be recorded to go along with the movie.
6. Compile a picture book of characters created by Hans Christian Andersen. Pictures can be drawn or cut out of magazines.

Special Events

7. With your class, plan a Hans Christian Andersen Festival as an assembly or a class program.
8. With your class, read some of Andersen's tales to some younger students.

Critical Thinking

9. Read the Hans Christian Andersen tale, "The Emperor's New Clothes." Write a brief paragraph about the lesson or moral of the story.
10. Select some of Hans Christian Andersen's most popular stories and, in one or two lines, describe what each tale is about.
11. Read some of Andersen's tales. Then choose your favorite. In a story review, explain why you found the tale so interesting and enjoyable.

QUESTIONS FOR CLASS DISCUSSION

1. When he was a boy, people said Hans Christian Andersen was fit for nothing except dreaming, yet he became a very successful author. Can you explain this?
2. Why is the ugly duckling story meaningful to people throughout the world?
3. Why are Hans Christian Andersen's works still popular today?
4. Andersen once explained that in the whole realm of prose, no domain is so boundless as a fairy tale. What do you think he meant?
5. In what ways is Hans Christian Andersen's sad early life reflected in his children's tales?
6. Do you think Andersen's stories are too frightening for children?
7. If Hans Christian Andersen were alive today, what kind of writing do you think he would be doing?

KEY VOCABULARY

ambition	imagination
author	legend
ballet	literature
character	moral
comedy	narration
critic	novel
dialogue	parable
drama	philosopher
fairy tale	play
fantasy	plot
fiction	poem
folklore	publish
headmaster	puppet
history	tale
humble	

RELATED CAREER EDUCATION TERMS

actor	playwright
actress	poet
artist	producer
author	publisher
critic	puppeteer
dancer	set designer
illustrator	storyteller
librarian	teacher
mime	translator
musician	

Booker T. Washington Born

Dignity, Efficiency, Discipline, Work, Commitment, Ideals

No race can prosper till it learns that there is as much dignity in tilling a field as in writing a poem.
—*Booker T. Washington*

Work is no disgrace; it is idleness which is a disgrace.
—*Hesiod*

It is work that gives flavor to life.
—*Amiel*

FASCINATING FACTS

Booker Taliaferro Washington was born a slave on a Virginia plantation. After the slaves were emancipated, his family moved to Malden, West Virginia. Poverty made it necessary for the 9-year-old Booker to work with his foster father in a salt furnace and later in a coal mine. In 1872, at the age of 16, he was so determined to secure an education that he walked 300 miles to enroll at Hampton Normal and Agricultural Institute in Hampton, Virginia, and worked as a janitor to help pay for his school expenses.

After graduation from Hampton, he became a teacher of his fellow African-Americans. He integrated practical work with academic subjects. Washington organized and served as the first president of Tuskegee Institute in Alabama. Tuskegee Institute started with 30 students in a shanty in 1881. Washington was the only teacher and the principal. When he died in 1915, 34 years later, Tuskegee had 2,000 acres of land, over 100 buildings, and 200 teachers, who taught thousands of students 38 different trades and professions. His success at Tuskegee gained him national acclaim. During his time,

Washington was regarded as the most influential spokesperson for African-Americans.

He wrote a dozen books, some of which were translated into more than 18 languages. He wrote an autobiography entitled *Up from Slavery.* Besides being an author, Washington is credited with starting rural extension work among blacks and creating the National Negro Business League. He received honorary degrees from Harvard University (1896) and Dartmouth College (1901). Booker T. Washington died at Tuskegee in 1915. There is a national monument in his honor near his birthplace, not far from Roanoke, Virginia.

ACTIVITIES FOR STUDENTS

Art and Visual Aids

1. With your class, make a bulletin-board display about famous African-Americans, with an emphasis on teachers.

Writing and Language Arts

2. Write a short biography of Booker T. Washington. Design a book jacket for a book-length biography of Washington.
3. An epitaph is an inscription written on a tomb or monument in memory of the person buried there. Write an appropriate epitaph for Booker T. Washington.
4. Write a dialogue that might have occurred between Booker T. Washington and a new student at Tuskegee in 1901.
5. Write an original proverb or slogan related to the theme of the Booker T. Washington story.
6. Booker T. Washington wrote two autobiographies. Write a publisher's advertisement or promotional announcement about one of his books.

Information Gathering and Sharing

7. Investigate what was said about Booker T. Washington when he was inducted into the New York University Hall of Fame for Great Americans in 1946.
8. Make a "Who's Who Book" containing brief biographies of important African-American contributors to U.S. history. Pictures and drawings should be included. Group the people included according to their fields of accomplishments.
9. Report on the facilities and the student enrollment at Tuskegee Institute today.

Critical Thinking

10. In a class discussion, list qualities and characteristics one needs in order to become an effective teacher.

For additional activities about African-American history, see "Benjamin Banneker" (pages 88-91), "Emancipation Proclamation Issued" (pages 146–148), "Martin Luther King, Jr." (pages 155–157), "Crispus Attucks" (pages 210–212), "Frederick Douglass" (pages 174–177), and "Harriet Tubman" (pages 216–218).

QUESTIONS FOR CLASS DISCUSSION

1. In what ways did Booker T. Washington overcome his disadvantages?
2. Why was Washington's story a model for all Americans?
3. Why was his idea to combine academic subjects with practical work a wise one for that period? Would it be effective today?
4. What is meant by the expression "Nothing truly worthwhile comes easily"?
5. If Booker T. Washington were alive today, what advice might he have for young people?
6. What type of school do you think Booker T. Washington would start today?
7. Washington could be considered a "frontier thinker." What does this term mean?
8. What kinds of schools are needed to help the less-privileged advance today?
9. Booker was an appropriate first name for Washington. What nicknames might have been appropriate for him?
10. Why did Booker T. Washington equate hard work and education as a first step to success?
11. Where do you think Washington received his motivation and determination to become educated?
12. It is said that "He who dares to teach must never cease to learn." How did Washington exemplify that saying?

KEY VOCABULARY

academic	ideal
apprentice	institute
career	intellectual
degree	job
determination	profession
dignity	rural
educator	self-made man
epitaph	skill
faculty	slave
graduation	trade

KEY VOCABULARY CONTINUED

training	work
vocation	

RELATED CAREER EDUCATION TERMS

advocate	home economics agent
agricultural agents	miner
author	principal
custodian	school administrator
educator	
farmer	

Thomas Jefferson Born

Humanitarianism, Foresight, Ideals, Liberty, Justice

Give the people light, and they will find their way.
—*Thomas Jefferson*

The God who gave us life, gave us liberty at the same time.
—*Thomas Jefferson*

To do injustice: more disgraceful than to suffer it.
—*Plato*

We hold these truths to be self-evident; that all...are created equal; that they are endowed by their creator with certain unalienable rights; that among these are life, liberty, and the pursuit of happiness; that to secure these rights, governments are instituted... deriving their just powers from the consent of the governed; that whenever any form of government becomes destructive to these ends, it is the right of the people to alter or to abolish it, and to institute new government, laying its foundation on such principles, and organizing its powers in such form, as to them shall seem most likely to effect their safety and happiness.
—*Thomas Jefferson*
(Declaration of Independence)

Liberty without learning is always in peril and learning without liberty is always in vain.
—*John F. Kennedy*

Above all other things is justice: success is a good thing; wealth is good also; honor is better, but justice excels them all.
—*D. D. Field*

FASCINATING FACTS

Thomas Jefferson was born in 1743 into a family that owned a large Virginia plantation. As a boy, he loved animals, enjoyed music, played the violin, and liked to read by himself in the woods. He liked to talk to people, but he was reserved in manner. His father died when he was 14, but the young Jefferson was able to continue his schooling because an overseer was appointed to manage the plantation.

Jefferson graduated from college at age 19 and became a successful lawyer. He was described as being tall, straight-bodied, and always walking erectly.

He served in the Virginia legislature, where he became a radical leader in protest against British colonial policies. At the age of 33, Jefferson was well known as an accomplished writer and, at the Second Continental Congress, he was asked to draft the Declaration of Independence, one of the world's greatest documents for freedom.

Jefferson would go on to serve his country in Congress, as a foreign minister, Secretary of State, Vice President, and later as President for two terms. He was nicknamed the

"Father of the Patent Office" because he administered the first patent laws in his role as Secretary of State. Although he owned slaves, as was the custom of the times, he was opposed to slavery. During his presidency, Congress passed a law banning slavery in the Northern states.

Jefferson was not only a statesman and President, but an agriculturist, scientist, architect, and able linguist. As an agriculturist, he improved the moldboard plow, introduced the threshing machine in the United States, and was one of the first Americans to use crop rotation and contour plowing. As a scientist, he encouraged the invention of the stopwatch, submitted to inoculation for smallpox, and believed in the possibility of the submarine. Some of the items Jefferson invented or designed and used in Monticello, his home, were the seven-day clock, an octagonal filing table, a coffee urn, a portable writing desk, a music stand for a quartet, and a dumb waiter that brought wine from the cellar.

As an architect, he designed not only Monticello, but also the building used as the capitol in Richmond, Virginia, and many buildings for the University of Virginia. As a linguist, Jefferson was fluent in Greek, Latin, and Spanish, and was a pioneer in making written records of Native American languages. After he retired from public life, he devoted much of his energy to establishing the University of Virginia.

Prior to his death in 1826, Jefferson wrote his own epitaph: "Here was buried Thomas Jefferson, author of the Declaration of American Independence, of the statute of Virginia for religious freedom, and father of the University of Virginia."

History has recognized Thomas Jefferson as one of the greatest Americans ever to hold public office, and a great champion of freedom and human rights.

ACTIVITIES FOR STUDENTS

Dramatics and Role-Playing

1. With your class, role-play a committee of reporters interviewing Jefferson about the Louisiana Purchase.

2. With a small group, give an imaginary guided tour of Monticello, Jefferson's home.

Writing and Language Arts

3. Write a newspaper editorial about the election of Thomas Jefferson as President.
4. Write and deliver an Independence Day speech that Jefferson would have enjoyed.

Information Gathering and Sharing

5. With your class, make a list or a pictorial timeline of important events in the United States and Europe during Jefferson's administration.
6. Report on the general growth of public education from Jefferson's day to the present.
7. Make a list of places and things in the United States named in honor of Thomas Jefferson.
8. Construct a list that summarizes all of Jefferson's abilities, talents, inventions, designs, and accomplishments.

Art and Visual Aids

9. Construct a diorama showing some of the new ideas Jefferson developed in farming, such as contour plowing.
10. Construct a model of the Jefferson Memorial. Use dowels for the columns, a ball cut in half for the dome, and your imagination!
11. Make a simple pictorial timeline of Jefferson's life.

QUESTIONS FOR CLASS DISCUSSION

1. In what ways was Jefferson a "versatile genius"?
2. In what ways did Jefferson's home at Monticello reflect his personality, interests, and ideals?
3. Jefferson is considered by many historians to be the greatest of all Americans. Why would you agree or disagree with this notion?

4. What are some titles or nicknames suitable for describing Thomas Jefferson?
5. Which of Jefferson's designs and inventions are forerunners of things used today?
6. Find out what Jefferson wanted inscribed on his tombstone. Why do you think he preferred such a simple statement?
7. What one achievement or contribution do you consider Jefferson's most important?
8. What were the major differences and similarities between Jefferson and Alexander Hamilton? Between Jefferson and Benjamin Franklin? Between Jefferson and Booker T. Washington?
9. Why do some people feel that Jefferson was the greatest friend of the public schools?
10. Sometimes people of great wealth dedicate their lives to improving the lot of poor people. How do you account for this?
11. Prove the statement that Thomas Jefferson was the author of human freedom.
12. What adjectives best describe Jefferson's philosophy of life? What adjectives best tell about his personality and contributions?
13. How might the course of history in the United States have been different had Jefferson never lived?

KEY VOCABULARY

administration	liberty
agriculturist	linguist
architect	monarchy
author	Monticello
capitol	patent
contour plowing	pioneered
crop rotation	planner
declaration	plantation
diplomat	principle
embargo	reserved
founder	scientist
genius	versatile
innovator	visionary
inventive	

RELATED CAREER EDUCATION TERMS

agriculturist	linguist
architect	musician
diplomat	patent attorney
farmer	politician
inventor	scientist
lawyer	writer

Pan-American Day

Appreciation, Fidelity,
Understanding, Peacefulness,
Neighborliness

We have learned that we cannot
live alone, at peace; that our own
well-being is dependent on the well-
being of other nations, far away.
—*Franklin D. Roosevelt*

In time of need—we must all
stand together, or we may all stand
alone.
—*Franklin D. Roosevelt*

God has made us neighbors; let
justice make us friends.
—*William Jennings Bryan*

FASCINATING FACTS

Pan is a Greek word meaning "all." The Pan-American movement began in the 1800s, when many Latin American countries were struggling for their independence from Spain. The leaders of the independent nations of Latin America, such as the Venezuelan general, Simón Bolívar, agreed that they would benefit from closer economic and political cooperation. The First International Conference of American States was held in Washington, D.C., in 1889. It created a permanent organization, which was renamed the Pan-American Union in 1910. The Pan-American Union has facilitated postal and radio agreements and coordinated the building of the Pan-American Highway, which links the United States, Mexico, and Central and South America.

The first Pan-American Day was observed in 1931. The flag of the Americas, representing all the American nations, was first raised in 1932 on October 12 (Columbus Day). The flag has three wine-colored crosses on a white field, symboliz-ing Columbus' ships. It also has a bronze sun of the Incas, representing the Native Americans.

In 1948, representatives of the Pan-American Union met in Bogotá, Columbia, and founded the Organization of American States (OAS). The OAS charter states that the organization sup-ports the principles of international law, social justice, economic cooperation, and the equality of all people. The OAS is a regional organization that works within the United Nations. It func-tions through several bodies—major political decisions are made in the General Assembly and urgent problems of defense and peace in the Americas are handled by the Meeting of Consultation of Ministers of Foreign Affairs. Meetings of the 32 member nations can also be called to settle urgent security problems. The Permanent Council, with headquarters in Washington, D.C., acts as the executive body of the organization.

New York City has a unique monument to the Americas. The flags of the countries of Latin

America are mounted along Sixth Avenue, which is also known as the Avenue of the Americas.

ACTIVITIES FOR STUDENTS

Critical Thinking

1. With your class, discuss ways students can be good neighbors.

Information Gathering and Sharing

2. If you have a collection of stamps, dolls, or other items from various countries in the Americas, bring it in to share with the class.
3. Write to the Organization of American States (1889 F St., NW, Washington, D.C. 20006) for information. Also write airlines that fly to Latin America for information about the countries they serve. Or visit a travel agency for free travel brochures.
4. Trace the route of the Alcan–Pan-American Highway on a globe and a map.
5. Report on the Panama Canal and its significance.
6. Report on the animals and plants native to one of the countries in the Americas.
7. Report on the famous Avenue of the Americas (Sixth Avenue) in New York City.

Art and Visual Aids

8. With your class, make a display of flags of the Pan-American countries. Flags may be constructed out of paper or cloth and mounted or stapled on dowels.
9. Design a tile or a mosaic using a Latin American motif.
10. Construct a model or a diorama of a typical Latin American market.
11. With your class, design a mural showing typical scenes in various countries of the Americas. Or make a series of three-dimensional dioramas.

Dramatics and Role-Playing

12. With your class, role-play travel agents and potential travelers. Each "travel agent" selects a country and gathers brochures and information about it. Take turns being potential travelers and inquiring about an imaginary trip to a country in the Americas.
13. With your class, put on an imaginary radio or television show about the Pan-American countries.

Writing and Language Arts

14. List some of the early European explorers of the Americas. Write entries in an imaginary diary of one of their trips. Trace the route on a large map.

Music

15. Listen to a radio or television concert of Latin American music. Discuss how the concert made you feel.
16. Make a Latin American instrument out of a gourd, such as a maraca, a cabaca, or a guiro. Research these instruments in the library.

Special Project

17. With your class, plan a Latin American fiesta, with special songs, dances, Latin American food, decorations, and music. Invite your parents and friends to attend. Write the invitations in Spanish.

QUESTIONS FOR CLASS DISCUSSION

1. What effect has the completion and improvement of the Pan-American Highway had on our relationships with Latin American countries?
2. Do you think the Monroe Doctrine is still a wise policy to follow today? Why or why not?
3. Why do so many people from North America visit Latin America? What benefits for all the countries can be derived from these visits?
4. What can we learn from the Latin Americans? What can they learn from us?
5. What products would North America have

to do without if we were unable to trade with Latin American countries?

6. What are some Latin American customs and styles that have been adopted by people in the United States?

7. Why do we need a good-neighbor policy and a Pan-American organization for the Americas?

8. It has been said that South Americans need trade, not aid. Why is this so?

9. What single improvement would be the most important for most Latin Americans?

10. Why has there been so much misery, poverty, and unrest in Latin America?

11. Why do the Latin American nations need to have closer ties and cooperation with one another?

12. What can go wrong in a country when there is too much reliance on a single crop or produce? How can this be prevented?

13. What do you think the future has in store for most Latin American nations?

14. Why do the Brazilians speak Portuguese while most other Latin American nations converse in Spanish?

15. Identify the "ABC" nations of South America. Why are they called the ABC nations?

16. Why has there been so much immigration to the United States from Latin American countries in recent years?

17. Why does the United States promote a good-neighbor policy with Latin American nations?

KEY VOCABULARY

Andes Mountains	market
cathedral	mestizo
Central America	Monroe Doctrine
conference	nation
continent	neighbor
cooperation	Organization of American States
dispute	
embassy	Pan-American
empire	plantation
export	policy
fiesta	relations
foreign policy	republic
friendliness	revolution
good-neighbor policy	siesta
	Spanish
hacienda	tariff
hemisphere	totalitarian
Hispanic	tourist
import	trade
inter-American	treaty
intervention	tropics
investment	union
Latin America	

RELATED CAREER EDUCATION TOPICS

ambassador	farmer
banker	importer
customs agent	investor
diplomat	translator
exporter	travel agent

Arbor Day

THEMES AND THOUGHTS

Nature, Conservation, Legacy, Volunteering, Caring

I think that I shall never see
A poem lovely as a tree. . . .
Poems are made by fools like me,
But only God can make a tree.
—*Joyce Kilmer*

It is our task in our time and in our generation to hand down undiminished to those who come after us, as was handed down to us by those who went before, the natural wealth and beauty which is ours.

—*John F. Kennedy*

I think I shall never see
A billboard lovely as a tree.
Indeed, unless the billboards fall
I'll never see a tree at all.
—*Ogden Nash*

Of all the tress that grow so fair,
Old England to adorn,
Greater are none beneath the Sun,
Than Oak, and Ash, and Thorn.
—*Rudyard Kipling*

Today I have grown taller from walking with the trees.
—*Karle Wilson Baker*

Woodman, spare that tree!
Touch not a single bough!
In youth it sheltered me,
And I'll protect it now.
—*George Pope Morris*

FASCINATING FACTS

Arbor means "tree" in Latin. Arbor Day was started by J. Sterling Morton, a Nebraska newspaper publisher who encouraged Nebraskans to plant trees to beautify and enrich the treeless state. He offered prizes for the most trees planted on April 10, 1877, Nebraska's first Arbor Day. Over a million trees were planted on that day.

After Arbor Day was made a legal holiday in Nebraska in 1885, agricultural associations and town councils spread the idea of Arbor Day in other states. A campaign was also inaugurated to make Arbor Day a school festival. Now, with activities that range from the planting of a single tree to the beautification of public grounds, children are learning the importance of forestry and reforestation.

Most states now observe Arbor Day, but it is celebrated on different dates throughout the country, depending on the climate. The most common date is the last Friday in April. In Nebraska, however, Arbor Day is now celebrated on April 22, the date of Morton's birthday. California celebrates Arbor Day on March 7, horticulturist Luther Burbank's birthday.

In many countries a tree is planted whenever there is a birth in the family. For instance, in Israel in a celebration called Tu B'Shebat, a cedar tree is planted for a boy and a cypress tree is planted for a girl.

Famous trees in America include the following:

1. Charter Oak in Hartford, Connecticut—the charter of the Connecticut colony was hidden here.
2. General Stewart Sequoia in Sequoia National Park, California—the oldest and biggest tree in the park. It is wide enough for a camper truck to drive through.
3. Kilmer Oak in the Douglass Campus of Rutgers University, New Brunswick, New Jersey—the huge, 300-year-old oak may have inspired the famous poem "Trees" by Joyce Kilmer, the soldier-poet. It was so weakened by age and disease that it had to be removed in 1963.

There is also a Road of Remembrance in Seattle, Washington—one thousand elms are planted along this road in memory of native sons who died in wars.

How to plant a tree:

(1) dig a hole large enough for all the roots to fit below ground level;

(2) put a shallow layer of topsoil in the hole;

(3) set the tree so that the roots are all in the hole, but not too deep;

(4) cover the roots with topsoil, peat moss, or subsoil mixed with humus;

(5) pack firmly;

(6) water well; and

(7) mulch.

ACTIVITIES FOR STUDENTS

Special Projects

1. With permission from your principal, plant a tree or shrub on the school grounds, in a park, or in the woods and fields. Start a schoolroom planter for transplanting or for room beautification.
2. "Adopt" a tree and take care of it.
3. With your class, take a nature walk and identify the various trees.

Information Gathering and Sharing

4. Invite a local landscaper or tree expert to give a talk to the class on the care and planting of a tree.
5. With your class, discuss the parts of a tree, the types of trees, and the value of trees. Demonstrate how to tell the age of a tree by its rings.
6. List as many products and uses of trees as you can.
7. With your class, report on the kinds of trees typical of the different regions of the United States. The information may be shared in booklets, on a bulletin-board display, or in oral or written reports.
8. Report on reforestation and land reclamation in the United States. Or report on tree planting on arid land, such as in Israel. Find out about the Kennedy Forest.
9. Give a simulated demonstration on how to plant and care for a large tree.
10. Can you think of ways fauna (animals) and flora (plants) need each other? Select an animal (a pet or a common animal in your area) and find out how that animal and plants need one another.
11. Brainstorm with your parents (and other relatives) to find out ways in which wood products are used in their jobs. Share your findings with your class in a discussion (you might call it "Sawdust Information Bowl"). You might also discuss substitutes for the wood products mentioned in order to promote conservation of this natural resource.
12. Read the story of Johnny Appleseed.

Writing and Language Arts

13. Learn and recite poems about trees. With a small group, perform a choral recitation of Joyce Kilmer's "Trees."
14. Write a description of the most beautiful tree you have ever seen.
15. Write riddles about trees, such as "What is

the tree that cries?" (Answer: weeping willow)

16. Write a poem about Arbor Day.
17. Write an imaginative composition about living in a country without trees.
18. Write a "Conservation Pledge," starting with "I give my pledge as an American to. . . ."
19. Write a short essay about the need to keep surroundings beautiful by protecting and conserving natural resources.

Art and Visual Aids

20. Make a step-by-step flow chart of the development of a specific wood product from the forest to the consumer.
21. Draw a pictorial map that uses symbols to show the location of the predominant tree types in your state, the United States, or the world.
22. Make a pictorial chart about the "friends" and "foes" of trees.
23. Make a pictorial chart to illustrate the various tree types and the special use or purpose of each one.
24. Make a display of things in your home made of wood. Use pictures or the actual items.

QUESTIONS FOR CLASS DISCUSSION

1. In what ways can too few or too many trees cause problems?
2. What causes a timberline on the slopes of mountains?
3. Name ten items made of wood in your home. Do the same in your classroom.
4. Identify the various parts of a tree. Are there any similarities between the structure of a tree and the structure of a person?
5. What are some unusual products made from trees?
6. What are some ways people abuse trees? How can we prevent these abuses?
7. What is implied by the saying "Plant a tree in your youth so that you can rest under its shade in old age"?
8. Why should you not take shelter under a

tree during an electrical storm? What alternatives are better?
9. Why do we use the word *tree* when we trace family, national, and ethnic histories?
10. Why is the taiga of Siberia often referred to as the "green ocean"?
11. What is an accepted way to approximate the age of a tree?
12. What is the relationship between the availability and type of trees found in a region and the building materials used in that area?

KEY VOCABULARY

arbor	needle
arboretum	oasis
branch	plant
by-product	pulp
cone	reforestation
coniferous	ring
conservation	root
deciduous	seed
ecology	seedling
evergreen	shade
fauna	soil
flora	sylvan
forest	timber
leaves	timberline
lumber	trunk
mill	

RELATED CAREER EDUCATION TERMS

agriculturist	landscaper
botanist	lumberjack
conservationist	scientist
environmentalist	sprayer
farmer	tree farmer
forest ranger	tree surgeon
gardener	

May

First Week:

International Music Week
National Postcard Week
National Wildflower Week
Kentucky Derby (the 1st Saturday in May)

National Pet Week (the 1st full week of May)
National Letter Writing Week
PTA Teacher Appreciation Week (the 1st full
   week of May)

1
May Day
Loyalty Day (Law Day) designated by Congress, 1958
Mother Goose Day

2
Hudson's Bay Company chartered, 1670

3
First U.S. school of medicine established, in Philadelphia, 1765

4
Horace Mann, educator, born, 1796

5
*Cinco de Mayo
First suborbital space flight, made by Alan B. Shepard, 1961

6
Robert E. Peary, Arctic explorer, born, 1856
First postage stamp issued, in England, 1840

7
Lusitania sunk in Atlantic, 1915

*A teaching unit is included on the following pages for each starred entry.

Second Week:

*Mother's Day (the 2nd Sunday in May)
Police Week (the week including May 15)
National Nursing Home Week (starting on Mother's Day)
National Hospital Week (the week including May 12)

8

President Harry S. Truman born, 1884
V-E Day—World War II ended in Europe, 1945

9

James Pollard Espy, meteorologist who started scientific weather prediction, born, 1785
John Brown, abolitionist, born, 1800

10

Golden Spike Day—completion of first transcontinental railroad, 1869

11

Ottmar Merganthaler, inventor of Linotype, born, 1854

12

Florence Nightingale, English founder of modern nursing, born, 1820
Limerick Day

13

U.S. declared war on Mexico, 1846
Jamestown, Virginia, first permanent English settlement in North America, founded, 1607

14

*Gabriel D. Fahrenheit born, 1686
Lewis and Clark began trip up Missouri River, 1804

15

First air-mail service flight, 1918

Third Week:

National Transportation Week (the week including the 3rd Friday)
Armed Forces Day (the 3rd Saturday in May)

16 Elizabeth Peabody, founder of the first U.S. kindergarten, born, 1804

17 Future Nurses' Day
Father Jacques Marquette and Louis Joliet began exploring the Mississippi River, 1673

18 Mount St. Helens erupted, causing loss of life, fires, mud slides, and floods, 1980
Visit Your Relatives Day

19 The Ringling Brothers Circus opened, in Baraboo, Wisconsin, 1884

20 *Homestead Act signed, 1862

21 *American Red Cross organized, 1881
First bicycles imported into the U.S., 1891
Charles A. Lindbergh completed first solo transatlantic flight, 1927

22 National Maritime Day—S.S. *Savannah* began first transoceanic voyage of a steam-powered ship, 1819

23 South Carolina admitted to the Union, 1788

Fourth Week:

*Memorial Day (the last Monday in May)

24 Samuel F. B. Morse sent the first telegraph message, 1844

25 Ralph Waldo Emerson, philosopher and writer, born, 1803

26 Last Confederate troops in the Civil War surrendered in Shreveport, Louisiana, 1865

27 Golden Gate Bridge, San Francisco, opened, 1937
Julia Ward Howe, author of the "Battle Hymn of the Republic," born, 1819
Isadora Duncan, dancer, born, 1878

28 John Muir formed the Sierra Club, 1892

29 President John F. Kennedy born, 1917
Patrick Henry, American Revolution leader and orator, born, 1736

30 Christopher Columbus began third voyage, 1498

31 Walt Whitman, poet, born, 1819
Indianapolis 500 Race Day
U.S. copyright law enacted, 1790

Cinco de Mayo

THEMES AND THOUGHTS

¡No Pasarán!

They shall not pass!
—*A Mexican battle cry*

Yo no quiero oro, ni quiero plata.
¡Yo lo que quiero es quebrar la
piñata!

Gold and silver do not matter.
All I want is to break the piñata!
—*Traditional saying*

El respeto al derecho ajeno es
lapaz.

Respecting other people's rights
creates an atmosphere of peace.
—*Benito Juárez*

¡Ay, ay, ay, ay! canto no llores,
porque candando se alegran
cielito lindo los corazones.

Sing and do not cry,
because with singing
the heart becomes happy.
—*Lyrics from "Cileto Lindo"*

FASCINATING FACTS

One of more than 365 festivals celebrated by people of Mexican descent, Cinco de Mayo (the Fifth of May) commemorates the victory of a group of untrained and poorly armed Mexican soldiers against thousands of well-armed, professional French soldiers at Puebla, Mexico, on May 5, 1862. The French defeat must have surprised Napoleon III, the ruler of France, who was attempting to annex Mexico by taking advantage of the destruction and bankruptcy that existed there. Mexico's condition at that time was the result of the War of Reform (1858-1860), an internal political, economic, and religious struggle. At the end of this civil war, Mexico owed more than $80,000,000 to foreigners. France invaded Mexico, using debt collection as an excuse. Napoleon III's true motivation, however, was total control of Mexico and its potential wealth!

An important patriotic celebration, the fiesta of Cinco de Mayo often includes speeches by government officers, fireworks, and a military parade. Lively dances and games, mariachi music, traditional foods, and colorful decorations provide additional enjoyment for festival participants.

Information Gathering and Sharing

1. Write to the Chambers of Commerce in the following cities to request information about that particular city's annual Cinco de Mayo festivals. Share the information you gather with the class. If possible, visit one of the festivals.

Albuquerque	Sacramento
Denver	San Diego
Los Angeles	San Francisco
Mexico City	Tucson
Phoenix	

2. Invite someone who has participated in a Cinco de Mayo festival to come speak to the class about this celebration.

3. Gather books and pictures about Cinco de Mayo. Display these materials in a classroom learning center. Libraries such as the Chicano Resource Center, 4801 E. Third Street, Los Angeles, CA 90022 (213-263-5087) and the Southern California Library for Social Studies and Research, 6120 S. Vermont, Los Angeles, CA 90044 (213-759-6063) can be of assistance.

Writing and Language Arts

4. Learn more about the names and sounds of the letters in the Spanish alphabet. Then use a Spanish/English dictionary to choose nouns with a Cinco de Mayo theme that begin with each letter. Extend this activity by including Spanish words now common to the English language. Include words such as *adobe, bonanza, bronco, burro, canyon, chili, fiesta, mesa, mustang, patio, rodeo, sierra,* and *tomato.*

5. Puebla is famous not only for the Cinco de Mayo victory that occurred there, but also for a festive dish called *mole poblano de guajolote* (turkey in chocolate and chili sauce). Prepare a report about Mexican chocolate. Include its source, history, use during festivals, and recipes.

Special Projects

6. The basis for many Mexican fiesta dishes is the tortilla, an unleavened cornmeal pan-cake. Try to make tortillas by grinding corn with a metate (flat rock) and molino de mano (roller) or by using a tortilla press and masa harina (cornmeal).

7. Plan a Cinco de Mayo party. Investigate the history and significance of the piñata. Make a piñata out of cardboard and colorful crepe paper or make it out of papier-mâché using an inflated balloon as the form. Decorate the piñata in bright colors or shape it into the form of an animal or other shape associated with the holiday. Remember to leave an opening for candy or prizes. Once the piñata is ready, hang it from a rope or heavy string. Each person then takes a turn hitting the piñata with a stick while blindfolded. When the piñata breaks, the participants dash for the candy or prizes that have fallen to the ground. In addition to piñata fun, teach the children nursery rhymes like "Tortillitas para Mama" ("Little Tortillas for Mother") and "Rima de Chocolate" ("Chocolate Rhyme"). Play games, such as the Mexican version of "London Bridge Is Falling Down," "A la Víbora" ("To the Viper").

Art and Visual Aids

8. Draw a large wall map of Mexico. Include and label the Sierra Madre Occidental, Sierra Madre Oriental, Sierra Madre del Sur, Central Plateau, Yucatán Peninsula, Pacific Ocean, Gulf of Mexico, Puebla, and Mexico City.

9. Many Mexicans celebrate Cinco de Mayo in villages that include a central plaza (mini-park) and a nearby mercado (market). Construct models of these two places during the Cinco de Mayo holiday.

10. Study pictures of the historical murals by artists Diego Rivera, Jose Clemente Orozco, and David Alfaro Siqueiros. Create a classroom mural depicting the battle at Puebla on May 5, 1862.

11. No Cinco de Mayo celebration is complete without mariachi music. Present information about the origin and nature of this type of music in an imaginary interview between a talk-show host and a mariachi musician. Or create six to eight paper doll mariachi players. Make traditional traje de charro

costumes for the players. Construct violins, horns, and guitars. Listen to records and performances of mariachi music. Include two early mariachi songs, such as "Las Olas" ("The Waves") and "La Mujer Negra" ("The Dark Woman").

12. Watch Mexican folklore dance groups. Learn Mexican folk dances, such as "La Cucaracha" and "La Raspa."

Dramatics and Role-Playing

13. Role-play the experiences of two families celebrating Cinco de Mayo in a traditional Mexican village.
14. Write a play about the events leading up to the Battle of Puebla.

Critical Thinking

15. Study ancient civilizations and their contributions to the world. Create an Ancient Civilizations timeline. Highlight or emphasize the Aztec and Mayan civilizations.
16. Create a chart that compares and contrasts the customs of the festival of Las Posadas with those of Cinco de Mayo.
17. Compare and contrast Cinco de Mayo celebrations in rural and urban areas. Vote to determine which location or celebration your class prefers.

QUESTIONS FOR CLASS DISCUSSION

1. Why do people other than the citizens of Mexico celebrate Cinco de Mayo?
2. Mexicans place great value on the family unit. What aspects of Cinco de Mayo benefit the family?
3. Are all Mexican fiestas patriotic and national? Identify and describe several religious and regional festivals of Mexico.
4. What contributions did the Indians, Spanish, and French make to Mexican countries?
5. Why do people continue to celebrate events that occurred long ago?
6. What event or events do you celebrate each year? How do you celebrate them?

KEY VOCABULARY

adobe	mesa
annex	metate
bankruptcy	motivation
bonanza	mural
bronco	mustang
burro	participant
celebration	patio
charro	patriotic
commemorate	piñata
canyon	plaza
chili	regional
economic	rodeo
festival	rural
fiesta	sierra
folklore	tomato
invasion	tortilla
mano	traditional
mariachi	unleavened
masa harina	urban
mercado	

RELATED CAREER EDUCATION TERMS

craftsmaker	mariachi musician
farmer	market vendor
festival organizer	mural artist
fireworks manufacturer	piñata maker
folklore dancer	soldier
government official	Spanish linguist
historian	

Mother's Day

THEMES AND THOUGHTS

Appreciation, Love, Respect,
Helpfulness, Caring, Compassion

All I am or can be I owe to my
angel Mother.
—*Abraham Lincoln*

God could not be everywhere
and therefore he made mothers.
—*Jewish Proverb*

What is home without a mother?
—*Alice Hawthorne*

For the hand that rocks the
cradle is the hand that rules the
world.
—*William Ross Wallace*

Who ran to help me when I fell,
And would some pretty story tell,
Or kiss the place to make it well?
My mother.
—*Ann Taylor*

A mother is not a person to lean
on, but a person to make leaning
unnecessary.
—*Dorothy Canfield Fisher*

By and large, mothers…are the
only workers who do not have
regular time off. They are the great
vacationless class.
—*Anne Morrow Lindbergh*

That best academy, a mother's
knee.
—*James Russell Lowell*

FASCINATING FACTS

This family day is celebrated on the second Sunday in May—a time when flowers are in bloom. Mother's Day is a special day for children to honor their mothers (as well as grandmothers and other "mothers") and show appreciation for their love and caring.

Honoring mothers is a tradition long observed in many European countries, such as England and Yugoslavia. In England, the day is called Mothering Sunday and comes in the middle of Lent.

Julia Ward Howe, social reformer and poet, made the first suggestion for a Mother's Day in the United States. In 1872, she suggested Mother's Day be on June 2 and that it be a day dedicated to peace. She sponsored Mother's Day meetings in Boston for several years, and people in other towns began to do the same. In 1907, Anna Jarvis of Grafton, West Virginia, began a campaign for a nationwide observance of Mother's Day. She also began the custom of wearing a carnation on that day—a colored carnation if one's mother is living and a white carnation if one's mother has died. On May 9, 1914, President Woodrow Wilson signed a joint resolution of Congress authorizing federal agencies to observe Mother's Day. The following year, Mother's Day was proclaimed as an annual national holiday.

Mothers are often taken out for dinner, given greeting cards, flowers, candy, or handmade gifts as expressions of love and appreciation to "moms" of all ages.

ACTIVITIES FOR STUDENTS

Critical Thinking

1. With your class, discuss the responsibilities of family living and the mother's role in the family.
2. With your class, make a chart that lists ways children can help their mothers.

Art and Visual Aids

3. Make a Mother's Day gift and card.
4. Make a portrait of your mother.

Writing and Language Arts

5. Write a thank-you letter to your mother.
6. Compile a list of words describing your mother.
7. Compose a poem or write a story in tribute to your mother.
8. Compose a simple proverb or maxim about mothers.

Information Gathering and Sharing

9. Make a list of some famous mothers living today.
10. Make a list of the word for "mother" in other countries. Investigate how children in these nations honor their mothers.
11. In the *Guinness Book of World Records,* look up motherhood records, such as the mother with the most children and the oldest mother.
12. With your class, compile a scrapbook of Mother's Day advertisements, magazine and newspaper articles, tributes, pictures, and stories a week before Mother's Day.

Special Projects

13. Do a good deed for your mother.

For additional activities, see Father's Day (pages 300–302) and Grandparents' Day (pages 21–23).

QUESTIONS FOR CLASS DISCUSSION

1. In what ways do you observe Mother's Day?
2. Why do we set one particular day aside to honor our mothers?
3. In what special ways do we show our appreciation on Mother's Day? How can we show our appreciation throughout the year?
4. How have the responsibilities of motherhood changed from "grandma's" time to the present?
5. Who were some outstanding mothers in history who influenced their children in special ways?
6. If one wish could be granted, what would you wish for your mother?
7. Why is nature often referred to as "Mother Nature"?
8. What is meant by each of the following terms: motherland, mothering, mother-in-law, motherhood, motherly, and mother-tongue?
9. Who were Mother Hubbard, Mother Goose, and Grandma Moses? Can you name other well-known "mothers"—real or fictional?
10. It is often recognized that mothers show great courage. Explain how this might be so.
11. What does the expression "Mother knows best" imply?

KEY VOCABULARY

affection	corsage
appreciation	custom
bouquet	floral
caring	gratitude
carnation	guidance

Key Vocabulary Continued

- honor
- kindness
- love
- loyalty
- maternal
- matriarch
- motherhood
- motherly
- nurture
- observe
- parent
- rearing
- recognition
- remembrance
- respect
- tradition
- tribute

Related Career Education Terms

- confectioner
- florist
- greeting card designer
- restauranteur

Gabriel D. Fahrenheit Born

THEMES AND THOUGHTS

Integrity, Initiative,
Innovativeness, Accuracy

Necessity is the mother of
invention.
—*Anonymous Latin saying*

Numerical precision is the very
soul of science.
—*Sir D'Arcy Wentworth Thompson*

Some are weatherwise, some are
otherwise.
—*Benjamin Franklin*

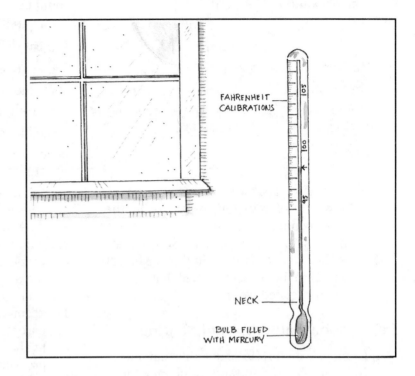

FAHRENHEIT
CALIBRATIONS

NECK

BULB FILLED
WITH MERCURY

FASCINATING FACTS

Gabriel Fahrenheit was born in Danzig, Germany (now Gdansk, Poland) in 1686, but for most of his life, he lived in Amsterdam, the Netherlands. Fahrenheit , who also studied with Sir Isaac Newton, is most famous for his improvements on the thermometer. Galileo, the Italian astronomer, had invented the thermometer in 1593. A more accurate thermometer, which used alcohol, was developed in 1641. In 1714, Fahrenheit replaced the alcohol with mercury, which enabled even more accurate readings, and he established a temperature scale. On the Fahrenheit scale, water freezes at 32° and boils at 212°. As a maker of meteorological instruments, Fahrenheit also invented a hydrometer and a new type of barometer.

The finer gradations of Fahrenheit's scale allow for more accurate readings than the Celsius, or centigrade, scale, which was invented later in the 1700s by a Swedish astronomer. But because the centigrade scale has 0° as the freezing point and 100° as the boiling point,

it is easier to use for mathematical calculations. In the United States, the Fahrenheit scale is used in daily life to measure body temperature, air temperature, and cooking temperature—the centigrade scale is used for scientific applications. The centigrade scale is almost universally used in Europe today. The formula for converting centigrade degrees (C) to Fahrenheit degrees (F) is 5/9 (F – 32) = C. The reciprocal formula is 9/5 (C + 32) = F.

Thermo is derived from the Greek word for "heat" and *meter* comes from the Greek word for "measure." Thus, a thermometer is an instrument used to measure heat.

ACTIVITIES FOR STUDENTS

Writing and Language Arts

1. Research and explain the meaning of the following weather terms:

accumulation	dust devil	leeward	smog
advection	elevation	lightning	snowfall
blizzard	flood	low pressure system	squall
Chinook wind	fog	nimbus	stratus
cirrus	freezing rain	precipitation	thunder
cloud	front	radiation	tornado
cloud cover	frost	rain gauge	wind direction
convection	haze	rain shower	wind velocity
cumulus	high pressure system	relative humidity	windchill factor
dew point	hurricane	sensible temperature	windward
drizzle	ice	sleet	

2. Study a newspaper weather map and write a TV weather forecaster's report, using the weather conditions given.

3. Make a list of place names and words that have the root word *therm-* in them. You can also make a list of place names that contain a weather-related word.

Information Gathering and Sharing

4. Demonstrate how to read a thermometer. Regulate the heat of water or change the position of the thermometer in the room to show variations in temperature. Take the thermometer outside for a reading.

5. With your class, keep temperature records and other weather data on a large calendar using a code you have developed.

6. Record and report the temperature outside your home at given intervals over a period of time. With your class, construct a graph of all your home temperatures. Discuss the reasons for the differences.

7. Exchange records of daily local temperature conditions for a given period of time with a school or class in a different state or country.

8. Compare actual temperature conditions with the forecasts from the weather bureau or the *Farmer's Almanac*. Make a chart that shows the reliability of weather forecasts.

9. Make a booklet about temperature and weather records around the world.

10. Refer to the climatic data for U.S. cities in an almanac. Make climate graphs, plotting the monthly temperature averages of a few selected cities on a line graph (with 5-degree intervals) and the monthly precipitation averages for the same cities on a bar graph (with 1-inch units). You can also plot the annual temperature and precipitation averages.

11. Record readings from a barometer or barometric weather reports. Make a chart to show the relationship between low pressure (below 29.92 inches, or 1013.2 millibars) and storm periods.

12. Construct a Fahrenheit-Celsius conversion chart or table.

13. Research how wind direction and barometric pressure reflect weather changes. Construct a "How to Forecast the Weather" chart.

Art and Visual Aids

14. With a small group, construct a classroom thermometer. Draw a large scale on oaktag and make a slot at the top and another at the bottom. Insert an elastic strip or ribbon that is half red and half white into the slots. Sew or staple the ribbon so that the red "bar of mercury" can be moved up and down to show the reported temperature of the day.

15. Collect pictures, articles, and advertisements that illustrate how temperature plays an important part in science and daily life.

16. With your class, make a mural or frieze that shows how climate affects the way people live in certain regions of the world.

17. With your class, draw and color a local weather board (about 50 inches high) on oaktag. Take turns attaching appropriate weather symbols to the board each morning.

Critical Thinking

18. Correlate temperature and weather conditions in different places and in different seasons with types of clothing, sports, occupations, and homes. Chart the comparisons.
19. Make a list of occupations that rely on thermometers.
20. Make a chart of ways transportation is affected by weather conditions. Include land, sea, and air vehicles.

Special Projects

21. With your class, set up a weather bureau, equipped with appropriate student-made or commercial instruments. Take turns being the daily weather forecaster and recording and reporting the weather data.
22. With your class, take a field trip to a nearby weather or agricultural station where weather instruments are housed.

QUESTIONS FOR CLASS DISCUSSION

1. Why are both the centigrade and Fahrenheit scales being used throughout the world?
2. Why do doctors and meteorologists in the United States usually use the Fahrenheit scale instead of the centigrade scale?
3. How do temperature and other weather factors affect us?
4. How do latitude, elevation, and surface features affect temperature?
5. How does temperature change affect wind, precipitation, seasons, and climate in general?
6. Are greater extremes of temperature observed during a series of clear days and nights or during a cloudy period? Explain.
7. What do you think weather forecasting will be like in the year 2050?
8. Do you think it will be possible for scientists to someday control the weather?
9. What are the differences between an alcohol-filled and a mercury-filled thermometer?
10. Why are the inventions of Gabriel Fahrenheit, such as the hydrometer, barometer, and thermometer, so closely related to one another?

KEY VOCABULARY

alcohol	instrument shelter
barometer	inversion
boiling point	liquid
Celsius	maximum
centigrade	measurement
chart	mercury
condensation	meteorologist
conversion	millibar
degree	minimum
dew point	observation
experiment	physics
Fahrenheit	range of
forecast	temperature
freezing point	reading
front	scale
frost	temperature
hydrometer	thermograph
hygrometer	thermometer
instrument	thermostat

RELATED CAREER EDUCATION TERMS

instrument maker	physicist
inventor	scientist
meteorologist	

Homestead Act Signed

THEMES AND THOUGHTS

Opportunity, Initiative, Courage, Exploration, Neighborliness

'Mid pleasures and palaces though we may roam,
Be it ever so humble, there's no place like home.
—*John Howard Payne*

Property has its duties as well as its right.
—*Disraeli*

Give me a home where the buffalo roam and the skies are not cloudy all day.
—*"Home on the Range"*

In the United States there is more space where nobody is than where anybody is.
This is what makes America what it is.
—*Gertrude Stein*

FASCINATING FACTS

The word *homestead* comes from the German words that mean "home" and "place." The homestead is the place where a family makes its home, including the house, the land, and any outbuildings, such as a barn.

As U.S. territory grew during the 1800s, farmers and other citizens wanted the government to give public land, or at least sell it cheaply, to people who would improve it. Some felt the Eastern states were becoming too crowded, others wanted the opportunity for better farms, and some simply wanted the adventure of frontier life. Congress considered various proposals for homesteading programs in the 1850s and 1860s, but there was bitter disagreement about whether slavery should be permitted in homesteading areas.

After the Southern states seceded from the Union in 1860–1861, the remaining members of Congress, who were opposed to slavery, soon passed the Homestead Act. The act allowed each head of a family to become the owner of 160 acres (a quarter section) of land, provided he or she lived on the land for five years and improved it or paid $1.25 an acre for it.

Most of the land settled under the Homestead Act was in the Great Plains. This was a difficult place to start new farms, for a number of reasons. Because there was generally less rainfall than in the East, many farmers had to learn how to use irrigation. Homesteaders also needed to build fences to protect their crops, because cattle ranchers in Texas often drove their cattle northward through homesteaders' land to reach the railroads in Kansas and Nebraska. Many Native American tribes lived on land that was granted to the homesteaders, and some tribes took up arms to keep their land intact. The Great Plains was an inhospitable place for many homesteading families.

Over 400,000 families received land under the Homestead Act between 1862 and 1900—about 20 percent of these families were headed by women. In all, over a quarter of a billion acres of land were distributed under the Homestead Act and its amendments. As a result of amendments to the Homestead Act, however, about 80 percent of the land was sold to the railroads and to business people who wanted the land's minerals, oil, and other natural resources.

The government ended the homesteading program in all states but Alaska in 1976. Homesteading there was ended in 1986. The Homestead National Monument in southeastern Nebraska marks one of the first claims made.

ACTIVITIES FOR STUDENTS

Critical Thinking

1. With your class, discuss the similarities and differences in our present way of life and that of a homesteader in the 1860s. Compare and contrast food, clothing, shelter, and activities.

Dramatics and Role-Playing

2. With your class, put on an assembly program or a play depicting the search for choice land and early settlement.
3. With a small group, role-play a round-table discussion in which a panel of members of Congress discuss the significance and importance of the Homestead Act.
4. With a small group, role-play some games and activities that homesteaders' children might have played. Also role-play a family situation on a homestead.

Art and Visual Aids

5. Design a three-dimensional layout of a newly claimed homestead plot for a family in the 1860s.
6. Design an advertisement that might have appeared in a local paper in 1862 to advertise the Homestead Act.
7. With a small group, design and make a panorama depicting the story of a homesteader's life. A panorama is a long picture containing several scenes. It is exhibited by being unrolled a section at a time. Unroll your panorama before your class or a school assembly.
8. Make a poster extolling the advantages of the Homestead Act that might have appeared in eastern cities in 1863.
9. With your class, create a mural or frieze—half of which depicts a typical scene on a homestead, the other half depicting a comparable scene today.
10. Make a seed mosaic out of dried weed seeds, beans, cereals, and any other seeds that might be brought to class. Glue the seeds to construction paper and cover your creation with clear shellac.
11. Draw pictures that show the evolution of selected farm implements.

Writing and Language Arts

12. Write a report about a book that depicts life on the frontier.
13. Pretend you are a recently arrived homesteader and write a letter to a friend back home.
14. Write two weeks of entries in the diary of a typical homesteader.

Information Gathering and Sharing

15. Compile a simple gazetteer containing geographical terms and maps of the Old West.
16. Make a pictorial timeline of the history of a typical Great Plains city from 1800 to the present.
17. Investigate the story of the "sooners" and the Oklahoma Territory.

Music

18. Learn the words to a number of western, cowboy, and classic regional songs, such as "I've Been Working on the Railroad,"

"My Old Kentucky Home," "The Old Chisholm Trail," "Oklahoma," "California, Here We Come," and "Home on the Range."

Special Projects

19. With your class, put on a homestead festival. Wear the attire of the era and provide food, entertainment, and music that might have been found at a homestead picnic.
20. Locate possible "homestead" sites in town. Describe them and explain why they would be suitable places to live.

QUESTIONS FOR CLASS DISCUSSION

1. What were the unexpected hardships and problems encountered by the homesteaders?
2. In what ways do the place names of the Great Plains area indicate the origin and impact of the Homestead Act?
3. Which promises proved true and which expectations proved false for the early homesteaders?
4. Where is the United States' frontier today? Explain your answer.
5. Why was barbed wire important to the early homesteader? Who was opposed to it?
6. Why were railroads built on lands out West even before the arrival of the settlers?
7. Do you think that first-time settlers anywhere in the world (or in space) face similarly harsh environmental conditions? Why or why not?
8. Why did President Lincoln sponsor the Homestead Act in 1862?
9. If you were a new homesteader, how would you order your work and building schedule?
10. What were some advantages and some disadvantages of the coming of the railroads to the open lands of the Midwest and West?
11. What are our newest frontiers? How do they compare to the old frontiers? How are they different?

12. How do you think the Homestead Act affected the Native American tribes living in the Great Plains area?

KEY VOCABULARY

acre	prairie
act (noun)	production
barbed wire	prospector
barn raising	ranch
claim	range
cultivation	residence
drought	resource
environment	settler
freehold	sod house
frontier	soil
grant	speculator
grazing	squatter
Great Plains	stake
homestead	territory
homesteader	trail
livestock	trek
pasture	watering hole
pioneer	well (noun)
plains	windmill

RELATED CAREER EDUCATION TERMS

architect	geologist
banker	government official
builder	lawyer
cartographer	notary public
construction worker	rancher
contractor	real-estate agent
county clerk	real-estate developer
deed-recording clerk	sheriff
engineer	surveyor
farmer	title searcher
	well-driller

American Red Cross Organized

THEMES AND THOUGHTS

Volunteering, Mercy, Commitment, Service

Those who bring sunshine to the lives of others cannot keep it from themselves.
—*James Matthew Barrie*

After the verb to love, to help is the most beautiful verb in the world.
—*Bertha von Suttner*

Service to others is our creed
Anxious to assist in time of need
Providing health, welfare, and peace of mind
Helpful work for all mankind
We pledge ourselves to promote good relations
Amongst fellow Americans and all the nations.
—*A Young Person's Red Cross Creed*

FASCINATING FACTS

Jean Henri Dunant, a Swiss philanthropist, was traveling through Italy during the Austro-Sardinian War in 1859. He arrived at a battle site the day after 40,000 people had been killed or wounded. Many of the wounded soldiers were still lying there, and he was distressed to see their suffering. He quickly organized some volunteers to help them, regardless of which side they had fought on.

Dunant went on to press for the formation of voluntary aid societies that would help wounded soldiers and remain neutral—that is, they would not favor any side. In 1863, a conference of delegates from 16 nations and several organizations took the first steps toward establishing the Red Cross. In 1864, delegates of 12 European nations met in Geneva, Switzerland, to draft an international law that would enable the Red Cross to function as a neutral agency during

wartime. This law, the first Geneva Convention, called for the humane treatment of sick and wounded soldiers during times of war. Eventually, all the European nations, the United States, and some Asian and South American countries adopted the convention. In later years, additional provisions were added to cover naval personnel, prisoners of war, and civilians. In 1901, Dunant won the first Nobel Peace Prize for his accomplishments.

The organization's name is derived from its flag—a red cross on a white background. In tribute to Dunant, the banner is the reverse of the flag of Switzerland, the homeland of the Red Cross. The association flags in most Moslem nations show a red crescent on a white background, and the groups are known as the Red Crescent Societies. In Israel, a red six-pointed star denotes the helping organization.

The Red Cross movement exists in over 120 nations. The American Association of the Red Cross was established by a nurse, Clara Barton, in 1881. Barton had become well known for her work nursing wounded men on Civil War battlefields. When the war ended, she set up a service to search for missing men. In 1869, she went to Europe as a battlefield nurse and saw the work of the International Committee of the Red Cross during the Franco-Prussian War. When she returned home four years later, she began to work for the establishment of a branch of the Red Cross in the United States. She became its first president and held that post until 1904. She broadened the mission of the Red Cross to provide help in times of natural calamities and epidemics, as well as in times of war. The American Red Cross grew quickly during World War I, when it served troops both in the United States and overseas.

In the United States, the President acts as honorary chairman of the American Red Cross. The Red Cross has a continuous service program operating at all times, and its main purpose is to prevent and alleviate human suffering. The relief work of the American Red Cross includes aiding victims of fires, floods, tornadoes, hurricanes, major transportation accidents, and other emergencies. The Red Cross also sponsors nursing services, blood donor services, swimming instruction, first-aid and CPR instruction, international communication with prisoners of war, dislocated persons assistance, recreational programs for armed services personnel, and numerous other forms of assistance to distressed persons. Schoolchildren can join the Junior Red Cross and perform volunteer services in hospitals and participate in international friendship ventures.

ACTIVITIES FOR STUDENTS

Information Gathering and Sharing

1. Contact your local American Red Cross chapter for materials describing the work of the American Red Cross, the League of Red Cross Societies, and the International Committee of the Red Cross. Request information about school-to-school exchanges and examples of international projects.
2. With your class, subscribe to *Junior Red Cross* magazine.
3. Ask your local American Red Cross chapter to provide a speaker for the school or class to describe the organization and its activities.
4. Bring in newspaper items that mention American Red Cross activities, such as providing aid during a flood, hospital projects, and water-safety programs.
5. With your class, present an international program about the work of the Red Cross in the style of a television documentary. Divide the class into committees representing various Red Cross countries. Each committee will present the accomplishments and the functions of the Red Cross in that particular country. The presentations may be illustrated with pictures.
6. After your class studies the functions of the Red Cross, a panel may be selected to answer questions from the class audience concerning the organization. Students may take turns on the panel.
7. Research and write a report about the life of Clara Barton.

Art and Visual Aids

8. Design a poster, using colored construction paper and paints, depicting the activities of the Red Cross.
9. With your class, design and make large posters depicting the story and achievements of the American Red Cross. Distribute the posters to various stores, public buildings, and churches for display.

Critical Thinking

10. Through a class discussion, formulate the main functions and contributions of the Red Cross. List these on the chalkboard. Students can select what they see as the single most important function and then defend their choices.
11. Compare the work of the Salvation Army to that of the Red Cross.

Writing and Language Arts

12. Write a newspaper article about the history, program, and achievements of the Red Cross.
13. Imagine you were one of the victims of a recent natural disaster. Write a thank-you letter to the Red Cross director for the organization's assistance.

Special Projects

14. With your class, undertake a "Good Health Habit" project, such as selling carrot sticks or apples at lunchtime. The money raised may be donated to the American Red Cross Youth Fund, a fund for the health and educational needs of children around the world. Contact the local American Red Cross chapter for specific details.
15. With your class, arrange with the local chapter of the Red Cross for a weekly Red Cross–approved first-aid course (complete or adapted) at your school.
16. With your class, sponsor a fund drive or a paid-admission student program for a worthy Red Cross–sponsored program.
17. With your class, participate in a community, school, or class project in health and safety or international friendship.

does that apply to the Red Cross program?

8. Can you think of other helping organizations similar to the Red Cross whose purpose is also to assist the needy? Why are such organizations often considered the "unsung heroes" of disaster missions?
9. Why is the Red Cross so concerned about quick and efficient transportation services in times of disaster-relief assignments?
10. What kinds of buildings does the Red Cross require in emergency situations? With which organizations do they need to work closely?
11. In what ways has the world of technical and medical science made the job of the Red Cross easier? How has the Red Cross helped the scientific world?
12. What are some general guidelines to remember for emergency first-aid needs?
13. Why do Red Cross members hold frequent meetings and conventions? Why do they work closely with government agencies?
14. What kinds of problems do Red Cross workers encounter during an emergency situation? What kind of training do they need?
15. Why is it appropriate that the Red Cross is an organization that knows no state or international boundaries?

QUESTIONS FOR CLASS DISCUSSION

1. What valuable services does the Red Cross provide? Why is the Red Cross needed?
2. In what ways does the Red Cross continue its idea of "We serve" in today's world?
3. Can you think of an appropriate slogan for the American or International Red Cross?
4. How is the Red Cross making great contributions toward peace and good feeling among all peoples?
5. The Red Cross relies on many volunteer workers to get the job done. What are the advantages and disadvantages of such a system?
6. Why is there rarely a dull moment in Red Cross work?
7. What is meant by the saying "An ounce of prevention is worth a pound of cure"? How

KEY VOCABULARY

ambulance	lifesaving
association	paramedic
blood bank	philanthropist
canteen	plasma
chapter	prisoner of war
charity	relief
disaster	service
emergency	society
field worker	victim
first aid	volunteer
Gray Ladies	wounded
international	

RELATED CAREER EDUCATION TERMS

administrator

civilian relief
 personnel

disaster aid
 director

doctor

fund-raiser

government
 benefits
 consultant

health services
 personnel

medical technician

missing-persons
 locator

nurse

paramedic

radio operator

recreational worker

rehabilitation
 worker

Memorial Day

THEMES AND THOUGHTS

Remembrance, Appreciation,
Gratefulness, Patriotism

Your silent tents of green
We deck with fragrant flowers;
Yours has the suffering been,
The memory shall be ours.
          —*Henry Wadsworth Longfellow*

Soldier, rest! thy warfare o'er,
Sleep the sleep that knows not breaking,
Dream of battled fields no more.
Days of danger, nights of waking.
          —*Sir Walter Scott*

In Flanders fields the poppies blow
Between the crosses, row on row.
          —*John McCrae*

And so, my fellow Americans: ask not what your country can do for you—ask what you can do for your country.
          —*John F. Kennedy*

FASCINATING FACTS

We give thanks on Memorial Day that we live in a free nation and honor those who gave their lives for that blessing. Memorial Day is also called Decoration Day. Since World War I, it has also been called Poppy Day. Volunteers sell small, red artificial flowers as a fund-raiser for disabled veterans.

The location of the first observance of Memorial Day is in dispute. Some claim the custom of honoring war dead began in Boalsburg, Pennsylvania. Others claim the custom was originated by some Southern women who placed flowers on the graves of both Union and Confederate soldiers after the Civil War. According to one writer, the first

Memorial Day service took place on May 30, 1866, on Belle Isle, a burial ground for Union soldiers in the St. James River, at Richmond, Virginia. The school superintendent and the mayor planned the program of hymns and speeches and had the burial ground decorated with flowers. In 1966, however, the U.S. government proclaimed that Waterloo, New York, was the birthplace of Memorial Day. On May 5, 1865, the people of Waterloo had honored soldiers who had died in the Civil War.

In 1868, General John A. Logan, commander-in-chief of the Grand Army of the Republic (an organization of Union veterans of the Civil War), named May 30 as a special day to honor the graves of Union soldiers. The selection of May 30 is attributed to a Virginian of French descent, Cassandra Oliver Moncure, who may have selected this date because it was "The Day of Ashes" in France—the day that Napoleon's remains were returned to France from St. Helena.

The custom of placing flowers on graves is an old one that exists in many countries. Today, almost everywhere around the globe, people have a special day to honor not only those who gave their lives in battle, but also family members and friends whom they wish to remember.

The Northern states and some Southern states celebrate Memorial Day on the last Monday in May. This date was made a federal holiday in 1971. Some Southern states have Memorial Day celebrations to honor Confederate soldiers who died in the Civil War. Mississippi and Alabama celebrate Confederate Memorial Day on the last Monday in April. In Florida and Georgia, the date is April 26. May 10 is Memorial Day in North and South Carolina, and the holiday is June 3 in Kentucky, Louisiana, and Tennessee. Texas observes Confederate Heroes Day on January 19 (Robert E. Lee's birthday).

ACTIVITIES FOR STUDENTS

Writing and Language Arts

1. Write a creative story or an essay on the traditional freedoms of the United States.
2. With a small group, compose original lyrics for a song about the theme of Memorial Day.
3. Write an editorial about the need for peace for the school newspaper or a newspaper in your community.

Information Gathering and Sharing

4. Divide your class into groups to compile a list of the wars in which the United States has been involved. Report on the numbers who have died in each war and describe how each war was declared.
5. Report on the Tomb of the Unknown Soldier.

6. Divide your class into small groups to prepare scenarios about memorial customs in a variety of other cultures, such as the Druids, the ancient Greeks, the Japanese, and the French. Discuss the similarities to our Memorial Day customs.
7. Research the famous Vietnam War Memorial in Washington, D.C., which lists all the members of the U.S. armed forces who were killed in that war. Compose a poem about that dramatic memorial.
8. Invite a member of a local American Legion or Veterans of Foreign Wars post (or other veterans' service organization) to address your class about the meaning of Memorial Day.

Art and Visual Aids

9. Design a peace emblem or symbol.

Critical Thinking

10. With your class, discuss and make a list of the ways Memorial Day should be observed.

Special Projects

11. With your class, put on a program of patriotic songs and music, ending your presentation with "Taps."
12. With your class, make table favors, placemats, and room decorations (such as a paperweight or small flower arrangement) for distribution to veterans' hospitals.
13. With your class, design and draw a parade float honoring some military or community subject. Construct the float as a class project and participate in the local Memorial Day parade.

QUESTIONS FOR CLASS DISCUSSION

1. In what ways does your community observe Memorial Day?
2. Why is the reading of the "Gettysburg Address" appropriate for a Memorial Day service?

3. Why is Memorial Day also called Decoration Day and Poppy Day?
4. Why do some states observe this holiday on different dates?
5. Why do we honor the Tomb of the Unknown Soldier in Arlington Cemetery on Memorial Day?
6. Why do we need the armed forces?

RELATED CAREER EDUCATION TERMS

armed forces personnel	historian
flagmaker	musician
florist	Parks Commissioner

KEY VOCABULARY

appreciation	military exercise
artificial poppy	monument
cemetery	parade
changing of the guard	patriotism
commemorate	recognize
deceased	remember
decorate	reminiscent
eternal light (or flame)	sacrifice
formation	serve
grave	serviceman
honor	servicewoman
honor roll	Tomb of the Unknown Soldier
inscription	tribute
marker	valiant
memorial	

June

Dairy Month
National Rose Month
National Arts and
    Crafts Month
*Carnival and Circus
    Month

National Adopt-a-Cat
    Month
National Pest Control
    Month
Zoo and Aquarium Month
American Rivers Month

First Week:

National Theatre Week
Teacher "Thank You" Week (the 1st full week of June)
Teacher's Day (the 1st Sunday in June)
Family Day (the 1st Sunday in June)
National Safe Boating Week

1

Jacques Marquette, French explorer, born, 1637
Brigham Young, leader of the Mormons, born, 1801

2

John Randolph, statesman, born, 1773
Alexander Graham Bell heard a sound on his invention, the telephone, 1875

3

Jefferson Davis, President of the Confederate States of America, born, 1808
Dr. Charles Drew, blood plasma researcher, born, 1904

4

Buckle Up for Safety Day

5

World Environment Day
Senator Robert F. Kennedy shot by assassin, 1968
First hot-air balloon flight, by Montgolfier brothers, in France, 1783

6

D-Day, on Normandy coast of France, 1944
*Nathan Hale born, 1755

7

Freedom of the Press Day

*A teaching unit is included on the following pages for each starred entry.

Second Week:

Children's Day (the 2nd Sunday in June)
Heritage Week
National Flag Week (the week including June 14)

8

Frank Lloyd Wright, architect, born, 1869

9

Senior Citizens Day
Cole Porter, composer, born, 1893

10

State and National Park Day

11

Summer Hobby Day

12

*Celebration of the invention of baseball

13

Department of Labor created, 1888
Yukon Territory organized, 1898
"Red" Grange, football hero, born, 1903

14

*Flag Day
Harriet Beecher Stowe, author of Uncle Tom's Cabin, born, 1811
Congress established U.S. Army, 1775

15

Ben Franklin's historic kite-flying experiment, proving lightning was composed of electricity, 1752
Magna Carta granted by King John, 1215
First nonstop transatlantic flight arrived in Ireland, 1919
Smile Power Day

Third Week:

Little League Baseball Week (the 2nd or 3rd week of June)
*Father's Day (the 3rd Sunday in June)
Amateur Radio Week

16

Ford Motor Company founded, 1903
National Juggling Day

17

Battle of Bunker Hill, 1775
John Hersey, novelist, born, 1914

18

Napoleon defeated at Waterloo, 1815

19

Statue of Liberty arrived in New York harbor from France, 1885

20

Congress adopted design for Great Seal of the U.S., 1782
Eli Whitney applied for the patent on the cotton gin, 1793

21

Daniel Carter Beard, naturalist, writer, and illustrator, who started Boy Scouts in the
    U.S., born, 1850
Summer begins (traditional date)
Summer Safety Day

22

Department of Justice founded, 1870
Voting age lowered from 21 to 18 in the U.S., 1970

23

William Penn signed treaty with Indians, 1683

Every Day's a Holiday

24
John Cabot discovered North American mainland, 1497
Henry Ward Beecher, clergyman and orator, born, 1813

25
Sioux Indians massacred General George Custer and his troops at Battle of Little Bighorn, 1876
Korean War began, 1950

26
United Nations charter signed, 1945
Pearl S. Buck, novelist, born, 1892

27
*Helen Keller born, 1880
Paul Laurence Dunbar, poet, born, 1872

28
Archduke Francis Ferdinand of Austria assassinated, starting World War I, 1914
Versailles Treaty signed, ending World War I, 1918

29
George W. Goethals, engineer who supervised building of the Panama Canal, born, 1858
William James Mayo, surgeon who helped establish the Mayo Foundation, born, 1861

30
Pure Food and Drug Act signed, 1906
Establishment of the U.S. Fish and Wildlife Service, 1940

Carnival and Circus Month

THEMES AND THOUGHTS

Cooperation, Teamwork, Caring,
Courage

How the grand band-wagon
shown with a splendor all its own,
And glittered with a glory that
our dreams had never known!
—*James Whitcomb Riley*

An ounce of mirth is worth a
pound of sorrow.
—*Richard Baxter*

Music has charms to soothe a
savage breast.
—*William Congreve*

The most wasted day of all is
that on which we have not laughed.
—*Sébastien Roch Nicholas Chamfort*

Laugh and the world laughs with
you.
—*Ella Wheeler Wilcox*

A good laugh is sunshine in a
house.
—*William Thackeray*

FASCINATING FACTS

A carnival was originally the feasting and merrymaking on the three days before Lent. The word *carnival* is derived from the Latin *carnem levare*, meaning "to put away meat," a common practice during Lent in Catholic countries. The most famous early carnivals were held in Rome and Venice. The Mardi Gras in New Orleans is the most famous carnival in the United States.

A carnival can also be a form of outdoor amusement. The major attractions of this type of carnival are its thrill rides, such as the Ferris wheel and the roller coaster. A carnival can also include games, exhibits, and shows. Today, there are about 500 traveling carnivals in the United States. Many of the features of the carnival can also be found in amusement parks.

Circus is a Latin word that means "circle" or "racecourse." The circus had its beginnings in ancient Rome chiefly as a place for chariot races and other exhibitions of horsemanship. Roman circuses were also the site of gladiator contests and beast hunts.

John Bill Ricketts, a famous English rider, brought the first circus to the United States. In 1793, George Washington went to Ricketts' circus in Philadelphia and rode with Ricketts in the show. It is recorded that George Washington sold Ricketts a horse.

The traveling circus in the United States

came into existence in the early 1800s. The show usually consisted of a fiddler, a juggler, a tightrope walker, an acrobat, and a clown who would sing and tell jokes. After the show, a collection was taken and the performance then moved on to the next village green. The full-tent circus was started by some New Englanders, who added animal exhibitions to the show.

In the 1870s, there were about ten major circuses touring the United States. They traveled from town to town in colorful wagons. When the circus came to town, the performers and the animals would parade through the streets before setting up the tents. Now most circuses travel by train or truck, perform indoors, and have a parade as an opening act before each performance.

In 1881, two of the biggest circuses merged. P. T. Barnum and James A. Bailey formed Barnum and Bailey's Greatest Show on Earth. In 1884, the five Ringling brothers in Wisconsin started another famous circus. They bought the Barnum and Bailey show in 1907, and in 1919, combined the two circuses to form the largest and most famous circus ever, the Ringling Brothers and Barnum & Bailey Circus.

Small circuses travel by truck and perform in a different city or town every day for about seven months a year. Ringling Brothers and Barnum & Bailey Circus travels in its own railroad cars and may perform in a city for a week or more. It's on the road for about 10 1/2 months a year; its winter quarters are in Venice, Florida. When circuses are not touring, the performers and crew are still busy. The performers are practicing and planning new acts. The crew members are making and buying new costumes and pieces of equipment and repairing old ones. And of course, the animals need to be exercised and cared for.

Circus history is on display at the Ringling Museum of the Circus in Sarasota, Florida, and the Circus World Museum in Baraboo, Wisconsin.

ACTIVITIES FOR STUDENTS

Information Gathering and Sharing

1. With your class, set up a display of books with the theme of carnivals or circuses.

Construct a three-dimensional "big top" out of striped wrapping paper. Arrange the tent and the books on a table with a sign that says "What's Under the Big Top?"
2. Try to find real circus or carnival posters or promotional announcements for display.
3. Report on a famous carnival or circus personality, such as P. T. Barnum, the Wallendas, Emmett Kelly, Jumbo, or Tom Thumb.
4. With your class, write to the Sarasota Chamber of Commerce (1551 2nd St., Sarasota, Florida 34236) for brochures and information about the Circus Hall of Fame, the Ringling Museum of Art, and the Ringling Museum of the Circus.
5. With your class, discuss each of the following topics about circus animals:

   • How are the animals captured?

   • Where are most of the animals found?

   • What do the animals eat?

   • How are the animals trained?

   • Why do some animals sleep all winter and how do they wake up?
6. Research and report to your class how people learn to become circus performers, such as clowns, animal trainers, acrobats, or jugglers.
7. Research and report to your class how some amusement rides, such as the roller coaster and the Ferris wheel, are designed and constructed.

Writing and Language Arts

8. With your class, discuss and list circus and carnival words. Place them on a chart for classroom use, or alphabetize them and compile them into a large classroom dictionary.
9. With your class, discuss the various workers needed in a circus, such as trainers, animal keepers, clowns, and trick riders. Write a report about one of the kinds of workers.

Art and Visual Aids

10. Research the early Roman circus. With a small group, construct a diorama or a bulletin-board display of a chariot race or

an animal exhibition.

11. Draw a clown on construction paper and decorate it with colored paper and scraps of material. Use heavy colored yarn to connect the class' pictures to make a display with the following poem:

> Big clowns,
> Little clowns,
> Fat clowns,
> Thin clowns,
> Sad clowns,
> Funny clowns,
> Clowns, clowns—
> Just look around!

12. Design a poster or banner to advertise a circus, carnival, or rodeo.

13. With a group, make free-standing circus animals by drawing them on colored index cards and cutting them out. Display the animals in cages made of shoeboxes and drinking straws. Name the animals.

14. With your class, make a frieze or a large illustrated book about circus animals.

Dramatics and Role-Playing

15. With your class, set up a colorful ticket booth. Using props, such as a hat, a microphone, and a cane, take turns pretending to be a circus or carnival barker selling curios or advertising a particular sideshow or thrill ride.

Special Projects

16. Visit a circus or carnival if there is one nearby.

17. Plan a circus day program to present to parents, another classroom, or to the school. Design posters to advertise the event. Include clowns, jugglers, gymnasts, an imaginary animal act, and a ringmaster. Serve popcorn and juice. If weather permits, the program can be held outdoors.

18. With your class, have a quiz show based on questions and riddles about circus animals.

QUESTIONS FOR CLASS DISCUSSION

1. Do you think the circus is as exciting to watch today as it was many years ago? Is it as important a form of entertainment today?
2. What were some of the prejudices people had against circus and carnival people in the United States in the 1800s?
3. What were some of the problems of the traveling circus?
4. What is the real purpose of a clown?
5. Who has the hardest job of all in the circus?
6. What happens to the circus during the winter months?
7. Why have many tent circuses gone out of business?
8. Why are sea lions good to have in a circus? What are some other performing circus animals?
9. What is meant when someone in a circus says "The circus is my life"?
10. Why do circus people seem to speak a language of their own?
11. What would be the advantages and disadvantages of growing up in a circus or carnival family?
12. What is meant by the expression "The circus gets in your blood"?

KEY VOCABULARY

acrobat	clown
act	exhibit (noun)
animal trainer	Ferris wheel
announcer	fortuneteller
bareback rider	game
barker	giant
big top	high-wire act
billboard	juggler
brass ring	Mardi Gras
carnival	midway (noun)
carousel	mirth
circus	music

Every Day's a Holiday

KEY VOCABULARY CONTINUED

performer
popcorn
poster
publicity
ride (noun)
ringmaster
rodeo
roller coaster
sideshow
state fair

stunt
tamer
tent
three-ring circus
tradition
trainer
trampoline
trapeze
van
vendor

RELATED CAREER EDUCATION TERMS

acrobat
advertiser
amusement ride
    designer
animal trainer
booking agent
clown
costumer
equestrian
equipment
    manufacturer

juggler
lighting technician
manufacturer of
    food for animals
promoter
stuntman
stuntwoman
talent agent
vendor
veterinarian

Nathan Hale Born

THEMES AND THOUGHTS

Obedience, Loyalty, Commitment,
Honor, Sacrifice

I only regret that I have but one
life to lose for my country.
—*Nathan Hale*

The greatest test of courage on
the earth is to bear defeat without
losing heart.
—*R. G. Ingersoll*

Courage conquers all things: it
even gives strength to the body.
—*Ovid*

It is the cause, not the death that
makes the martyr.
—*Napoleon Bonaparte*

The martyr cannot be dishonored.
—*Ralph Waldo Emerson*

They never fail who die in a great
cause.
—*Lord Byron*

FASCINATING FACTS

Posing as a harmless Dutch schoolteacher, Nathan Hale crossed the British lines to obtain information for General Washington during the Revolutionary War, but he was captured and hanged as a spy by the British.

Nathan Hale was born in Coventry, Connecticut, into a family of 12 children. At the age of 18, he graduated from Yale, where he distinguished himself for his interest in reading and his athletic ability. He was only 21 when he was hanged in 1776, one day after his capture. Hale had taught school for a year after graduating from college, and he had been a successful teacher. He became caught up in the spirit of the American Revolution and joined the colonial troops.

He fought in the siege of Boston and was then transferred to New York. He was promoted to the rank of captain in an elite troop called the Rangers, who were known for their daring exploits on dangerous missions. General George Washington asked the commander of the Rangers to obtain information on British fortifications in New York, and Hale volunteered for the job. He succeeded in crossing the British lines and obtaining information about the British position. He hid notes, written in Latin, in the sole of his shoe. He was captured on his way back to Washington's headquarters and was taken before General William Howe, who condemned him to hang the next day, September 22, 1776.

Many believe that a pro-British cousin betrayed Hale. Hale showed his courage by making a speech just before his execution. Although no one recorded the speech, it is said that he ended with the words, "I only regret that I have but one life to lose for my country." It is said that his captors refused his last request—a Bible and the services of a minister.

Hale is remembered as a courageous martyr for the cause of the colonies' independence. There are several monuments to Hale (including one at the site of his capture near Huntington, New York, and the Nathan Hale Homestead in South Coventry, Connecticut), and many schools in the United States are named for this one-time schoolteacher.

ACTIVITIES FOR STUDENTS

Information Gathering and Sharing

1. Investigate modern intelligence techniques and report on the general objectives of the Central Intelligence Agency (CIA) and Army Intelligence.

Writing and Language Arts

2. Write a diary entry for a day in Nathan Hale's life.
3. Write and deliver a speech that Nathan Hale might have given.
4. Write a eulogy about Nathan Hale that might have appeared in a colonial newspaper.
5. An acrostic is a list of words whose first letters form a motto, phrase, name, or word. Write an acrostic for Nathan Hale.
6. Write a brief biography of a famous spy and try to uncover the factors in the person's background that may have led him or her to become a spy for his or her country.

Critical Thinking

7. With your class, have a debate on the issue of spying.

Dramatics and Role-Playing

8. With a group of classmates, write and act out a play about Nathan Hale.

QUESTIONS FOR CLASS DISCUSSION

1. What evidence do you think the British found on Nathan Hale to convict him as a spy?
2. Just before Nathan Hale mounted the gallows, he wrote two letters which were later destroyed by the British. Why do you suppose they did not allow Hale's letters to be delivered?
3. What kind of person would want to volunteer to be a spy for his country?
4. What five adjectives would you select to best describe Nathan Hale's character?
5. What kind of teacher do you think Nathan Hale was? Why?

KEY VOCABULARY

agent	hero
betray	informer
carrier pigeon	intelligence
clandestine	intrigue
code	loyalty
counterspy	martyr
covert	message
cryptogram	microfilm
cryptography	mission
decipher	operation
decoy	pose
device	reconnoiter
devotion	sabotage
disguise	sacrifice
double agent	secret
enemy	secret service
espionage	spy
execute	spy apparatus
gallows	surveillance

RELATED CAREER EDUCATION TERMS

CIA agent
cryptologist
detective
electronics expert
FBI agent
make-up artist

minister
pilot
professional soldier
schoolteacher
secret service
   agent

Celebration of the Invention of Baseball

THEMES AND THOUGHTS

Teamwork, Sportsmanship,
Winning, Spirit

The game isn't over till it's over.
—*Yogi Berra*

Whoever wants to know the heart and mind of America had better learn baseball, the rules and realities of the game—and do it by watching first some high school or small-town teams.
—*Jacques Barzun*

The cheerful loser is a winner.
—*Elbert Hubbard*

In play there are two pleasures for your choosing—
The one is winning, and the other is losing.
—*Lord Byron*

FASCINATING FACTS

Baseball was named for the four bases the batter must make to score a run. The game developed from the English games of cricket and rounders. The principal difference between rounders and baseball is that fielders throw the ball at runners, rather than tagging them, for an out. In colonial times, children in Boston played games similar to baseball, including games called One-o-cat, Two-o-cat, Town Ball, and the New York Game.

In 1906, a commission appointed by major league officials declared that Abner Doubleday invented the game of baseball in Cooperstown, New York, in 1839. Historians today believe that there is no good evidence to support the claim for Doubleday. Nevertheless, the name of Cooperstown is still synonymous with baseball

because the National Baseball Hall of Fame and Museum is located there. (In order to be named to the Hall of Fame, a player who has been in the major leagues for at least ten years must be elected by three-quarters of the members of the Baseball Writers' Association of America and the Committee of Veterans.) The annual celebration of the invention of baseball takes place in Cooperstown.

The first set of formal rules for baseball were established by a commission headed by Alexander J. Cartwright in 1845. Cartwright started the first organized baseball team, the Knickerbocker Base Ball Club of New York, in 1845. On June 19, 1846, the Knickerbocker Club met the New York Nine in Hoboken, New Jersey, for what many historians believe was the first baseball game between organized teams. During the Civil War, the game spread across the country because many soldiers played it for recreation.

In Cartwright's day, the rules for baseball were somewhat different from what we know today. The first team with 21 or more runs at the end of an inning won the game. The pitcher stood only 45 feet (rather than 60 feet 6 inches) from home plate and had to throw the ball underhand. A fielder could put a batter out by catching a fly on the first bounce. There was no such thing as a strike or a walk.

The Red Stockings of Cincinnati became the first paid—or professional—team in 1869. In 1876, eight professional teams formed the first major league, the National League. The American League was formed in 1900. The first World Series was played in 1903 between Boston, an American League team, and Pittsburgh, a National League team. Boston won the game, 5–3.

On April 14, 1910, William Howard Taft was the first President to pitch a ball for the season's opening game. A crowd of 12,226 witnessed Washington beat Philadelphia, 3–0. Today, it is a tradition for the President of the United States, or another celebrity, to open the major league season by throwing out the first ball.

Today, 24 professional baseball teams are located in cities throughout the United States. There is also an American League team in Toronto, Canada, and a National League team in Montreal. Each year, an All-Star game between teams of players chosen from all the teams in both leagues is played in a host city. Over 50 million spectators attend professional baseball games every year. Some of the stars earn more than $1 million for a season of play.

Teams of boys and girls play Little League baseball in practically every community across the country. Little Leaguers hold a world championship game each summer in Williamsport, Pennsylvania.

Baseball is considered to be our "national pastime," and it is also very popular in Latin America and parts of Asia.

BASIC RULES OF THE GAME

1. The bat is not to exceed 2 3/4 inches in diameter, nor more than 42 inches in length.
2. The ball should weigh between 5 and 5 1/4 ounces and be 9 to 9 1/4 inches in circumference.
3. The game is to have nine innings unless called after four and a half innings by the umpire, or until a tie score is broken after nine complete innings.
4. Each team has three outs per inning.
5. Nine players constitute a team, but many specialized substitutes are carried on a squad.

ACTIVITIES FOR STUDENTS

Sports and Games

1. With your class, discuss the rules for playing baseball. Challenge another class to a baseball game.
2. Divide the class into two teams and play baseball with a school subject. A spelling word is "pitched" to the batter, who gets a "hit" if the word is spelled correctly. The "bases" could be the corners of the room. A "run" is scored after a player makes the circuit of the bases. The team with the most "runs" wins.
3. On the school grounds, demonstrate specific baseball terms or plays.

Information Gathering and Sharing

4. Invite a Little League or high-school baseball coach to speak to the class about the game of baseball.
5. Measure diameters, weights, and lengths of some balls and bats.
6. Report on a famous baseball player in the Hall of Fame, such as Babe Ruth, Joe DiMaggio, or Roger Hornsby.
7. With a committee, research and report on the history of baseball or on colorful baseball stories.

8. Research the way baseballs, bats, and gloves are manufactured.

Art and Visual Aids

9. With your class, make a table display of baseball equipment.
10. With your class, make a display of reference and library books about baseball and baseball players. Arrange the display like a baseball diamond, with a book for each plate. Use an appealing slogan, such as "Don't strike out—Make a run for these books!" or "Score by reading!"
11. Find out the exact dimensions of an official baseball diamond. With permission from your principal, plot a diamond on the playground. Line the base paths.
12. Make an exhibit of baseball cards, pictures, and books about baseball and popular players.
13. Investigate baseball "firsts" and league records. Report your findings and post the reports on a bulletin-board display entitled "Did You Know?"

Dramatics and Role-Playing

14. Read the poem "Casey at the Bat" by Ernest L. Thayer. With your class, dramatize the poem. Find other poems about baseball for choral-speaking exercises.
15. The All-Star game is played in July. With a group, role-play television and radio sportscasters reporting on an imaginary All-Star game. Or write up the game for a sports column or a newspaper article.

Writing and Language Arts

16. Write a sports story that incorporates a series of baseball news items that have occurred over the years since the start of professional baseball.
17. Compile a list of baseball vocabulary, like foul, home plate, run, and double play. Alphabetize these words for a baseball dictionary.

Critical Thinking

18. With your class, discuss the safety precau-

tions and equipment used to play baseball.
19. With your class, discuss these sports-related expressions:
  - Success is never accidental.
  - The one who is pulling the oars has no time to rock the boat.
  - Athletes are dedicated people of the highest order.
  - A winner never quits, and a quitter never wins.
  - It is no disgrace to be defeated, but it is a disgrace to stay defeated.
  - When the going gets tough, the tough get going.
  - Athletes are their own police.

Mathematics

20. Learn how to calculate a batting average. Check the sports pages for actual averages.

QUESTIONS FOR CLASS DISCUSSION

1. Why do you think baseball is considered to be our national pastime?
2. What qualities does a player need to be a professional?
3. Why must there be a set of rules for a game or sport?
4. The players on the first professional team in 1869 earned $600 to $1,400. How do you explain the fabulous salaries some baseball players receive today?
5. In what ways can baseball players become national heroes?
6. In what ways is baseball a team game?
7. How can baseball, or any other sport, promote respect and good feeling among players of different backgrounds?
8. Why is football becoming at least as popular as baseball?
9. Why are fans so loyal to their hometown teams?
10. What are the advantages of Little League and Pony League teams?
11. What changes are needed to improve the game of baseball as it is presently played?

12. Why has night baseball become so popular with the professionals?
13. What are the benefits of having international baseball competition?
14. Baseball is sometimes called a game of inches. It is also referred to as a game of science. Explain what is meant by these two descriptions.
15. Some people think that today's baseball is too commercial. Why do they make that charge? Explain your opinion.
16. Which position on the team do you feel is the most vital? Is it more important to have a better hitting or a better fielding team?
17. How has the airplane aided professional teams?
18. Why is record keeping so important for the players?
19. Why is baseball today so highly organized, with professional scouts, farm teams, record keeping, and other business practices?
20. Why are so many professional athletes so highly paid?
21. What do the team members and fans demand of a player?
22. Why must professional players maintain good conduct and proper living on and off the field?

KEY VOCABULARY

ball	manager
base	mask
bat	no-hitter
batter	out
batting average	outfield
box score	pick off
bullpen	plate
bunt	play
catcher	runs batted in (RBI)
coach	score
diamond	series
double play	shin guards
fair play	sign
fan	spectator
fly	spikes
glove	squeeze play
hit	steal
home run	strike
infield	strikeout
inning	Texas leaguer
league	umpire
line drive	walk
lineup	World Series

RELATED CAREER EDUCATION TERMS

club owner	scout
coach	sporting goods and uniform manufacturer
equipment manager	
groundskeeper	
lighting contractor	sports announcer
maintenance worker	sports artist
manager (front office or field)	sports reporter
	statistician
player	trainer
public address announcer	umpire
public relations person	vendor

Flag Day

Patriotism, Respect, Loyalty, Service

The flag is the embodiment, not of sentiment, but of history. It represents the experiences made by men and women . . . who . . . live under that flag.
—*Woodrow Wilson*

I believe in the United States of America as a Government of the people, by the people, for the people; whose just powers are derived from the consent of the governed; a democracy in a republic, a sovereign Nation of many sovereign States; a perfect Union one and inseparable; established upon those principles of freedom, equality, justice and humanity for which American patriots sacrificed their lives and fortunes. I therefore believe it is my duty to my country to love it, to support its Constitution, to obey its laws, to respect its flag, and to defend it against all enemies.
—*William Tyler Page*
("The American's Creed," adopted by the House of Representatives, April 3, 1918)

One flag, one land, one heart, one hand. One Nation evermore.
—*Oliver Wendell Holmes*

When I think of the flag, . . . I see alternate stripes of parchment upon which are written the rights of liberty and justice, and stripes of blood to vindicate those rights, and then, in the corner, a prediction of the blue serene into which every nation may swim which stands for those great things.
—*Woodrow Wilson*

Flags have been used as symbols since ancient times. The first flags were probably the banners that the ancient Egyptians carried into battle. Throughout history, flags have been important in battles because they show the positions of the opposing forces. Flags have become symbols of national pride the world over—in times of peace, as well as in times of war.

Although it is not in official records, it is thought that Betsy Ross was commissioned to design and make the first American flag. It is confirmed, though, that George Washington, as General of the First Continental Army, raised the first Union flag on January 1, 1776, on Prospect Hill in Somerville, Massachusetts. Known as the Grand Union Flag, it symbolized the unity of all the colonies' militias as one fighting army. The British Union Jack appeared in the upper left corner of this flag, because the colonies had not yet agreed to declare their independence from England.

After the Declaration of Independence was signed, the Union Jack had to be replaced. On June 14, 1777, the Continental Congress adopted a new flag, which it described as "13 stripes alternate red and white, and . . . 13 stars white in a blue field representing a new constellation."

The 13 stripes and the 13 stars in the flag represented the 13 original states. The Continental Congress did not leave a record of why it chose the colors red, white, and blue. But in 1782, the Congress of the Confederation chose the same colors for the Great Seal of the United States and explained that the red is for hardiness and courage; the white is for purity and innocence; and the blue is for vigilance, perseverance, and justice.

When Vermont and Kentucky joined the Union in 1794, Congress added two stars and two stripes to the flag. Five more states had been added by 1817, but it was agreed that 20 stripes were too many for an attractive design. Congress decided in 1818 to adopt a design with 13 stripes—one for each of the original states—and a star for each state. This design could easily be altered whenever new states were added to the Union.

The nickname the "Stars and Stripes" is the most popular nickname for the flag that stands for the land, the people, the government, and the ideals of the United States. Francis Scott Key called our flag the "Star-Spangled Banner" in 1814, when he wrote the poem that is now the U.S. national anthem. "Old Glory" was a name given in 1824 by William Driver, a sea captain from Salem, Massachusetts.

Some other flags also represent the United States or various government agencies. For example, a blue flag with white stripes, the "Navy Jack," represents the United States on Navy ships.

A department store in Detroit, Michigan, the J. L. Hudson Company, owns the world's largest U.S. flag, which is 104 feet wide and 235 feet long.

Flag Day is not an official national holiday, but it is proclaimed by the President each year as a public observance.

ACTIVITIES FOR STUDENTS

Art and Visual Aids

1. With your class, make replicas of flags in U.S. history. Use colored paper, or if you can sew, make your flag out of fabric.

Information Gathering and Sharing

2. Trace the history of the U.S. flag from 1776 to today.
3. Compile a list of rules for displaying and honoring a flag. Display the list in your classroom.
4. Make a study of various kinds of flags and how they are used today.
5. Invite a veteran, a member of the military, or a government official to speak to your class about how and why the flag has become increasingly important to him or her. Prepare "interview" questions to pose to the speaker.
6. There have been many dramatic incidents involving the U.S. flag, such as the first U.S. flag raised on the moon. Go to the library and research these events (you might look under the heading "Flags, U.S."). Report to the class about one of these incidents.
7. Research and list various terms that have been used to refer to our flag.
8. Research and list the days that the U.S. flag should especially be displayed.
9. Research the origin of the Pledge of Allegiance.

Dramatics and Role-Playing

10. With some classmates, pantomime the story of George Washington and Betsy Ross planning our first flag.
11. With your class, give a choral recitation of the pledge to the flag. Discuss and analyze the pledge.

Special Projects

12. With your class, have a Flag Day marching parade, using flags that you have made.

Music

13. Learn some songs about our flag.

Critical Thinking

14. With your class, study displays of flags

from various countries, and identify those that have characteristics similar to those of the U.S. flag.

For additional activities, see "Francis Scott Key" (pages 27–28) and "Betsy Ross" (pages 149–150).

QUESTIONS FOR CLASS DISCUSSION

1. The Stars and Stripes is the most popular name for the national flag of the United States. Can you think of an original and different nickname for our flag?
2. Why do we need a flag? What purpose does a flag serve for a country?
3. During the Civil War, President Abraham Lincoln refused to have the stars for Southern states taken from the flag. Why do you think he refused?
4. Can you think of any other appropriate meanings for the colors in our flag that will tell something about the United States?
5. What is the correct manner of disposing of a U.S. flag after it has been worn and tattered?

KEY VOCABULARY

allegiance	official
banner	Old Glory
British Union Jack	original
citizen	patriotism
display	pledge
equality	proclaim
flag	republic
indivisible	spangled
justice	staff
legal	stars
national	stripes
oath	symbol
observance	vigilance

RELATED CAREER EDUCATION TERMS

distributor	steeplejack
dyer	tailor
flag designer	textile worker
manufacturer	

Father's Day

THEMES AND THOUGHTS

Honor, Respect, Love,
Devotion, Family

Honor Thy Father. . .
—*Exodus 20:12*

It is a wise father that knows his own child.
—*William Shakespeare
(Merchant of Venice)*

FASCINATING FACTS

Father's Day is a special day to honor and appreciate fathers. Mrs. Sonora Louise Smart Dodd is generally credited with establishing Father's Day. Her father, William Smart, had raised his six young children alone. To recognize her father's devotion and love for his family, Mrs. Dodd suggested to her minister that the congregation honor all fathers. She selected the third Sunday in June because her father's birthday was in June. Because of Mrs. Dodd's efforts, the first Father's Day was observed in Spokane, Washington, on June 19, 1910.

The white or red rose is the official flower for Father's Day. This, too, was Mrs. Dodd's idea. She suggested people wear a white rose to honor a father who was deceased and a red rose for a father who was living.

In 1916, President Woodrow Wilson approved the idea to observe Father's Day. He marked the event by pressing a special button on his desk in the White House that unfurled a flag at a Father's Day celebration in Spokane, Washington. From that year on, church services and special ceremonies were held on Father's Day throughout the country. But Father's Day did not become a national holiday until 1972, when President Richard Nixon signed the congressional resolution permanently establishing the third Sunday in June as Father's Day.

Harry C. Meek is also given credit for the idea of Father's Day. Mr. Meek, as president of a Lions Club in Chicago, gave speeches to various clubs in the United States about the need to honor fathers. In appreciation for his work, the Lions Clubs of America presented him with a gold watch, with the inscription "Originator of Father's Day," on his birthday, June 20, 1920.

Writing and Language Arts

1. Write a letter of thanks to your father or a friend who has been especially helpful to you.
2. Make a list of alternative words for the word *father* in English. Make a second list of words for the word *father* in various foreign languages.
3. List phrases and expressions with the word *father* in them (or referring to a father), such as "fatherly advice," "in his (or her) father's footsteps," "like father, like son," "a chip off the old block," "grandfather clock," "Father Time," "fatherland," "father confessor," and "father figure."

Information Gathering and Sharing

4. Make a list of famous fathers—such as Dr. Jonas Salk and John F. Kennedy—and their contributions to our nation and to the world.

Critical Thinking

5. With your class, compile a list of things you could do to show appreciation and respect for your fathers on Father's Day.
6. Select five prominent men or men in your family and describe an appropriate Father's Day gift for each of them.
7. Write an ending to each of the following statements:

   - Things that I like to do best with my father are . . .
   - The best day I ever spent with my father was . . .
   - The reasons I respect and listen to my father are . . .
   - The reason I love my father so much is that he . . .
   - The reason I admire my father so much is that he . . .

Art and Visual Aids

8. Design, draw, color, and cut out a paper tie or another item to be given as a Father's Day gift.
9. Trace, cut out, and sew a kitchen or barbecue apron for Dad. The apron can be made out of an old bed sheet. A marking pen may be used to print personalized and humorous sayings on the apron.
10. With your class, make a montage of line drawings or magazine pictures that depict what you think fathers may enjoy doing in their leisure time. Or, individually, make a montage for your own father and present it to him on Father's Day.

For additional activities, see National Grandparents' Day (pages 21–23) and Mother's Day (pages 266–268).

1. What does the expression "Follow in your father's footsteps" mean? Why is this not as true today as it may have been years ago?
2. The role of the father has changed over the years. Why?
3. What are some ways that a son or daughter can show respect for a father on Father's Day? On any day?
4. What are some adjectives that best describe the ideal father?
5. "A man never knows how to be a son until he has become a father" and "Father knows best" are two familiar expressions. What does each mean?
6. How are Father's Day and Mother's Day alike? How are they celebrated differently?
7. Why should children be happy to accept fatherly advice?
8. Why do our teachings tell us to honor our fathers and our mothers? Why is it important to be obedient and respectful and to follow their wishes and instructions?
9. How do you think the words *pa, papa,* and *pop* originated?
10. Many children have father substitutes who love them very much and are often responsible for their upbringing. How is this beneficial to the children, the mother, and even the father substitute?

11. Other than your own father or father substitute, who would you vote for as "Father of the Year"?
12. Why do fathers sometimes enjoy doing "kid" activities with their children?
13. What might be some chores that children could do around the house to make Father's Day a day of leisure for their fathers?
14. Mothers are often sent flowers and gifts and are taken out to dinner on Mother's Day. What are the special and unique ways we pay tribute to our fathers on "their day"?

RELATED CAREER EDUCATION TERMS

clothing manufacturer	florist
clothing-store clerk	greeting-card designer
	restauranteur

KEY VOCABULARY

appreciate	inspiration
aspire	loving
celebrate	loyal
dedication	observance
dependent	parent
devotion	provider
emulate	related
gift	respect
gratitude	stepfather
honor	

Helen Keller Born

Perseverance, Sacrifice, Devotion, Kindness, Courage

It is only with the heart that one can see rightly; what is essential is invisible to the eye.
—*Antoine de Saint-Exupéry*

How to reconcile this world of fact with the bright world of my imagining? My darkness has been filled with the light of intelligence, and, behold, the outer day-lit world was stumbling and groping in social blindness.
—*Helen Keller*

I cannot do everything,
But still I can do something;
And because I cannot do everything,
I will not refuse to do the something that I can do.
—*Edward Everett Hale*

Literature is my Utopia. Here I am not disfranchised. No barrier of the senses shuts me out from the sweet, gracious discourse of my book friends. They talk to me without embarrassment or awkwardness.
—*Helen Keller*

FASCINATING FACTS

Helen Keller lost her sight and hearing due to a serious illness before she was 2. Before her illness, she was just learning how to talk. But after she lost her hearing, she lost the ability to speak because she could not hear herself or others. She was completely cut off from the world.

When Helen was 7, Anne Sullivan Macy, a graduate of Boston's Institution for the Blind, was hired as Helen's teacher. Helen already had a "vocabulary" of about 60 pantomime gestures. She would, for example, pile her hair on top of her head to express "mother" and make the motion of turning the crank on an ice-cream maker and shiver a little to express "ice cream." For several months, Anne constantly spelled words for familiar objects into Helen's hand in sign language. Helen could imitate the gestures, but she did not understand that they were words for real things. One day, Anne held Helen's hand under the stream of water gushing from a pump and spelled w-a-t-e-r into her hand again and again. Helen suddenly realized that water was the name of the cool, smooth substance flowing over her hand. She immediately began to run about and touch everything, demanding that her teacher give her the words for each item. Thus began Helen's endless search for knowledge. Anne Sullivan had rescued Helen from a life of darkness, and she remained her teacher-companion for nearly 50 years.

At the age of 10, Helen Keller could read and write in braille, and she began to learn to speak by taking lessons from a teacher of the deaf. She did her writing on a special typewriter. At the age of 16, she entered preparatory school and then went on to graduate from Radcliffe in 1904. Throughout her schooling, Anne Sullivan was Keller's constant companion, spelling the lectures and lessons into her hand.

After college, Keller became active in improving conditions for the blind and the deaf-blind. She gave lectures, wrote books and articles, and spoke before legislatures. She also raised money for foundations for the blind. She was concerned about conditions for the blind not only in the United States, but also in developing and war-torn countries. She lectured in more than 25 countries, had her books published in more than 50 languages, and worked with soldiers who had been blinded during World War II. When Anne Sullivan died in 1936, Mary Agnes "Polly" Thompson became Keller's aide. Helen Keller died at the age of 88 in 1968.

ACTIVITIES FOR STUDENTS

Information Gathering and Sharing

1. With your class, discuss the importance of caring for our five senses. Invite the school nurse to tell about habits we can acquire to take good care of our senses. Make a list of guidelines and post it in the classroom.
2. Obtain copies of books written in braille from the library. With your class, discuss the distinctions between the letters.
3. Read and report on a book written by or about Helen Keller.
4. Compile a list of accomplishments of famous people who have handicaps. (See pages 46 and 47.)
5. Write a report on ways in which today's

scientists and doctors are attempting to aid the physically handicapped.
6. Prepare a report about seeing-eye dogs.
7. Write a comprehensive, illustrated report on the history and use of sign language.
8. Obtain a copy of a book on sign language. As a class, learn to sign the alphabet.

Dramatics and Role-Playing

9. With some classmates, plan a pantomime—a dramatic performance using rhythmic expressions and gestures, but no speech. Props, backdrops, and costumes may be used with pantomimes.

Critical Thinking

10. Read *The Miracle Worker*. With your class, discuss the main characters and their relationships.
11. With your class, compile a list of helpful rules for people to follow when they encounter seriously handicapped persons.

Writing and Language Arts

12. Write an essay entitled "The Sense I Rely on Most."

Art and Visual Aids

13. Collect and draw pictures to illustrate the use of the five senses. These may be placed in a booklet or a chart entitled "Which Senses?"

Special Projects

14. With a small group, collect items for a sensory recognition test. Have the rest of your classmates wear blindfolds and try to identify the items by only touch, sound, smell, or taste—or a combination of two or more of those senses.
15. With your class, write letters, make gifts, perform, or participate in some other social service activity for shut-ins, the Red Cross, Community Chest, youth centers, hospitals, or nursing homes.

For additional activities, see "National Employ the Handicapped Week" (pages 46–48) and "Thomas Edison" (pages 183–186).

QUESTIONS FOR CLASS DISCUSSION

1. Which sense is the most necessary to you? Explain your choice.
2. What qualities did Helen Keller possess that enabled her to overcome her physical handicaps?
3. In what ways did Helen Keller help others?
4. What progress in science and medicine has been made to help the blind? To help the deaf?
5. Why do some companies make a special effort to hire the handicapped?
6. What is meant by the phrase "A friend in need is a friend indeed"?
7. Why is it often common that people who have an impairment of one of their senses possesses a superior ability in other senses?
8. What are some general rules to remember in order to conserve the gifts of our senses?
9. Why should Helen Keller be considered a fighter?
10. Can you name the five senses?
11. What are some ways in which you can be misled by your senses? How do you account for this?
12. Some people think that Helen Keller "saw" more of life than most people with normal vision. How can you explain that?
13. In which occupations is the sense of sight or of hearing seriously at risk?
14. Do you think your senses can change temporarily from time to time? How could this occur?
15. What are some common adjectives used with certain senses?
16. What is extrasensory perception, sometimes called "the sixth sense"?

KEY VOCABULARY

author	inspiration
autobiography	instinct
blind	lecturer
braille	olfactory
cane	pantomime
companion	reader
compassion	rhythmic
compensation	seeing-eye dog
courage	sensation
deaf	senses
dependent	sightless
deprived	signing
disability	tactile
faith	touch
handicap	vision
impaired	

RELATED CAREER EDUCATION TERMS

fund-raiser	speech therapist
ophthalmologist	surgeon
public speaker	teacher
seeing-eye dog trainer	tutor
signer	writer

July

First Week:

National Tom Sawyer Days (July 4–8)

1

First U.S. postage stamps issued, 1847
Battle of Gettysburg began, 1863
Dominion Day—Dominion of Canada established, 1863

2

Continental Congress declared U.S. independence, 1776
President James Garfield assassinated, 1881

3

John Singleton Copley, painter, born, 1738
George M. Cohan, composer, born, 1878
Idaho admitted to the Union, 1890

4

Independence Day—Declaration of Independence adopted, 1776
Stephen Foster, composer, born, 1826
President Calvin Coolidge born, 1872

5

David G. Farragut, first admiral of the U.S. Navy, born, 1801
Phineas Taylor Barnum, showman and circus promoter, born, 1810

6

John Paul Jones, naval hero, born, 1747
Republican Party named, 1854
Beatrix Potter, creator of Peter the Rabbit, born, 1866

7

Hawaii annexed by the U.S., 1898

Second Week:

8
Liberty Bell cracked, tolling death of Chief Justice John Marshall, 1835

9
John D. Rockefeller, Sr., industrialist and philanthropist, born, 1839
Elias Howe, inventor of sewing machine, born, 1819

10
Washington, D.C., chosen as site of nation's capital, 1790
James McNeill Whistler, painter, born, 1834
Mary Bethune, educator, born, 1875
Wyoming admitted to the Union, 1890
First interactive communications satellite, Telstar, launched, 1962

11
President John Quincy Adams born, 1767
U.S. Air Force Academy established, 1955

12
George Eastman, photography pioneer, born, 1854
Medal of Honor established, 1861
Aaron Burr killed Alexander Hamilton in duel, 1804

13
Congress passed Northwest Ordinance, 1787
Women began competing in Olympics, 1908

14
Bastille Day (Independence Day in France), 1789
Edwin James made ascent of Pikes Peak, 1820

15
Wiley Post began his first round-the-world solo flight, 1933
Clement Moore, author of *A Visit from St. Nicholas,* born, 1779

Third Week:

Space Week (the week including July 20)

16

Roald Amundsen, Norwegian explorer and discoverer of the South Pole, born, 1872
First atomic bomb exploded in Alamogordo, New Mexico, desert, 1945

17

John Jacob Astor, financier and fur merchant, born, 1763
Spain ceded Florida to the U.S., 1819

18

Tennis introduced in the U.S., 1874
Presidential Succession Act signed, 1947

19

First women's rights convention, held in Seneca Falls, New York, 1848
Samuel Colt, inventor of repeating pistol, born, 1814

20

First draft number of World War I drawn, 1917
Georgia joined the colonies, 1770
Space Milestone Moon Day—Apollo 11's lunar module "Eagle," landed on the moon;
    astronauts Armstrong and Aldrin walked on the moon, 1969

21

First Battle of Bull Run, 1861
U.S. Veteran's Administration established, 1930

22

Alexander MacKenzie, first man to cross North America, reached the Pacific, 1793

23

First typewriter patented, 1829
Bunker Hill Monument completed, 1841
General William Booth founded the Salvation Army, in England, 1865
Ice-cream cone introduced, at St. Louis World's Fair, 1904

Every Day's a Holiday

Fourth Week:

24
Amelia Earhart, aviator, writer, and lecturer, born, 1897
Mormons founded Salt Lake City, 1847

25
Antarctica discovered, 1820

26
U.S. Postal Service began, 1775
New York admitted to the Union, 1788

27
First successful transatlantic cable completed, 1866
U.S. State Department established, 1789
Korean Armistice signed, 1953

28
World War I began, 1914
14th Amendment to the Constitution effective, 1868
National Joseph Lee Day, honoring the founder of playgrounds

29
Booth Tarkington, novelist, born, 1869

30
First representative assembly in America, at Jamestown, Virginia, 1619
Henry Ford, auto manufacturer and philanthropist, born, 1863
"In God We Trust" became an official U.S. motto, 1956

31
First U.S. patent granted, 1790

August

National Water Quality Month
Ostomy Awareness Month

First Week:

National Smile Week
National Clown Week
Friendship Day (the 1st Sunday in August)

1

Army Air Force established, 1907
Herman Melville, novelist, born, 1819
Colorado admitted to the Union, 1876
Francis Scott Key, author of "The Star-Spangled Banner," born, 1779

2

U.S. bought the first military plane from the Wright Brothers, 1909
Rodeo Day

3

Columbus sailed westward from Palos, Spain, 1492
U.S.S. *Nautilus* became first ship to reach the North Pole, 1958

4

U.S. Coast Guard established, 1790

5

National Greeting Card Day
Federal income tax introduced by Abraham Lincoln, 1861

6

Atomic bomb dropped on Hiroshima, Japan, 1945
Gertrude Ederle became first woman to swim the English Channel, 1926

7

International Peace Bridge dedicated, commemorating long-lasting peace between the U.S. and Canada, 1927
George Stephenson invented steam locomotive, 1815
Ralph Bunche, statesman, born, 1904

Every Day's a Holiday

Second Week:

8
Intertribal Indian Ceremonial Day, Gallup, New Mexico
International Good Character Day
Marjorie Kinnan Rawlings, novelist, born, 1896

9
Izaak Walton, English writer, known as the "father of angling," born, 1593

10
President Herbert C. Hoover born, 1874
Smithsonian Institution established in Washington, D.C., 1846

11
The Clermont, Robert Fulton's steamboat, made successful run up the Hudson River, 1807
National Night Out—community residents throughout the nation turn on lights in
    solidarity against crime (date may vary among communities or states)

12
First police force established in America, 1658
Thomas Edison invented the phonograph, 1877

13
Manila surrendered to U.S. forces, 1898
Lucy Stone, women's rights leader, born, 1818
Annie Oakley, sharpshooter, born, 1860

14
Japan surrendered and World War II ended, 1945
Social Security Act approved, 1935

15
Panama Canal opened, 1914
Napoleon Bonaparte born, 1769
National Relaxation Day

Third Week:

16 Battle of Bennington, Vermont, 1777

17 Davy Crockett, frontiersman, scout, and politician, born, 1786
Hot-air balloon crossed the Atlantic, landing in France, 1978
Gold discovered in the Klondike, 1896

18 Virginia Dare, first English child born in America, 1587
Meriwether Lewis, explorer, born, 1774

19 National Aviation Day—Orville Wright, inventor and airplane manufacturer, born, 1871
Victory of "Old Ironsides," the U.S.S. *Constitution*, 1812

20 President Benjamin Harrison born, 1833
Pennsylvania-Dutch Days begin, Hershey, Pennsylvania
Oliver H. Perry, naval hero, born, 1785

21 Admission Day—Hawaii became 50th state to enter the Union, 1959
Lincoln-Douglas debates began, 1858

22 First local chapter of American Red Cross founded by Clara Barton, 1881

23 Edgar Lee Masters, poet and biographer, born, 1869

Fourth Week:

Arts and Crafts Week

24 White House burned by British troops, 1814

25 Bret Harte, author and poet, born, 1836
Peace Treaty with Germany signed, 1921
Leonard Bernstein, composer and conductor, born, 1918

26 Women's Equality Day—19th Amendment, granting women the right to vote, adopted, 1920
First automobile trip across the U.S. arrived in New York City after 52 days, 1903

27 First radio message sent from an airplane, 1910
President Lyndon B. Johnson born, 1908
Petroleum Day—first oil well drilled in the U.S., at Titusville, Pennsylvania, 1859

28 First U.S. commercial radio broadcast, 1922
First coal mined in the U.S., 1806

29 Oliver Wendell Holmes, poet and essayist, born, 1809

30 Mary Wollstonecraft Shelley, author of *Frankenstein*, born, 1797

31 Agricultural Hall of Fame established, 1960

Every Day's a Holiday

Additional Resources for Teaching Special Days and Holidays

The following instructional resources are available in most educational libraries, media, or curriculum materials centers. They are especially useful for enhancing the teaching of special days and holidays:

Chase's Annual Events: Special Days, Weeks and Months. Compiled by William D. and Helen M. Chase. Chicago: Contemporary Books. This invaluable resource includes an almanac and survey of the year; a calendar of holidays, holy days, national and ethnic days; seasons; astronomical phenomena; festivals and fairs; anniversaries; birthdays; special events and traditional observances of all kinds from the world over.

Educators Guide to Free Films and *Educators Guide to Free Audio and Video Materials.* Randolph, Wisconsin: Educators Progress Service. Annotated lists of resources that include source, availability, and terms of loan. Entries are arranged by subject, and the guides have subject and title indexes. The same publisher offers an annual series of guides to free materials for various subjects, including *Educators Guide to Free Guidance Materials; Educators Guide to Free Social Studies Materials; Educators Guide to Free Health, Physical Education and Recreation Materials; Educators Guide to Free Science Materials;* and *Elementary Teachers Guide to Free Curriculum Materials.*

Other Resources for the Classroom

Druse, Kenneth. *Free Things for Gardeners.* Edited by Susan Osborn. New York: Putnam Publishing Group, 1982.

Ewing, S. A. *Guide to Over One Thousand Things You Can Get Free.* Lynn, Massachusetts: Sunnyside, 1984.

Feinman, Jeffrey, and Betty Schwartz. *Freebies for Kids.* New York: Simon & Schuster, 1983.

Hendrickson, Marilyn and Robert. *Two Thousand and One Free Things for the Garden.* New York: St. Martin's Press, 1983.

Osborn, Susan. *Free Things for Teachers.* New York: Putnam Publishing Group, Perigee, 1987.